D1517793

MISCELLANEOUS READINGS

EDITED BY

LEWIS B. MONROE.

Granger Index Reprint Series

 BOOKS FOR LIBRARIES PRESS

FREEPORT, NEW YORK

First Published 1872
Reprinted 1972

INTERNATIONAL STANDARD BOOK NUMBER:
0-8369-6335-0

LIBRARY OF CONGRESS CATALOG CARD NUMBER:
71-38603

PRINTED IN THE UNITED STATES OF AMERICA
BY
NEW WORLD BOOK MANUFACTURING CO., INC.
HALLANDALE, FLORIDA 33009

PREFACE.

IN my position as teacher of elocution, I have been
the recipient of numerous letters from amateur
Readers, members of literary clubs, and others, asking
me to name some piece appropriate to a given occasion. Teachers have desired choice readings for school
exhibitions. My own public entertainments have been
followed by verbal or written requests for copies of
selections which excited the interest of hearers. Such
appeals were usually for pieces which were not common or familiar, and of which I possessed perhaps but
a manuscript copy. I was therefore put to the task
of transcribing the desired pieces over and over again,
or forced to the ungracious duty of denying the very
proper request, for want of time to comply with it.
These solicitations were very frequently accompanied by
offers of compensation; but manifestly no price could be
set on what — though costing much time and trouble
when so multiplied — was in any individual case a mere
courtesy. I was led, therefore, to think that a book made
up in the main of selections which had proved entertain-
ing to public audiences, or literary or social circles, might
be acceptable to the public at large.

The unexpectedly cordial welcome extended to my first volume — Humorous Readings — encourages me to follow out my intentions by adding the present one. The selections herein are mostly of a serious character, — patriotic, pathetic, tragic, — with now and then the contrast of a lively narrative or choice bit of humor. While a few established favorites are included in this collection, by far the largest part is made up of pieces not to be found in any other compilation. My object has been, not to furnish a volume of familiar elegant extracts for the student, or rhetorical compositions for declaimers, but to bring together mostly fresh and rare productions which afford gratification when read or recited aloud. I trust that the volume may prove serviceable in promoting intelligent recreation in the social and public assembly.

In compliance with many requests it is my purpose, in completing the series, to prepare a volume of fresh and sparkling dialogues and brief dramas.

L. B. M.

CONTENTS.

———◆———

THE POOR FISHER FOLK. — Victor Hugo.

Translated by Rev. H. W. Alexander.

'TIS night; within the close-shut cabin-door
    The room is wrapped in shade, save where there fall
Some twilight rays that creep along the floor,
    And show the fisher's nets upon the wall.

In the dim corner, from the oaken chest
    A few white dishes glimmer; through the shade
Stands a tall bed with dusky curtains dressed,
    And a rough mattress at its side is laid.

Five children on the long low mattress lie, —
    A nest of little souls, it heaves with dreams;
In the high chimney the last embers die,
    And redden the dark roof with crimson gleams.

The mother kneels and thinks, and, pale with fear,
    She prays alone, hearing the billows shout;
While to wild winds, to rocks, to midnight drear,
    The ominous old ocean sobs without.

Poor wives of fishers! Ah, 't is sad to say,
    Our sons, our husbands, all that we love best,
Our hearts, our souls, are on those waves away, —
    Those ravening wolves that know nor ruth nor rest.

Think how they sport with those beloved forms,
And how the clarion-blowing wind unties
Above their heads the tresses of the storms :
Perchance even now the child, the husband dies !

For we can never tell where they may be
Who, to make head against the tide and gale,
Between them and the starless, soundless sea,
Have but one bit of plank, with one poor sail.

Terrible fear ! We seek the pebbly shore,
Cry to the rising billows, "Bring them home."
Alas ! what answer gives their troubled roar
To the dark thought that haunts us as we roam ?

Janet is sad : her husband is alone,
Wrapped in the black shroud of this bitter night :
His children are so little, there is none
To give him aid. "Were they but old, they might."
Ah, mother, when they too are on the main,
How wilt thou weep, "Would they were young again ! "

She takes her lantern, — 't is his hour at last ;
She will go forth, and see if the day breaks,
And if his signal-fire be at the mast ;
Ah no, — not yet ! — no breath of morning wakes.

No line of light o'er the dark waters lies ;
It rains, it rains, — how black is rain at morn !
The day comes trembling, and the young dawn cries, —
Cries like a baby fearing to be born.

Sudden her human eyes, that peer and watch
Through the deep shade, a mouldering dwelling find.
No light within, — the thin door shakes, — the thatch
O'er the green walls is twisted of the wind,

Yellow and dirty as a swollen rill.
"Ah me," she saith, "here doth that widow dwell;
Few days ago my good man left her ill;
I will go in and see if all be well."

She strikes the door, she listens; none replies,
And Janet shudders. "Husbandless, alone,
And with two children, — they have scant supplies, —
Good neighbor!   She sleeps heavy as a stone."

She calls again, she knocks; 't is silence still, —
No sound, no answer; suddenly the door,
As if the senseless creature felt some thrill
Of pity, turned, and open lay before.

She entered, and her lantern lighted all
The house so still, but for the rude waves' din.
Through the thin roof the plashing rain-drops fall,
But something terrible is couched within.

Half clothed, dark-featured, motionless lay she,
The once strong mother, now devoid of life;
Dishevelled spectre of dead misery, —
All that the poor leaves after his long strife.

The cold and livid arm, already stiff,
Hung o'er the soaked straw of her wretched bed.
The mouth lay open horribly, as if
The parting soul with a great cry had fled, —

That cry of death which startles the dim ear
Of vast eternity.   And all the while
Two little children, in one cradle near,
Slept face to face, on each sweet face a smile.

The dying mother o'er them, as they lay,
Had cast her gown, and wrapped her mantle's fold;

Feeling chill death creep up, she willed that they
Should yet be warm while she was lying cold.

Rocked by their own weight, sweetly sleep the twain,
With even breath, and foreheads calm and clear;
So sound that the last trump might call in vain,
For, being innocent, they have no fear.

Still howls the wind, and ever a drop slides
Through the old rafters, where the thatch is weak.
On the dead woman's face it falls, and glides
Like living tears along her hollow cheek.

And the dull wave sounds ever like a bell.
The dead lies still, and listens to the strain;
For when the radiant spirit leaves its shell,
The poor corpse seems to call it back again.

It seeks the soul through the air's dim expanse,
And the pale lip saith to the sunken eye,
"Where is the beauty of thy kindling glance?"
"And where thy balmy breath?" it makes reply.

Alas! live, love, find primroses in spring,
Fate hath one end for festival and tear.
Bid your hearts vibrate, let your glasses ring;
But as dark ocean drinks each streamlet clear,

So for the kisses that delight the flesh,
For mother's worship, and for children's bloom,
For song, for smile, for love so fair and fresh,
For laugh, for dance, there is one goal, — the tomb.

And why does Janet pass so fast away?
What hath she done within that house of dread?
What foldeth she beneath her mantle gray?
And hurries home, and hides it in her bed?
With half-averted face, and nervous tread,
What hath she stolen from the awful dead?

The dawn was whitening over the sea's verge
As she sat pensive, touching broken chords
Of half-remorseful thought, while the hoarse surge
Howled a sad concert to her broken words.

"Ah, my poor husband! we had five before;
Already so much care, so much to find,
For he must work for all.   I give him more.
What was that noise?   His step?   Ah no, the wind.

"That I should be afraid of him I love!
I have done ill.   If he should beat me now,
I would not blame him.   Did not the door move?
Not yet, poor man."   She sits with careful brow,
Wrapped in her inward grief; nor hears the roar
Of winds and waves that dash against his prow,
Nor the black cormorant shrieking on the shore.

Sudden the door flies open wide, and lets
Noisily in the dawn-light scarcely clear,
And the good fisher dragging his damp nets
Stands on the threshold with a joyous cheer.

"'T is thou!" she cries, and eager as a lover
Leaps up, and holds her husband to her breast;
Her greeting kisses all his vesture cover.
"'T is I, good wife!" and his broad face expressed

How gay his heart that Janet's love made light.
"What weather was it?"   "Hard."   "Your fishing?"   "Bad.
The sea was like a nest of thieves to-night;
But I embrace thee, and my heart is glad.

"There was a devil in the wind that blew;
I tore my net, caught nothing, broke my line,
And once I thought the bark was broken too;
What did you all the night long, Janet mine?"

She, trembling in the darkness, answered, " I ?
O, naught! I sewed, I watched, I was afraid ;
The waves were loud as thunders from the sky :
But it is over."　Shyly then she said : —

" Our neighbor died last night ; it must have been
When you were gone.　She left two little ones,
So small, so frail, — William and Madeline ;
The one just lisps, the other scarcely runs."

The man looked grave, and in the corner cast
His old fur bonnet, wet with rain and sea ;
Muttered awhile, and scratched his head, — at last,
" We have five children, this makes seven," said he.

" Already in bad weather we must sleep
Sometimes without our supper.　Now —　Ah, well,
'T is not my fault.　These accidents are deep ;
It was the good God's will.　I cannot tell.

" Why did he take the mother from those scraps,
No bigger than my fist ?　'T is hard to read ;
A learned man might understand perhaps, —
So little, they can neither work nor need.

" Go fetch them, wife ; they will be frightened sore,
If with the dead alone they waken thus ;
That was the mother knocking at our door,
And we must take the children home to us.

" Brother and sister shall they be to ours,
And they shall learn to climb my knee at even.
When He shall see these strangers in our bowers,
More fish, more food will give the God of heaven.

" I will work harder ; I will drink no wine —
Go fetch them.　Wherefore dost thou linger, dear ?
Not thus were wont to move those feet of thine."
She drew the curtain, saying, " They are here."

A YOUNG DESPERADO. — T. B. ALDRICH.

WHEN Johnny is all snugly curled up in bed, with his
rosy cheek resting on one of his scratched and grimy
little hands, forming altogether a perfect picture of peace
and innocence, it seems hard to realize what a busy, restive,
pugnacious, badly ingenious little wretch he is! There is
something so comical in those funny little shoes and stockings
sprawling on the floor, — they look as if they could jump
up and run off, if they wanted to, — there is something so
laughable about those little trousers, which appear to be
making vain attempts to climb up into the easy-chair, — the
said trousers still retaining the shape of Johnny's little legs,
and refusing to go to sleep, — there is something, I say,
about these things, and about Johnny himself, which makes
it difficult for me to remember that, when Johnny is awake,
he not unfrequently displays traits of character not to be
compared with anything but the cunning of an Indian warrior, combined with the combative qualities of a trained prize-
fighter.

I 'm sure I don't know how he came by such unpleasant
propensities. I am myself the meekest of men. Of course,
I don't mean to imply that Johnny inherited his warlike disposition from his mother. She is the gentlest of women.
But when you come to Johnny—he 's the terror of the whole
neighborhood.

He was meek enough at first, — that is to say, for the
first six or seven days of his existence. But I verily believe
that he was n't more than eleven days old when he showed
a degree of temper that shocked me, — shocked me in
one so young. On that occasion he turned very red in
the face, — he was quite red before, — doubled up his ri-
diculous hands in the most threatening manner, and finally, in the impotency of rage, punched himself in the eye.
When I think of the life he led his mother and Su-
san during the first eighteen months after his arrival,

I shrink from the responsibility of allowing Johnny to call me father.

Johnny's aggressive disposition was not more early developed than his duplicity. By the time he was two years of age I had got the following maxim by heart : "Whenever J. is particularly quiet, look out for squalls." He was sure to be in some mischief. And I must say there was a novelty, an unexpectedness, an ingenuity, in his badness that constantly astonished me. The crimes he committed could be arranged alphabetically. He never repeated himself. His evil resources were inexhaustible. He never did the thing I expected he would. He never failed to do the thing I was unprepared for. I am not thinking so much of the time when he painted my writing-desk with raspberry jam, as of the occasion when he perpetrated an act of original cruelty on Mopsey, a favorite kitten in the household. We were sitting in the library. Johnny was playing in the front hall. In view of the supernatural stillness that reigned, I remarked, suspiciously, "Johnny is very quiet, my dear." At that moment a series of pathetic *mews* was heard in the entry, followed by a violent scratching on the oil-cloth. Then Mopsey bounded into the room with three empty spools strung upon her tail. The spools were removed with great difficulty, especially the last one, which fitted remarkably tight. After that, Mopsey never saw a work-basket without arching her tortoise-shell back, and distending her tail to three times its natural thickness. Another child would have squeezed the kitten, or stuck a pin in it, or twisted her tail ; but it was reserved for the superior genius of Johnny to string rather small spools upon it. He never did the obvious thing.

It was this fertility and happiness, if I may say so, of invention, that prevented me from being entirely dejected over my son's behavior at this period. Sometimes the temptation to seize him and shake him was too strong for poor human nature. But I always regretted it afterwards. When I saw him asleep in his tiny bed, with one tear dried on his plump velvety cheek and two little mice-teeth visible through the parted lips, I could n't help thinking what a little bit of a fellow he was, with his funny little fingers and his funny little nails; and it did n't seem to me that he was the sort of person to be pitched into by a great strong man like me.

"When Johnny grows older," I used to say to his mother, "I 'll reason with him."

Now I don't know when Johnny will grow old enough to be reasoned with. When I reflect how hard it is to reason with wise grown-up people, if they happen to be unwilling to accept your view of matters, I am inclined to be very patient with Johnny, whose experience is rather limited, after all, though he is six years and a half old, and naturally wants to know why and wherefore. Somebody says something about the duty of "blind obedience." I can't expect Johnny to have more wisdom than Solomon, and to be more philosophic than the philosophers.

At times, indeed, I have been led to expect this from him. He has shown a depth of mind that warranted me in looking for anything. At times he seems as if he were a hundred years old. He has a quaint, bird-like way of cocking his head on one side, and asking a question that appears to be the result of years of study. If I could answer some of those questions, I should solve the darkest mysteries of life and death. His inquiries, however, generally have a grotesque flavor. One night, when the mosquitoes were making lively raids on his person, he appealed to me, suddenly : "How does. the moon feel when a skeeter bites it ?" To his meditative mind, the broad, smooth surface of the moon presented a temptation not to be resisted by any stray skeeter.

I freely confess that Johnny is now and then too much for me. I wish I could read him as cleverly as he reads me. He knows all my weak points ; he sees right through me, and makes me feel that I am a helpless infant in his adroit hands. He has an argumentative, oracular air, when things have gone wrong, which always upsets my dignity. Yet how cunningly he uses his power ! It is only in the last extremity that he crosses his legs, puts his hands into his trousers-pockets, and argues the case with me. One day last week he was very near coming to grief. By my directions, kindling-wood and coal are placed every morning in the library grate, in order that I may have a fire the moment I return at night. Master Johnny must needs apply a lighted match to this arrangement early in the forenoon. The fire was not discovered until the blower was one mass of red-hot iron, and the wooden mantel-piece was smoking with the intense heat.

When I came home, Johnny was led from the store-room, where he had been imprisoned from an early period, and where he had employed himself in eating about two dollars' worth of preserved pears.

"Johnny," said I, in as severe a tone as one could use in addressing a person whose forehead glistened with syrup, — "Johnny, don't you remember that I have always told you never to meddle with matches?"

It was something delicious to see Johnny trying to remember. He cast one eye meditatively up to the ceiling, then he fixed it abstractedly on the canary-bird, then he rubbed his ruffled brows with a sticky hand ; but really, for the life of him, he could n't recall any injunctions concerning matches.

"I can't, papa, truly, truly," said Johnny at length. "I guess I must have forgot it."

"Well, Johnny, in order that you may not forget it in future — "

Here Johnny was seized with an idea. He interrupted me.

"I 'll tell you what you do, papa, — *you just put it down in writin'*."

With the air of a man who has settled a question definitely, but at the same time is willing to listen politely to any crude suggestions that you may have to throw out, Johnny crossed his legs, and thrust his hands into those wonderful trousers-pockets. I turned my face aside, for I felt a certain weakness creeping into the corners of my mouth. I was lost. In an instant the little head, covered all over with yellow curls, was laid upon my knee, and Johnny was crying, "I'm so very, very sorry!"

I have said that Johnny is the terror of the neighborhood. I think I have not done the young gentleman an injustice. If there is a window broken within the radius of two miles from our house, Johnny's ball, or a stone known to come from his dexterous hand, is almost certain to be found in the battered premises. I never hear the musical jingling of splintered glass, but my porte-monnaie gives a convulsive throb in my breast-pocket. There is not a doorstep in our street that has n't borne evidences in red chalk of his artistic ability; there is n't a bell that he has n't rung and run away from at least three hundred times. Scarcely a day passes but he falls out of something, or over something, or into something. A ladder running up to the dizzy roof of an unfinished building is no more to be resisted by him than the back platform of a horse-car, when the conductor is collecting his fare in front.

I should not like to enumerate the battles that Johnny has fought during the past eight months. It is a physical impossibility, I should judge, for him to refuse a challenge. He picks his enemies out of all ranks of society. He has fought the ash-man's boy, the grocer's boy, the rich boys over the way, and any number of miscellaneous boys who chanced to stray into our street.

I can't say that this young desperado is always victorious. I have known the tip of his nose to be in a state of unpleasant redness for weeks together. I have known him to come home frequently with no brim to his hat; once he presented himself with only one shoe, on which occasion his jacket was split up the back in a manner that gave him the appearance of an over-ripe chestnut bursting out of its bur. How he will fight! But this I can say, — if Johnny is as cruel as Caligula, he is every bit as brave as Agamemnon. I never knew him to strike a boy smaller than himself. I never knew him to tell a lie when a lie would save him from disaster.

At present the General, as I sometimes call him, is in hospital. He was seriously wounded at the battle of The Little Go-Cart, on the 9th instant. On returning from my office yesterday evening, I found that scarred veteran stretched upon a sofa in the sitting-room, with a patch of brown paper stuck over his left eye, and a convicting smell of vinegar about him.

"Yes," said his mother, dolefully, "Johnny's been fighting again. That horrid Barnabee boy (who is eight years old, if he is a day) won't let the child alone."

"Well," said I, "I hope Johnny gave that Barnabee boy a thrashing."

"Didn't I, though?" cries Johnny, from the sofa. "*I* bet!"

"O Johnny!" says his mother.

Now, several days previous to this, I had addressed the General in the following terms: —

"Johnny, if I ever catch you in another fight of your own seeking, I shall cane you."

In consequence of this declaration, it became my duty to look into the circumstances of the present affair, which will be known in history as the battle of The Little Go-Cart. After going over the ground very carefully, I found the following to be the state of the case.

It seems that the Barnabee Boy — I speak of him as if he were the Benicia Boy — is the oldest pupil in the Primary Military School (I think it *must* be a military school) of which Johnny is a recent member. This Barnabee, having whipped every one of his companions, was sighing for new boys to conquer, when Johnny joined the institution. He at once made friendly overtures of battle to Johnny, who, oddly enough, seemed indisposed to encourage his advances. Then Barnabee began a series of petty persecutions, which had continued up to the day of the fight.

On the morning of that eventful day the Barnabee Boy appeared in the school-yard with a small go-cart. After running down on Johnny several times with this useful vehicle, he captured Johnny's cap, filled it with sand, and dragged it up and down the yard triumphantly in the go-cart. This made the General very angry, of course, and he took an early opportunity of kicking over the triumphal car, in doing which he kicked one of the wheels so far into space that it has not been seen since.

This brought matters to a crisis. The battle would have taken place then and there; but at that moment the school-bell rang, and the gladiators were obliged to give their attention to Smith's Speller. But a gloom hung over the morning's exercises, — a gloom that was not dispelled in the back row, when the Barnabee Boy stealthily held up to Johnny's vision a slate, whereon was inscribed this fearful message : —

Johnny got it "put down in writin'" this time!

After a hasty glance at the slate, the General went on with his studies composedly enough. Eleven o'clock came, and with it came recess, and with recess the inevitable battle.

Now I do not intend to describe the details of this brilliant action, for the sufficient reason that, though there were seven young gentlemen (connected with the Primary School) on the field as war correspondents, their accounts of the engagement are so contradictory as to be utterly worthless. On one point they all agree, — that the contest was sharp, short, and decisive. The truth is, the General is a quick, wiry, experienced old hero; and it did n't take him long to rout the Barnabee

Boy, who was in reality a coward, as all bullies and tyrants ever have been, and always will be.

I don't approve of boys fighting; I don't defend Johnny; but if the General wants an extra ration or two of preserved pear, he shall have it!

I am well aware that, socially speaking, Johnny is a Black Sheep. I know that I have brought him up badly, and that there is not an unmarried man or woman in the United States who would n't have brought him up very differently. It 's a great pity that the only people who know how to manage children never have any! At the same time, Johnny is not a black sheep all over. He has some white spots. His sins — if wiser folks had no greater! — are the result of too much animal life. They belong to his evanescent youth, and will pass away; but his honesty, his generosity, his bravery, belong to his character, and are enduring qualities. The quickly crowding years will tame him. A good large pane of glass, or a seductive bell-knob, ceases in time to have attractions for the most reckless spirit. And I am quite confident that Johnny will be a great statesman, or a valorous soldier, or, at all events, a good citizen, after he has got over being A Young Desperado.

CHARLIE MACHREE. — William J. Hoppin.

A BALLAD.

COME over, come over
 The river to me,
If ye are my laddie,
Bold Charlie Machree.

Here 's Mary McPherson
And Susy O'Linn,
Who say, ye 're faint-hearted,
And darena plunge in.

But the dark rolling water,
Though deep as the sea,
I know willna scare ye,
Nor keep ye frae me;

For stout is yer back,
And strong is yer arm,
And the heart in yer bosom
Is faithful and warm.

Come over, come over
The river to me,
If ye are my laddie,
Bold Charlie Machree!

I see him, I see him.
He's plunged in the tide,
His strong arms are dashing
The big waves aside.

O the dark rolling water
Shoots swift as the sea,
But blithe is the glance
Of his bonny blue e'e;

And his cheeks are like roses,
Twa buds on a bough;
Who says ye're faint-hearted,
My brave Charlie, now?

Ho, ho, foaming river,
Ye may roar as ye go,
But ye canna bear Charlie
To the dark loch below!

Come over, come over
The river to me,

My true-hearted laddie,
My Charlie Machree!

He 's sinking, he 's sinking,
O, what shall I do!
Strike out, Charlie, boldly,
Ten strokes and ye 're thro'.

He 's sinking, O Heaven!
Ne'er fear, man, ne'er fear;
I 've a kiss for ye, Charlie,
As soon as ye 're here!

He rises, I see him, —
Five strokes, Charlie, mair, —
He 's shaking the wet
From his bonny brown hair;

He conquers the current,
He gains on the sea, —
Ho, where is the swimmer
Like Charlie Machree!

Come over the river,
But once come to me,
And I 'll love ye forever,
Dear Charlie Machree.

He 's sinking, he 's gone, —
O God, it is I,
It is I, who have killed him —
Help, help! — he must die.

Help, help! — ah, he rises, —
Strike out and ye 're free.
Ho, bravely done, Charlie,
Once more now, for me!

Now cling to the rock,
Now gie us yer hand, —
Ye 're safe, dearest Charlie,
Ye 're safe on the land !

Come rest in my bosom,
If *there* ye can sleep ;
I canna speak to ye,
I only can weep.

Ye 've crossed the wild river,
Ye 've risked all for me,
And I 'll part 'frae ye never,
Dear Charlie Machree !

———————

OUR FOLKS. — ETHEL LYNN.

"HI ! Harry Holly ! Halt, — and tell
        A fellow just a thing or two ;
You 've had a furlough, been to see
    How all the folks in Jersey do.
It 's months ago since I was there, —
    I, and a bullet from Fair Oaks.
When you were home, — old comrade, say,
    Did you see any of our folks ?

"You did ?   Shake hands, — O, ain't I glad ;
    For if I do look grim and rough,
I 've got some feelin' —
                        People think
    A soldier's heart is mighty tough ;
But, Harry, when the bullets fly,
    And hot saltpetre flames and smokes,
While whole battalions lie afield,
    One 's apt to think about his folks.

B

"And so you saw them — when? and where?
  The old man — is he hearty yet?
And mother — does she fade at all?
  Or does she seem to pine and fret
For me? And Sis? — has she grown tall?
  And did you see her friend — you know
That Annie Moss —

               (How this pipe chokes!)
Where did you see her? — tell me, Hal,
  A lot of news about our folks.

"You saw them in the church — yet say;
  It's likely, for they're always there.
Not Sunday? no? A funeral? Who?
  Who, Harry? how you shake and stare!
All well, you say, and all were out.
  What ails you, Hal? Is this a hoax?
Why don't you tell me, like a man,
  What is the matter with our folks?"

"I said all well, old comrade, true;
  I say all well, for He knows best
Who takes the young ones in his arms,
  Before the sun goes to the west.
The axe-man Death deals right and left,
  And flowers fall as well as oaks;
And so —

          Fair Annie blooms no more!
And that's the matter with your folks.

"See, this long curl was kept for you;
  And this white blossom from her breast;
And here — your sister Bessie wrote
  A letter, telling all the rest.
Bear up, old friend."

              Nobody speaks;

Only the old camp-raven croaks,
   And soldiers whisper :
                        "Boys, be still ;
There's some bad news from Grainger's folks."

He turns his back — the only foe
   That ever saw it — on this grief,
And, as men will, keeps down the tears
   Kind Nature sends to Woe's relief.
Then answers he :
                "Ah, Hal, I 'll try ;
But in my throat there's something chokes,
Because, you see, I 've thought so long
   To count her in among our folks.

"I s'pose she must be happy now,
   But still I will keep thinking too,
I could have kept all trouble off,
   By being tender, kind, and true.
But maybe not.
            She's safe up there,
And when the Hand deals other strokes,
She 'll stand by Heaven's gate, I know,
   And wait to welcome in our folks."

———————•———————

WHAT WILL BECOME OF THE CHILDREN? —
JENNIE JUNE.

"MRS. NIPKIN, WEST TWENTY-FIFTH STREET, has rooms on the third story, which she is desirous of letting, with board, for the winter, or permanently, to families without children.   References exchanged."

What a delightful woman this Mrs. Nipkin must be! Wonder if she ever had any children of her own, or felt her heart beat a single throb quicker at hearing tiny lips lisp

Mother. Only " families " *without* children can enjoy the pleasure of her society, or the luxury of her third-story front, — *families* which consist of " Mr. So-and-so and lady," or " Mr. So-and-so, lady, and servant " ; as if there could be a " family " without children ; as if children did not constitute the very life and hope and joy of a family circle ; as if the pain and sorrow which they bring had not its sacred use in rooting out hard, vile, selfish, and worldly passions ; as if the love they providentially bring with them, as safeguard and protection, did not, in its pure devotion and holy disinterestedness, link us to the divine more nearly than any other inspiration or instinct of which human nature is susceptible.

"Families without children." Do you know, Mrs. Nipkin, how harshly that would grate on the ears of the lately bereaved mother, how coldly and selfishly on the ears of the newly made father ? Is it conceivable that you were ever a child yourself, or, if you were, that you were other than a snarling, passionate little vixen, who had managed to daguerreotype the horror with which she inspired others upon her own heart and brain, and in later years exhibited the deformed and misshapen product to the world in the form of a stupid, unwomanly advertisement.

And yet it cannot be that yours is a " family without children," Mrs. Nipkin, or you would know the " aching void," the desolation of heart, the dreary loneliness of life, the vacant spot in the soul, which only the sweet smiles and merry laughter of a child can fill ; and you would pine for the presence of so pure and innocent a spirit, in order that it might serve as a link between your selfish worldliness and the holy, spotless character and attributes of your Maker.

It would be interesting to know where you desire to go when you die, Mrs. Nipkin ; not certainly to the kingdom over which Christ reigns, for he called little children to him and blessed them, and said of *such* is the kingdom of heaven ; so it is evident you could not make your living *there*, Mrs.

Nipkin, by furnishing rooms and board to "families without children."

We pity you, poor Mrs. Nipkin. You do not know the sweet pleasure of pressing a soft, tiny face against your own, of watching its cunning looks and pretty ways, of hearing its first effort to pronounce your name, of guiding its trembling little feet in their essay to preserve the giddy balance on the uncertain floor, of listening to the first lisped prayer to God to "bess fader, moder, ittle boder, and sister, and all 'lations, and fens, and all the world," even Mrs. Nipkin, who would not admit a little child in the dismal precincts of her third story.

Good by, Mrs. Nipkin; we have no ill-feeling against you; we only hope Heaven will send you a dear little baby to soften your heart, and show you the difference between families with and "families without children."

———◆———

THE STARLING. — ROBERT BUCHANAN.

THE little lame tailor sat stitching and snarling, —
   Who in the world was the tailor's darling?
     To none of his kind
     Was he well inclined,
But he doted on Jack the starling.

For the bird had a tongue, and of words a store,
And his cage was hung just over the door,
And he saw the people and heard the roar, —
Folk coming and going evermore, —
And he looked at the tailor, — and swore.

From a country lad the tailor bought him, —
His training was bad, for tramps had taught him;
On alehouse benches his cage had been,
While louts and wenches made jests obscene, —

But he learned, no doubt, his oaths from fellows
Who travel about with kettle and bellows,
And three or four, the roundest by far
That ever he swore, were taught by a tar.

And the tailor heard. "We'll be friends!" said he,
"You're a clever bird, and our tastes agree, —
We both are old, and esteem life base,
The whole world cold, things out of place,
And we're lonely too, and full of care, —
So what can we do but swear?

"The devil take you, how you mutter! —
Yet there's much to make you swear and flutter.
You want the fresh air and the sunlight, lad,
And your prison there feels dreary and sad,
And here I frown in a prison dreary,
Hating the town, and feeling weary:
We're too confined, Jack, and we want to fly,
And you blame mankind, Jack, and so do I!
And then, again, by chance as it were,
We learned from men how to grumble and swear;
You let your throat by the scamps be guided,
And swore by rote, — all just as I did!
And without beseeching, relief is brought us, —
For we're turning the teaching on those who taught us!"

A haggard and ruffled old fellow was Jack,
With a grim face muffled in ragged black,
And his coat was rusty and never neat,
And his wings were dusty from the dismal street,
And he sidelong peered, with eyes of soot too,
And scowled and sneered, — and was lame of a foot too!
And he longed to go from whence he came; —
And the tailor, you know, was just the same.

All kinds of weather they felt confined,
And swore together at all mankind;

For their mirth was done, and they felt like brothers,
And the swearing of one meant no more than the other's ;
'T was just a way they had learned, you see, —
Each wanted to say only this, — " Woe 's me !
  I 'm a poor old fellow,
   And I 'm prisoned so,
  While the sun shines mellow,
  And the corn waves yellow,
   And the fresh winds blow, —
And the folk don't care if I live or die,
But I long for air, and I wish to fly ! "
Yet unable to utter it, and too wild to bear,
They could only mutter it, and swear.

Many a year they dwelt in the city,
In their prisons drear, and none felt pity,
And few were sparing of censure and coldness,
To hear them swearing with such plain boldness ;
But at last, by the Lord their noise was stopt, —
For down on his board the tailor dropt,
And they found him dead, and done with snarling,
And over his head still grumbled the starling ;
But when an old Jew claimed the goods of the tailor,
And with eye askew eyed the feathery railer,
And, with a frown at the dirt and rust,
Took the old cage down, in a shower of dust, —
Jack, with heart aching, felt life past bearing,
And, shivering, quaking, all hope forsaking, died swearing.

———◆———

THE RELIEF OF LUCKNOW. — ROBERT LOWELL.

O THAT last day in Lucknow fort !
  We knew that it was the last,
That the enemy's mines had crept surely in,
  And the end was coming fast.

To yield to that foe meant worse than death,
    And the men and we all worked on ;
It was one day more of smoke and roar,
    And then it would all be done.

There was one of us, a corporal's wife,
    A fair, young, gentle thing,
Wasted with fever and with siege,
    And her mind was wandering.

She lay on the ground, in her Scottish plaid,
    And I took her head on my knee ;
"When my father comes home frae the pleugh," she said,
    "O, please then waken me ! "

She slept like a child on her father's floor,
    In the flecking of woodbine shade,
When the house-dog sprawls by the half-open door,
    And the mother's wheel is stayed.

It was smoke and roar, and powder stench,
    And hopeless waiting for death ;
But the soldier's wife, like a full-tired child,
    Seemed scarce to draw her breath.

I sank to sleep, and I had my dream
    Of an English village lane,
And wall and garden — till a sudden scream
    Brought me back to the rear again.

There Jessie Brown stood listening,
    And then a broad gladness broke
All over her face, and she took my hand,
    And drew me near and spoke :

"The Highlanders ! O, dinna ye hear
    The slogan far awa' ?

The McGregors? Ah! I ken it weel;
  It is the grandest of them a'.

" God bless the bonny Highlanders!
  We 're saved! we 're saved!" she cried;
And fell on her knees, and thanks to God
  Poured forth, like a full flood-tide.

Along the battery line her cry
  Had fallen among the men;
And they started, for they were to die:
  Was life so near them, then?

They listened, for life; and the rattling fire
  Far off, and the far-off roar
Were all, — and the Colonel shook his head,
  And they turned to their guns once more.

Then Jessie said, " The slogan 's dune,
  But can ye no hear them noo?
The Campbells are comin'! It 's nae a dream;
  Our succors hae broken through!"

We heard the roar and the rattle afar,
  But the pipers we could not hear;
So the men plied their work of hopeless war,
  And knew that the end was near.

It was not long ere it must be heard, —
  A shrilling, ceaseless sound;
It was no noise of the strife afar,
  Or the sappers underground.

It was the pipe of the Highlanders,
  And now they played " Auld Lang Syne ";
It came to our men like the voice of God,
  And they shouted along the line.
    2

And they wept and shook each other's hands,
   And the women sobbed in a crowd;
And every one knelt down where we stood,
   And we all thanked God aloud.

That happy day, when we welcomed them in,
   Our men put Jessie first;
And the General took her hand, and cheers
   From the men like a volley burst.

And the pipers' ribbons and tartan streamed,
   Marching round and round our line;
And our joyful cheers were broken with tears,
   And the pipers played " Auld Lang Syne."

THE BELLS OF SHANDON. — Rev. Francis Mahony.

> Sabata pango;
> Funera plango;
> Solemnia clango.
> *Inscription on an old Bell.*

WITH deep affection
   And recollection,
I often think of
   Those Shandon Bells,
Whose sounds so wild would,
In the days of childhood,
Fling round my cradle
   Their magic spell.

On this I ponder
Where 'er I wander,
And thus grow fonder,
   Sweet Cork, of thee,
With thy bells of Shandon
That sound so grand on

The pleasant waters
　Of the river Lee.

I 've heard bells chiming
Full many a clime in,
Tolling sublime in
　Cathedral shrine,
While at a glib rate
Brass tongues would vibrate ;
But all their music
　Spoke naught like thine.

For memory, dwelling
On each proud swelling
Of thy belfry, knelling
　Its bold notes free,
Made the bells of Shandon
Sound far more grand on
The pleasant waters
　Of the river Lee.

I 've heard bells tolling
Old Adrian's Mole in,
Their thunder rolling
　From the Vatican,
And cymbals glorious
Swinging uproarious
In the gorgeous turrets
　Of Notre Dame.

But thy sounds were sweeter
Than the dome of Peter
Flings on the Tiber,
　Pealing solemnly.
O the bells of Shandon
Sound far more grand on
The pleasant waters
　Of the river Lee !

There 's a bell in Moscow ;
While on tower and kiosko
In Saint Sophia
    The Turkman gets,
And loud in air
Calls men to prayer
From the tapering summit
    Of tall minarets.

Such empty phantom
I freely grant them ;
But there 's an anthem
    More dear to me :
'T is the bells of Shandon,
That sound so grand on
The pleasant waters
    Of the river Lee.

THE LARK IN THE GOLD–FIELDS. — CHARLES READE.

PART FIRST. — THE LARK.

" TOM, I invite you to a walk."

" Well, George! a walk is a great temptation this beautiful day."

It was the month of January, in Australia ; a blazing-hot day was beginning to glow through the freshness of morning ; the sky was one cope of pure blue, and the southern air crept slowly up, its wings clogged with fragrance, and just tuned the trembling leaves, — no more.

" Is not this pleasant, Tom, — is n't it sweet ? "

" I believe you, George ! and what a shame to run down such a country as this ! There they come home, and tell you the flowers have no smell ; but they keep dark about the trees and bushes being haystacks of flowers. Snuff the air as we go ; it is a thousand English gardens in one. Look at all those tea-scrubs, each with a thousand blossoms on it as sweet as honey ; and the golden wattles on the other side, and all smelling like seven o'clock.

"Ay, lad ! it is very refreshing ; and it is Sunday, and we have got away from the wicked for an hour or two. But in England there would be a little white church out yonder, and a spire like an angel's forefinger pointing from the grass to heaven, and the lads in their clean frocks like snow, and the lasses in their white stockings and new shawls, and the old women in their scarlet cloaks and black bonnets, all going one road, and a tinkle-tinkle from the belfry, that would turn all these other sounds and colors and sweet smells holy as well as fair on the Sabbath morn.   Ah, England ! Ah ! "

"You will see her again, — no need to sigh.   Prejudice be hanged, this is a lovely land."

"So 't is, Tom, so 't is.   But I 'll tell you what puts me out a little bit ; — nothing is what it sets up for here.   If you see a ripe pear and go to eat it, it is a lump of hard wood.   Next comes a thing the very sight of which turns your stomach, and that is delicious, — a loquot, for instance. There, now, look at that magpie ; well, it is Australia, so that magpie is a crow and not a magpie at all.   Everything pretends to be some old friend or other of mine, and turns out a stranger.   Here is nothing but surprises and deceptions. The flowers make a point of not smelling, and the bushes, that nobody expects to smell or wants to smell, they smell lovely."

"What does it matter where the smell comes from, so that you get it ? "

"Why, Tom," replied George, opening his eyes, " it makes all the difference.   I like to smell a flower, — a flower is not complete without smell ; but I don't care if I never smell a bush till I die.   Then the birds, — they laugh and talk like Christians ; they make me split my sides, bless their little hearts ! but they won't chirrup.   It is Australia ! where everything is inside-out and topsy-turvy.   The animals have four legs, so they jump on two. Ten foot square of rock lets for a pound a month ; ten acres of grass for a shilling a year. Roasted at Christmas, shiver o' cold on midsummer-day. The lakes are grass, and the rivers turn their backs on the sea and run into the heart of the land ; and the men would stand on their heads, but I have taken a thought, and I 've found out why they don't."

" Why ? "

" Because, if they did, their heads would point the same way a man's head points in England."

Tom Robinson laughed, and told George he admired the country for these very traits. " Novelty for me against the world. Who 'd come twelve thousand miles to see nothing we could n't see at home ? One does not want the same story always. Where are we going, George ? "

" O, not much farther, — only about twelve miles from the camp."

" Where to ? "

" To a farmer I know. I am going to show you a lark, Tom," said George, and his eyes beamed benevolence on his comrade.

Robinson stopped dead short. " George," said he, " no ! don't let us. I would rather stay at home and read my book. You can go into temptation and come out pure; I can't. I am one of those that if I go into a puddle up to my shoe, I must splash up to my middle."

" What has that to do with it ? "

" You 're proposing to me to go for a lark on the Sabbath day."

" Why, Tom, am I the man to tempt you to do evil ? " asked George, hurt.

" Why, no ! but you proposed a lark."

" Ay, but an innocent one, — one more likely to lift your heart on high than to give you ill thoughts."

" Well, this is a riddle ! " and Robinson was intensely puzzled.

" Carlo ! " cried George, suddenly, " come here ; I will not have you hunting and tormenting those Kangaroo rats to-day. Let us all be at peace, if *you* please.   Come, to heel."

The friends strode briskly on, and a little after eleven o'clock they came upon a small squatter's house and premises.   " Here we are," said George, and his eyes glittered with innocent delight.

The house was thatched and whitewashed, and English was written on it and on every foot of ground around it.   A furze-bush had been planted by the door.   Vertical oak palings were the fence, with a five-barred gate in the middle of them. From the little plantation all the magnificent trees and shrubs of Australia had been excluded with amazing resolution and consistency, and oak and ash reigned, safe from over-towering rivals.   They passed to the back of the house, and there George's countenance fell a little, for on the oval grass-plot and gravel-walk he found from thirty to forty rough fellows most of them diggers.

" Ah, well," said he, on reflection, " we could not expect to have it all to ourselves, and, indeed, it would be a sin to wish it, you know.   Now, Tom, come this way ; here it is, here it is, — there."   Tom looked up, and in a gigantic cage was a light-brown bird.

He was utterly confounded.   " What ! is it this we came twelve miles to see ? "

" Ay ! and twice twelve would n't have been much to me."

" Well, and now where is the lark you talked of ? "

" This is it."

" This ?   This is a bird."

" Well, and is n't a lark a bird ? "

" Oh ! ah, I see !   Ha, ha ! ha, ha ! "

Robinson's merriment was interrupted by a harsh remonstrance from several of the diggers, who were all from the other end of the camp.

" Hold your cackle ! " cried one ; " he is going to sing." And the whole party had their eyes turned with expectation towards the bird.

Like most singers, he˙ kept them waiting a bit. But at last, just at noon, when the mistress of the house had warranted him to sing, the little feathered exile began as it were to tune his pipes. The savage men gathered round the cage that moment, and amidst a dead stillness the bird uttered some very uncertain chirps ; but after a while he seemed to revive his memories, and call his ancient cadences back to him one by one, and string them *sotto voce.*

And then the same sun that had warmed his little heart at home came glowing down on him here, and he gave music back for it more and more, till at last, amidst breathless silence and glistening eyes of the rough diggers hanging on his voice, outburst in that distant land his English song.

It swelled his little throat, and gushed from him with thrilling force and plenty ; and every time he checked his song to think of its theme, — the green meadows, the quiet-stealing streams, the clover he first soared from, and the spring he loved so well, — a loud sigh from many a rough bosom, many a wild and wicked heart, told how tight the listeners had held their breath to hear him. And when he swelled with song again, and poured with all his soul the green meadows, the quiet brooks, the honey-clover, and the English spring, the rugged mouths opened and so stayed, and the shaggy lips trembled, and more than one tear trickled from fierce, unbridled hearts down bronzed and rugged cheeks.

Sweet home !

And these shaggy men, full of oaths and strife and cupidity, had once been white-headed boys, and most of them had strolled about the English fields with little sisters and little brothers, and seen the lark rise and heard him sing this very song. The little playmates lay in the churchyard, and they were full of oaths and drink, and lusts and remorses, but no note was changed in this immortal song.

And so, for a moment or two, years of vice rolled away like a dark cloud from the memory, and the past shone out in the song-shine : they came back bright as the immortal notes that lighted them, — those faded pictures and those fleeted days ; the cottage, the old mother's when he left her without one grain of sorrow, the village church and its simple chimes, — ding-dong-bell, ding-dong-bell, ding-dong-bell ; the clover-field hard by, in which he lay and gambolled while the lark praised God overhead ; the chubby playmates that never grew to be wicked ; the sweet, sweet hours of youth, innocence, and home.

George stayed till the lark gave up singing altogether, and then he said, " Now I am off. I don't want to hear bad language after that ; let us take the lark's chirp home to bed with us " ; and they made off. And true it was, — the pure strains dwelt upon their spirits, and refreshed and purified these sojourners in a godless place. Meeting these two figures on Sunday afternoon, armed each with a double-barrelled gun and a revolver, you would never have guessed what gentle thoughts possessed them wholly. They talked less than they did coming, but they felt so quiet and happy.

" The pretty bird," purred George (seeing him by the ear), " I feel after him — there — as if I had just come out o' church."

" So do I, George ; and I think his song must be a psalm, if we knew all."

" That it is, for Heaven taught it him. We must try and keep all this in our hearts when we get among the broken bottles and foul language and gold," says George. " How sweet it smells, — sweeter than before ! "

" That is because it is afternoon."

" Yes ! or along of the music ; that tune was a breath from home that makes everything please me now. This is the first Sunday that has looked and smelled and sounded like Sunday."

" George, it is hard to believe the world is wicked ; everything seems good and gentle, and at peace with heaven and earth."

2 *   c

THE LARK IN THE GOLD–FIELDS.

PART SECOND. — CARLO.

A JET of smoke issued from the bush, followed by the report of a gun, and Carlo, who had taken advantage of George's revery to slip on ahead, gave a sharp howl, and spun round upon all fours.

"The scoundrels!" shrieked Robinson. And in a moment his gun was at his shoulder, and he fired both barrels slap into the spot whence the smoke had issued.

Both the men dashed up and sprang into the bush, revolver in hand, but ere they could reach it the dastard had run; and the scrub was so thick, pursuit was hopeless. The men returned, full of anxiety for Carlo.

The dog met them, his tail between his legs; but at sight of George he wagged his tail, and came to him and licked George's hand, and walked on with them, licking George's hand every now and then.

"Look, Tom! he is as sensible as a Christian. He knows the shot was meant for him, though they did n't hit him."

By this time the men had got out of the wood and pursued their road, but not with tranquil hearts. Sunday ended with the noise of that coward's gun. They walked on hastily, guns ready, fingers on the trigger at war. Suddenly Robinson looked back and stopped, and drew George's attention to Carlo. He was standing with all his four legs wide apart, like a statue. George called him; he came directly and was for licking George's hand, but George pulled him about and examined him all over.

"I wish they may not have hurt him, after all, the butchers; — they have, too! See here, Tom! here is one streak of blood on his belly; nothing to hurt, though, I do hope. Never mind, Carlo!" cried George; "it is only a single shot, by what I can see. 'T is n't like when Will put the whole charge into you, rabbit-shooting, — is it, Carlo? No, says he; we don't care for this, — do we, Carlo?" cried George, rather boisterously.

" Make him go into that pool there," said Robinson ; " then he won't have a fever."

" I will. Here, — cess ! cess ! " He threw a stone into the pool of water that lay a little off the road, and Carlo went in after it without hesitation, though not with his usual alacrity. After an unsuccessful attempt to recover the stone, he swam out lower down, and came back to the men, and wagged his tail slowly and walked behind George.

They went on.

" Tom," said George, after a pause, " I don't like it."

" Don't like what ? "

" He never so much as shook himself."

" What of that ? He did shake himself, I should say."

" Not as should be. Who ever saw a dog come out of the water and not shake himself ? Carlo ! hie, Carlo ! " and George threw a stone along the ground. Carlo trotted after it, but his limbs seemed to work stiffly ; the stone spun round a sharp corner in the road, — the dog followed it.

" He will do now," said Robinson.

They walked briskly on. On turning the corner they found Carlo sitting up and shivering, with the stone between his paws.

" We must not let him sit," said Tom ; " keep his blood warm. I don't think we ought to have sent him into the water."

" I don't know," muttered George, gloomily. " Carlo ! " cried he, cheerfully, " don't you be down-hearted ; there is nothing so bad as faint-heartedness for man or beast. Come, up and away ye go, and shake it off like a man ! "

Carlo got up and wagged his tail in answer, but he evidently was in no mood for running ; he followed languidly behind.

"Let us get home," said Robinson ; " there is an old pal of mine that is clever about dogs ; he will cut the shot out, if there is one in him, and give him some physic."

The men strode on, and each, to hide his own uneasiness, chatted about other matters ; but, all of a sudden, Robinson cried out, "Why, where *is* the dog?" They looked back, and there was Carlo some sixty yards in the rear, but he was not sitting this time, — he was lying on his belly.

"O, this is a bad job!" cried George. The men ran up, in real alarm; Carlo wagged his tail as soon as they came near him, but he did not get up.

"Carlo!" cried George, despairingly, "you would n't do it, you could n't think to do it! O my dear Carlo! it is only making up your mind to live; keep up your heart, old fellow, — don't go to leave us alone among these villains. My poor, dear, darling dog! O no! he won't live, — he can't live! See how dull his poor, dear eye is getting. O Carlo, Carlo!"

At the sound of his master's voice in such distress, Carlo whimpered, and then he began to stretch his limbs out. At the sight of this, Robinson cried hastily, —

"Rub him, George! We did wrong to send him into the water."

George rubbed him all over. After rubbing him awhile, he said, —

"Tom, I seem to feel him turning to dead under my hand."

George's hand, in rubbing Carlo, came round to the dog's shoulder; then Carlo turned his head, and for the third time began to lick George's hand. George let him lick his hand and gave up rubbing, for where was the use? Carlo never left off licking his hand, but feebly, very feebly, — more and more feebly.

Presently, even while he was licking his hand, the poor thing's teeth closed slowly on his loving tongue, and then he could lick the beloved hand no more. Breath fluttered about his body a little while longer; but in truth he had ceased to live when he could no longer kiss his master's hand.

The poor single-hearted soul was gone.

George took it up tenderly in his arms. Robinson made an effort to console him.

"Don't speak to me, Tom, if you please," said George,

gently but quickly. He carried it home silently, and laid it silently down in a corner of the tent.

Robinson made a fire and put some steaks on, and made George slice some potatoes, to keep him from looking always at what so little while since was Carlo. Then they sat down silently and gloomily to dinner; it was long past their usual hour, and they were working men. Until we die we dine, come what may. The first part of the meal passed in deep silence. Then Robinson said sadly, —

"We will go home, George. I fall into your wishes now. Gold can't pay for what we go through in this hellish place."

"Not it," replied George, quietly.

"We are surrounded by enemies."

"Seems so," was the reply, in a very languid tone.

"Labor by day and danger by night."

"Ay!" but in a most indifferent tone.

"And no Sabbath for us two."

"No."

"I'll do my best for you, and when we have five hundred pounds, you shall go home."

"Thank you. He was a good friend to us that lies there under my coat; he used to lie over it, and then who dare touch it?"

"No! but don't give way to that, George; do eat a bit, — it will do you good."

"I will, Tom, — I will. Thank you kindly. Ah! now I see why he came to me and kept licking my hand so the moment he got the hurt. He had more sense than we had, — he knew he and I were to part that hour; and I tormented his last minutes sending him into the water and after stones, when the poor thing wanted to be bidding me good by all the while. O dear! O dear!" and George pushed his scarce-tasted dinner from him, and left the tent hurriedly, his eyes thick with tears.

Thus ended this human day so happily begun; and thus the poor dog paid the price of fidelity this Sunday afternoon.

Siste viator iter and part with poor Carlo, for whom there are now no more little passing troubles, no more little simple joys. His duty is performed, his race is run; peace be to him, and to all simple and devoted hearts! Ah me! how rare they are among men!

THE FACE AGAINST THE PANE. — T. B. ALDRICH.

MABEL, little Mabel,
　　With face against the pane,
Looks out across the night
And sees the Beacon Light
　　A-trembling in the rain.
She hears the sea-birds screech,
And the breakers on the beach
　　Making moan, making moan.
And the wind about the eaves
Of the cottage sobs and grieves;
　　And the willow-tree is blown
　　　　To and fro, to and fro,
Till it seems like some old crone
Standing out there all alone,
　　　　With her woe!
Wringing, as she stands,
Her gaunt and palsied hands,
While Mabel, timid Mabel,
　　With face against the pane,
Looks out across the night,
And sees the Beacon Light
　　A-trembling in the rain.

Set the table, maiden Mabel,
　　And make the cabin warm;
Your little fisher-lover
　　Is out there in the storm,
And your father — you are weeping!

O Mabel, timid Mabel,
  Go, spread the supper-table,
And set the tea a steeping.
Your lover's heart is brave,
  His boat is staunch and tight;
And your father knows the perilous reef
  That makes the water white.
— But Mabel, Mabel darling,
  With face against the pane,
Looks out across the night
  At the Beacon in the rain.

The heavens are veined with fire !
  And the thunder, how it rolls !
In the lullings of the storm
  The solemn church-bell tolls
  For lost souls !
But no sexton sounds the knell
  In that belfry old and high ;
Unseen fingers sway the bell
  As the wind goes tearing by !
How it tolls for the souls
  Of the sailors on the sea !
God pity them, God pity them,
  Wherever they may be !
God pity wives and sweethearts
  Who wait and wait in vain !
And pity little Mabel,
  With face against the pane.

A boom ! — the Lighthouse gun !
  (How its echo rolls and rolls !)
'T is to warn the home-bound ships
  Off the shoals !
See ! a rocket cleaves the sky
  From the Fort, — a shaft of light !
See ! it fades, and, fading, leaves

Golden furrows on the night !
What made Mabel's cheek so pale ?
  What made Mabel's lips so white ?
Did she see the helpless sail
  That, tossing here and there,
  Like a feather in the air,
Went down and out of sight ?
Down, down, and out of sight !
O, watch no more, no more,
  With face against the pane ;
You cannot see the men that drown
  By the Beacon in the rain !

From a shoal of richest rubies
  Breaks the morning clear and cold ;
And the angel on the village spire,
  Frost-touched, is bright as gold.
Four ancient fishermen,
  In the pleasant autumn air,
Come toiling up the sands,
With something in their hands, —
Two bodies stark and white,
Ah, so ghastly in the light,
  With sea-weed in their hair !
O ancient fishermen,
  Go up to yonder cot !
You 'll find a little child,
  With face against the pane,
Who looks toward the beach,
  And, looking, sees it not.
She will never watch again !
  Never watch and weep at night !
For those pretty, saintly eyes
Look beyond the stormy skies,
  And they see the Beacon Light.

THE LOVER AND BIRDS. — Wm. Allingham.

WITHIN a budding grove,
    In April's ear sang every bird his best;
But not a song to pleasure my unrest,
Or touch the tears unwept of bitter love.
Some spake, methought, with pity; some as if in jest.
        To every word
        Of every bird
I listened, and replied as it behove.

    Screamed Chaffinch, "Sweet, sweet, sweet!
O, bring my pretty love to meet me here!"
"Chaffinch," quoth I, "be dumb awhile, in fear
Thy darling prove no better than a cheat;
And never come, or fly when wintry days appear."
        Yet from a twig,
        With voice so big,
The little fowl his utterance did repeat.

    Then I: "The man forlorn
Hears earth send up a foolish noise aloft."
"And what 'll *he* do? what 'll *he* do?" scoffed
The Blackbird, standing in an ancient thorn,
Then spread his sooty wings and flitted to the croft,
        With cackling laugh:
        Whom I, being half
Enraged, called after, giving back his scorn.

    Worse mocked the Thrush: "Die! die!
O, could he do it? could he do it? Nay!
Be quick! be quick! Here, here, here!" went his lay.
"Take heed! take heed!" Then, "Why? why? why?
        why? why?
See-ee now! see-ee now!" he drawled. "Back! back! back!
        R-r-r-run away!"

O Thrush, be still !
Or, at thy will,
Seek some less sad interpreter than I !

"Air, air ! blue air and white !
Whither I flee, whither, O whither, O whither I flee !"
Thus the Lark hurried, mounting from the lea.
"Hills, countries, many waters glittering bright,
Whither I see, whither I see ! deeper, deeper, deeper ! whither
I see, see, see !"
"Gay Lark," I said,
"The song that's bred
In happy nest may well to heaven make flight."

"There's something, something sad,
I half remember," piped a broken strain.
Well sung, sweet Robin !   Robin sung again :
"Spring's opening cheerily, cheerily ! be we glad !"
Which moved, I wist not why, me melancholy mad,
Till now, grown meek,
With wetted cheek,
Most comforting and gentle thoughts I had.

THE HIGH TIDE. — Jean Ingelow.

THE old mayor climbed the belfry tower,
The ringers ran by two, by three ;
"Pull, if ye never pulled before,
Good ringers ; pull your best," quoth he.
"Play uppe, play uppe, O Boston bells !
Ply all your changes, all your swells, —
Play uppe ' The Brides of Enderby !'"

I sat and spun within the doore ;
My thread brake off, I raised myne eyes ;

The level sun, like ruddy ore,
    Lay sinking in the barren skies;
And dark against day's golden death
She moved where Lindis wandereth, —
My sonne's faire wife, Elizabeth.

"Cusha! Cusha! Cusha!" calling
Ere the early dews were falling,
Farre away I heard her song.
"Cusha! Cusha!" all along
Where the reedy Lindis floweth,
      Floweth, floweth;
From the meads where melick groweth,
Faintly came her milking-song.

"Cusha! Cusha! Cusha!" calling,
"For the dews will soone be falling;
Leave your meadow grasses mellow,
      Mellow, mellow;
Quit your cowslips, cowslips yellow;
Come uppe, Whitefoot; come uppe, Lightfoot;
Quit the stalks of parsley hollow,
      Hollow, hollow;
Come uppe, Jetty, rise and follow, —
From the clovers lift your head;
Come uppe, Whitefoot; come uppe, Lightfoot;
    Come uppe, Jetty, rise and follow,
Jetty, to the milking shed."

Alle fresh the level pasture lay,
And not a shadowe mote be seene,
Save where, full fyve good miles away,
    The steeple towered from out the greene;
And lo! the great bell farre and wide
Was heard in all the country-side,
That Saturday at eventide.

I looked without, and lo ! my sonne
   Came riding downe with might and main ;
He raised a shout as he drew on,
   Till all the welkin rang again,
" Elizabeth ! Elizabeth ! "
(A sweeter woman ne 'er drew breath
Than my sonne's wife, Elizabeth.)

" The olde sea-wall (he cried) is downe ;
   The rising tide comes on apace,
And boats adrift in yonder towne
   Go sailing uppe the market-place."
He shook as one that looks on death :
" God save you, mother ! " straight he saith ;
" Where is my wife, Elizabeth ? "

" Good sonne, where Lindis winds away,
   With her two bairns I marked her long ;
And ere yon bells beganne to play,
   Afar I heard her milking-song."
He looked across the grassy lea,
To right, to left, — " Ho, Enderby ! "
They rang " The Brides of Enderby ! "

With that he cried and beat his breast ;
   For lo ! along the river's bed
A mighty eygre reared his crest,
   And uppe the Lindis raging sped.
It swept with thunderous noises loud, —
Shaped like a curling snow-white cloud,
Or like a demon in a shroud.

So farre, so fast the eygre drave,
   The heart had hardly time to beat
Before a shallow, seething wave
   Sobbed in the grasses at our feet :
The feet had hardly time to flee

Before it brake against the knee,
And all the world was in the sea.

Upon the roofe we sate that night,
   The noise of bells went sweeping by ;
I marked the lofty beacon-light
   Stream from the church-tower, red and high, —
A lurid mark and dread to see ;
And awesome bells they were to mee,
That in the dark rang " Enderby."

They rang the sailor lads to guide
   From roofe to roofe who fearless rowed ;
And I — my sonne was at my side,
   And yet the ruddy beacon glowed ;
And yet he moaned beneath his breath,
" O, come in life, or come in death !
O, lost ! my love, Elizabeth ! "

And didst thou visit him no more ?
   Thou didst, thou didst, my daughter deare ;
The waters laid thee at his doore,
   Ere yet the early dawn was clear.
Thy pretty bairns in fast embrace,
The lifted sun shone on thy face,
Downe drifted to thy dwelling-place.

That flow strewed wrecks about the grass,
   That ebbe swept out the flocks to sea ;
A fatal ebbe and flow, alas !
   To many more than myne and me :
But each will mourn his own (she saith),
And sweeter woman ne'er drew breath
Than my sonne's wife, Elizabeth.

I shall never hear her more
By the reedy Lindis shore,
" Cusha ! Cusha ! Cusha ! " calling,

Ere the early dews be falling ;
I shall never hear her song,
" Cusha ! Cusha ! " all along
Where the sunny Lindis floweth,
      Goeth, floweth ;
From the meads where melick groweth,
Where the water, winding down,
Onward floweth to the town.

I shall never see her more
Where the reeds and rushes quiver,
      Shiver, quiver ;
Stand beside the sobbing river,
Sobbing, throbbing, in its falling
To the sandy, lonesome shore.

Abridged.

SANDALPHON, THE ANGEL OF PRAYER.—
H. W. LONGFELLOW.

HAVE you read in the Talmud of old,
  In the legends the Rabbins have told,
   Of the limitless realms of the air ?
Have you read it, — the marvellous story
Of Sandalphon, the Angel of Glory,
   Sandalphon, the Angel of Prayer ?

How, erect at the outermost gates
Of the City Celestial he waits,
   With his feet on the ladder of light,
That, crowded with angels unnumbered,
By Jacob was seen, as he slumbered,
   Alone in the desert at night ?

The Angels of Wind and of Fire
Chant only one hymn, and expire

With the song's irresistible stress, —
Expire in their rapture and wonder,
As harp-strings are broken asunder,
   By the music they throb to express.

But serene in the rapturous throng,
Unmoved by the rush of the song,
   With eyes unimpassioned and slow,
Among the dead angels, the deathless
Sandalphon stands listening, breathless,
   To sounds that ascend from below, —

From the spirits on earth that adore,
From the souls that entreat and implore,
   In the frenzy and passion of prayer, —
From the hearts that are broken with losses,
And weary with dragging the crosses
   Too heavy for mortals to bear.

And he gathers the prayers as he stands,
And they change into flowers in his hands,
   Into garlands of purple and red ;
And beneath the great arch of the portal,
Through the streets of the City Immortal,
   Is wafted the fragrance they shed.

It is but a legend, I know, —
A fable, a phantom, a show
   Of the ancient Rabbinical lore ;
Yet the old mediæval tradition,
The beautiful strange superstition,
   But haunts me and holds me the more.

When I look from my window at night,
And the welkin above is all white,
   All throbbing and panting with stars ; —
Among them majestic is standing

Sandalphon the angel, expanding
His pinions in nebulous bars.

And the legend, I feel, is a part
Of the hunger and thirst of the heart,
  The frenzy and fire of the brain,
That grasps at the fruitage forbidden,
The golden pomegranates of Eden,
  To quiet its fever and pain.

———◆———

'BIAH CATHCART'S PROPOSAL. — H. W. BEECHER.

THEY were walking silently and gravely home one Sunday afternoon, under the tall elms that lined the street for half a mile. Neither had spoken. There had been some little parish quarrel, and on that afternoon the text was, " A new commandment I write unto you, that ye love one another." But after the sermon was done the text was the best part of it. Some one said that Parson Marsh's sermons were like the meeting-house, — the steeple was the only thing that folks could see after they got home.

They walked slowly, without a word. Once or twice 'Biah essayed to speak, but was still silent. He plucked a flower from between the pickets of the fence, and unconsciously pulled it to pieces, as, with a troubled face, he glanced at Rachel, and then, as fearing she would catch his eye, he looked at the trees, at the clouds, at the grass, at everything, and saw nothing,— nothing but Rachel. The most solemn hour of human experience is not that of Death, but of Life,— when the heart is born again, and from a natural heart becomes a heart of Love ! What wonder that it is a silent hour and perplexed ?

Is the soul confused ? Why not, when the divine Spirit, rolling clear across the aerial ocean, breaks upon the heart's shore with all the mystery of heaven ? Is it strange that

uncertain lights dim the eye, if above the head of him that
truly loves hover clouds of saintly spirits ? Why should not
the tongue stammer and refuse its accustomed offices, when
all the world — skies, trees, plains, hills, atmosphere, and the
solid earth — springs forth in new colors, with strange mean-
ings, and seems to chant for the soul the glory of that mystic
Law with which God has bound to himself his infinite realm,
— the law of Love ? Then, for the first time, when one so
loves that love is sacrifice, death to self, resurrection, and
glory, is man brought into harmony with the whole universe ;
and, like him who beheld the seventh heaven, hears things
unlawful to be uttered.

The great elm-trees sighed as the fitful breeze swept
their tops. The soft shadows flitted back and forth beneath
the walker's feet, fell upon them in light and dark, ran over
the ground, quivered and shook, until sober Cathcart thought
that his heart was throwing its shifting network of hope and
fear along the ground before him !

How strangely his voice sounded to him, as, at length, all
his emotions could only say, " Rachel,— how did you like the
sermon ? "

Quietly she answered, —

" I liked the text."

" ' A new commandment I write unto you, that ye love one
another.' Rachel, will you help me keep it ? "

At first she looked down and lost a little color; then, raising her face, she turned upon him her large eyes, with a look
both clear and tender. It was as if some painful restraint
had given way, and her eyes blossomed into full beauty.

Not another word was spoken. They walked home hand
in hand. He neither smiled nor exulted. He saw neither the
trees, nor the long level rays of sunlight that were slanting
across the fields. His soul was overshadowed with a cloud as
if God were drawing near. He had never felt so solemn.
This woman's life had been intrusted to him !

Long years, — the whole length of life, — the eternal years
beyond, seemed in an indistinct way to rise up in his imagi-

3   D

nation. All that he could say, as he left her at the door, was, —

" Rachel, this is forever — forever."

She again said nothing, but turned to him with a clear and open face, in which joy and trust wrought beauty. It seemed to him as if a light fell upon him from her eyes. There was a look that descended and covered him as with an atmosphere ; and all the way home he was as one walking in a luminous cloud. He had never felt such personal dignity as now. He that wins such love is crowned, and may call himself king. He did not feel the earth under his feet. As he drew near his lodgings, the sun went down. The children began to pour forth, no longer restrained. Abiah turned to his evening chores. No animal that night but had reason to bless him. The children found him unusually good and tender. And Aunt Keziah said to her sister, —

" Abiah 's been goin' to meetin' very regular for some weeks, and I should n't wonder, by the way he looks, if he had got a hope. I trust he ain't deceivin' himself."

He had a hope, and he was not deceived ; for in a few months, at the close of the service one Sunday morning, the minister read from the pulpit : " Marriage is intended between Abiah Cathcart and Rachel Liscomb, both of this town, and this is the first publishing of the banns."

LANGLEY LANE. — Robert Buchanan.

IN all the land, range up, range down,
   Is there ever a place so pleasant and sweet
As Langley Lane in London town,
   Just out of the bustle of square and street ?
Little white cottages all in a row,
Gardens where bachelor's-buttons grow,
   Swallows'-nests in roof and wall,
And up above the still blue sky

Where the woolly white clouds go sailing by, —
   I seem to be able to see it all !

For now, in summer, I take my chair,
   And sit outside in the sun, and hear
The distant murmur of street and square,
   And the swallows and sparrows chirping near ;
And Fanny, who lives just over the way,
Comes running many a time each day,
   With her little hand's touch so warm and kind,
And I smile and talk, with the sun on my cheek,
And the little live hand seems to stir and speak, —
   For Fanny is dumb and I am blind.

Fanny is sweet thirteen, and she
   Has fine black ringlets and dark eyes clear,
And I am older by summers three, —
   Why should we hold one another so dear ?
Because she cannot utter a word,
Nor hear the music of bee or bird,
   The water-cart's splash or the milkman's call !
Because I have never seen the sky,
Nor the little singers that hum and fly,
   Yet know she is gazing upon them all !

For the sun is shining, the swallows fly,
   The bees and the blue-flies murmur low,
And I hear the water-cart go by,
   With its cool splash-splash down the dusty row ;
And the little one close at my side perceives
Mine eyes upraised to the cottage eaves,
   Where birds are chirping in summer shine,
And I hear, though I cannot look, and she,
Though she cannot hear, can the singers see, —
   And the little soft fingers flutter in mine !

Hath not the dear little hand a tongue,
   When it stirs on my palm for the love of me ?

Do I not know she is pretty and young?
   Hath not my soul an eye to see?
'T is pleasure to make one's bosom stir,
To wonder how things appear to her,
   That I only hear as they pass around;
And as long as we sit in the music and light,
She is happy to keep God's sight,
   And *I* am happy to keep God's sound.

Why, I know her face, though I am blind, —
   I made it of music long ago, —
Strange large eyes and dark hair twined
   Round the pensive light of a brow of snow;
And when I sit by my little one,
And hold her hand and talk in the sun,
   And hear the music that haunts the place,
I know she is raising her eyes to me,
And guessing how gentle my voice must be,
   And *seeing* the music upon my face.

Though, if ever the Lord should grant me a prayer,
   (I know the fancy is only vain,)
I should pray just once, when the weather is fair,
   To see little Fanny and Langley Lane;
Though Fanny, perhaps, would pray to hear
The voice of the friend that she holds so dear,
   The song of the birds, the hum of the street.
It is better to be as we have been, —
Each keeping up something, unheard, unseen,
   To make God's heaven more strange and sweet!

Ah, life is pleasant in Langley Lane!
   There is always something sweet to hear!
Chirping of birds or patter of rain!
   And Fanny, my little one, always near!
And though I am weakly and can't live long,
And Fanny my darling is far from strong,

And though we can never married be,
What then, since we hold one another so dear,
For the sake of the pleasure one cannot hear,
And the pleasure that only one can see?

AT THE GRINDSTONE; OR, A HOME VIEW OF THE BATTLE–FIELD. — ROBERT BUCHANAN.

GRIND, Billie, grind! And so the war's begun?
Flash, bayonets! cannons, call! dash down their pride!
If I was younger, I would grip a gun,
And die a-field, as better men have died;
I'd face three Frenchmen, lad, and feel no fear,
With this old knife that we are grinding here!

Why, I'm a kind of radical, and saw
Some fighting in the riots long ago;
But, Lord, am I the sort of chap to draw
A sword against old Mother England? No!
England for me, with all her errors, still, —
I hate them foreigners and always will!

There was our Johnnie, now! — as kind a lad
As ever grew in England; fresh and fair!
To see him in his regimentals clad,
With honest, rosy cheeks and yellow hair,
Was something, Billy, worthy to be seen;
But Johnnie's gone, — murdered at seventeen.

None of your fighting sort, but mild and shy,
Soft-hearted, full of wench-like tenderness,
Without the heart, indeed, to hurt a fly,
But fond, you see, of music and of dress;
We could not hold him in, dear lad, and so
He heard the fife, and would a-soldiering go.

And it was pleasant for a time to see
   Johnnie, our little drummer, go and come,
Holding his head up, proudly, merrily,
   Happy with coat o' red, and hat, and drum.
That was in peace ; but war broke out one day,
And Johnnie's regiment was called away.

He went ! he went ! he could not choose but go !
   And me and my old woman wearied here :
We knew that men must fall and blood must flow,
   But still had many a thought to lighten fear :
Those Russian men could never be so bad
As kill or harm so very small a lad, —

A lad that should have been at school or play !
   A little baby in a coat o' red !
What ! touch our Johnnie ? No, not they !
   Why, they had little ones themselves, we said.
Billie, the little lad we loved so well
Was slain among the very first that fell !

Mark that ! A bullet from a murderous gun
   Singled him out, and struck him to the brain ;
He fell, — our boy, our joy, our little one, —
   His bright hair dark with many a stain,
His clammy hands clenched tight, his eyes o' brown
Looking through smoke and fire to Stamford town.

What ! call that war ! to slay a helpless child
   Who never, never hurt a living thing !
Butchered, for what we know, too, while he smiled
   On the strange light all round him, wondering !
Grind, Billie, grind ! call, cannons ! bayonets thrust !
Would we were grinding all our foes to dust !

Bah ! Frenchman, Turk, or Russian, — all alike !
   All eaten up with slaughter, sin, and slavery !

Little care they what harmless hearts they strike, —
  They murder little lads, and call it bravery !
Down with them when they cross our path, I say ;
Give me old England's manhood and fair play !

THE PILOT. — J. B. Gough.

JOHN MAYNARD was well known in the lake district as a God-fearing, honest, and intelligent man. He was pilot on a steamboat from Detroit to Buffalo. One summer afternoon — at that time those steamers seldom carried boats —smoke was seen ascending from below, and the captain called out, " Simpson, go below and see what the matter is down there."

Simpson came up with his face pale as ashes, and said, " Captain, the ship is on fire."

Then " Fire ! fire ! fire ! " on shipboard.

All hands were called up, buckets of water were dashed on the fire, but in vain. There were large quantities of rosin and tar on board, and it was found useless to attempt to save the ship. The passengers rushed forward and inquired of the pilot, " How far are we from Buffalo ? "

" Seven miles."

" How long before we can reach there ? "

" Three quarters of an hour, at our present rate of steam."

" Is there any danger ? "

" Danger ! Here, see the smoke bursting out, — go forward if you would save your lives."

Passengers and crew — men, women, and children — crowded the forward part of the ship. John Maynard stood at the helm. The flames burst forth in a sheet of fire ; clouds of smoke arose.

The captain cried out through his trumpet, " John Maynard ! "

" Ay, ay, sir ! "

" Are you at the helm ?"

" Ay, ay, sir ! "

" How does she head ? "

" Southeast by east, sir."

" Head her southeast, and run her on shore," said the captain. Nearer, nearer, yet nearer, she approached the shore. Again the captain cried out, " John Maynard ! "

The response came feebly this time, " Ay, ay, sir ! "

" Can you hold on five minutes longer, John ? " he said.

" By God's help, I will."

The old man's hair was scorched from the scalp, one hand disabled ; — his knee upon the stanchion, and his teeth set, with his other hand upon the wheel, he stood firm as a rock. He beached the ship ; every man, woman, and child was saved, as John Maynard dropped, and his spirit took its flight to God.

WAINAMOINEN'S SOWING. — From the Finnish.

TRANSLATED BY JOHN A. PORTER, M. D.

ALL the ocean isles and islets
　　Had been duly made and fashioned ;
All the ocean reefs and ledges
Had been duly wrought and founded ;
All the shining silver pillars
Of the firmament uplifted,
And the hills with crystals sprinkled,
And the highlands water-channelled ;
All the prairies had been levelled,
And the meadows wide unfolded.

Then at last in lapse of ages,
By the will of mighty Ukko,
Ukko, mighty Lord above us,
To the world was born a minstrel,

Finland's mighty sage and singer,
Wise and prudent Wainamoinen,
Of a goddess fair descended,
Daughter of the air and ocean.

Full of glory grew the forest,
Leaf and branch in beauty flourished,
All the race of trees and grasses,
All the tribe of reeds and sedges.
Birds sang sweetly in the tree-tops,
Making music all the day long ;
Cheerily chirped the noisy throstle,
Sweetly sang the low-voiced cuckoo.

Berries grew upon the mountains,
Golden flowers adorned the meadows
Leaf and fruit of every flavor,
Bush and herb of every fashion ;
All things fair and lovely flourished,
All things save the one most precious
Fruit of fruits, the golden barley.

Then one morning Wainamoinen.
Taking from his pouch of leather
Six small seeds of golden barley,
Sallied forth the seed to scatter.
Six small seeds of golden barley,
He had found upon the sea-shore,
On the mighty water's edges,
And with loose and sandy pebbles
Had concealed them in his skin-pouch,
In his pouch of squirrel-leather.

As he sowed he chanted ever,
"Blessing to the seed I scatter,
For it falls upon the meadow,
By the grace of Ukko mighty,
3 *

Through the open finger-spaces
Of the hand that all things fashioned,
Falls to rise again in beauty,
Evermore to spring and flourish.

"Rise, O Earth! from out thy slumbers,
Bid the soil unlock her treasures,
Bid the blade arise in beauty,
Bid the stalk grow strong and stately;
On a thousand stems uplifted
Let the yellow harvest ripen,
Let it cover all my cornfields
Hundred-fold for seed I planted.

"Ukko mighty! God above us,
Gracious Ukko! Father in Heaven,
Thou who all the sky commandest,
For the fleecy clouds appointing
Every morn their course and pathway,
In thine airy realm consulting,
In thy kingdom taking counsel,
Send us clouds from east and northeast,
From the south and from the sunset;
Let them scatter drops refreshing;
Bid them all their sweetness sprinkle,
That the ear may lift its treasure
And the corn make haste to ripen."

Gracious Ukko, Father in Heaven,
Heard the prayer the minstrel lifted,
From the south a cloud commanded,
From the west despatched its fellow,
Bid one gather in the northwest,
And from out the east another;
Closing then their swarthy borders,
Crowding all in haste together,
Bade them all their sweetness sprinkle,

Scatter wide their drops refreshing,
That the ear might rise in beauty
And the corn make haste to ripen.
Soon from out the earth and darkness,
Lo, the tender blade uplifted,
And anon the ears unfolded,
Through the care of Wainamoinen.

Summer days had sped and vanished,
Days and nights a goodly number,
When the ancient Wainamoinen
Sought the field to see, if might be,
How his ploughing and his sowing
And his praying had been prospered.
Verily the corn had thriven
Wholly to the bard's contentment;
Lo, the ears, in six rows seeded,
Waved o'er all the callow cornfield,
And the straw, in three joints builded,
Covered all the teeming acres.

Glancing then a moment round him,
Near him, lo ! a little cuckoo.
And the birdling sang unto him,
Long the birch-tree first surveying :
  " Why, when all the wood has fallen,
Standeth there the slender birch-tree ?"

Spake in answer Wainamoinen :
" Therefore is the birch left standing,
That its summit, soaring skyward,
Make for thee, my pretty birdling,
Station for thy cheerful singing.
Warble here, my pretty birdling,
Silken throat and breast attuning,
Warble forth thy sweetest carol
Dulcet as a bell of silver.

"Sing at morn and sing at evening,
Sing when sunny noon is highest,
Blessing to these chosen places,
Growth and greenness to our forests,
Wealth along our ocean borders
For our garner's rich abundance."

THE WITCH'S DAUGHTER. — J. G. WHITTIER.

IT was the pleasant harvest-time,
   When cellar-bins are closely stowed,
And garrets bend beneath their load,
And the old swallow-haunted barns —
   Brown-gabled, long, and full of seams
   Through which the moted sunlight streams —
Are filled with summer's ripened stores,
   Its odorous grass and barley sheaves,
   From their low scaffolds to their eaves.

On Esek Harden's oaken floor,
   With many an autumn threshing worn,
   Lay the heaped ears of unhusked corn.
And thither came young men and maids,
   Beneath a moon that, large and low,
   Lit that sweet eve of long ago.
They took their places; some by chance,
   And others by a merry voice
   Or sweet smile guided to their choice.

How pleasantly the rising moon,
   Between the shadow of the mows,
   Looked on them through the great elm-boughs! —
On sturdy boyhood, sun-embrowned,
   On girlhood with its solid curves
   Of healthful strength and painless nerves!

And jests went round, and laughs that made
   The house-dog answer with his howl,
   And kept astir the barn-yard fowl.

But still the sweetest voice was mute
   That river-valley ever heard
   From lip of maid or throat of bird;
For Mabel Martin sat apart,
   And let the hay-mow's shadow fall
   Upon the loveliest face of all.
She sat apart, as one forbid,
   Who knew that none would condescend
   To own the Witch-wife's child a friend.

The seasons scarce had gone their round,
   Since curious thousands thronged to see
   Her mother on the gallows-tree.
Few questioned of the sorrowing child,
   Or, when they saw the mother die,
   Dreamed of the daughter's agony.

Poor Mabel from her mother's grave
   Crept to her desolate hearth-stone,
   And wrestled with her fate alone.
Sore tried and pained, the poor girl kept
   Her faith, and trusted that her way,
   So dark, would somewhere meet the day.
And still her weary wheel went round,
   Day after day, with no relief:
   Small leisure have the poor for grief.

So in the shadow Mabel sits;
   Untouched by mirth she sees and hears,
   Her smile is sadder than her tears.
But cruel eyes have found her out,
   And cruel lips repeat her name,
   And taunt her with her mother's shame.

She answered not with railing words,
  But drew her apron o'er her face,
  And, sobbing, glided from the place.
And only pausing at the door,
  Her sad eyes met the troubled gaze
  Of one who, in her better days,
Had been her warm and steady friend,
  Ere yet her mother's doom had made
  Even Esek Harden half afraid.

He felt that mute appeal of tears,
  And, starting, with an angry frown
  Hushed all the wicked murmurs down.
"Good neighbors mine," he sternly said,
  "This passes harmless mirth or jest;
  I brook no insult to my guest.

"She is indeed her mother's child;
  But God's sweet pity ministers
  Unto no whiter soul than hers.
Let Goody Martin rest in peace;
  I never knew her harm a fly,
  And witch or not, God knows, — not I.
I know who swore her life away;
  And, as God lives, I'd not condemn
  An Indian dog on word of them."

The broadest lands in all the town,
  The skill to guide, the power to awe,
  Were Harden's; and his word was law.
None dared withstand him to his face,
  But one sly maiden spake aside:
  "The little witch is evil-eyed!
Her mother only killed a cow,
  Or witched a churn or dairy-pan;
  But she, forsooth, must charm a man!"

Poor Mabel, in her lonely home,
　　Sat by the window's narrow pane,
　　White in the moonlight's silver rain.
She strove to drown her sense of wrong,
　　And, in her old and simple way,
　　To teach her bitter heart to pray.

Poor child! the prayer, begun in faith,
　　Grew to a low, despairing cry
Of utter misery : "Let me die!
Oh! take me from the scornful eyes,
　　And hide me where the cruel speech
　　And mocking finger may not reach!

" I dare not breathe my mother's name :
　　A daughter's right I dare not crave
　　To weep above her unblest grave!
Let me not live until my heart,
　　With few to pity, and with none
　　To love me, hardens into stone.
O God! have mercy on thy child,
　　Whose faith in thee grows weak and small,
　　And take me ere I lose it all."

A shadow on the moonlight fell,
　　And murmuring wind and wave became
　　A voice whose burden was her name.
Had then God heard her? Had he sent
　　His angel down? In flesh and blood,
　　Before her Esek Harden stood!

He laid his hand upon her arm :
　　" Dear Mabel, this no more shall be ;
　　Who scoffs at you, must scoff at me.
You know rough Esek Harden well ;
　　And if he seems no suitor gay,
　　And if his hair is mixed with gray,

The maiden grown shall never find
   His heart less warm than when she smiled
   Upon his knees, a little child!"

Her tears of grief were tears of joy,
   As folded in his strong embrace,
   She looked in Esek Harden's face.
"O truest friend of all!" she said,
   "God bless you for your kindly thought,
   And make me worthy of my lot!"

He led her through his dewy fields,
   To where the swinging lanterns glowed,
   And through the doors the huskers showed.
"Good friends and neighbors!" Esek said,
   "I'm weary of this lonely life;
   In Mabel see my chosen wife!

"She greets you kindly, one and all;
   The past is past, and all offence
   Falls harmless from her innocence.
Henceforth she stands no more alone;
   You know what Esek Harden is; —
   He brooks no wrong to him or his."

Now let the merriest tales be told,
   And let the sweetest songs be sung,
   That ever made the old heart young!
For now the lost has found a home;
   And a lone hearth shall brighter burn,
   As all the household joys return!

O, pleasantly the harvest moon,
   Between the shadow of the mows,
   Looked on them through the great elm-boughs!
On Mabel's curls of golden hair,
   On Esek's shaggy strength, it fell;
   And the wind whispered, "It is well!"

Abridged.

THE HORSEBACK RIDE. — GRACE GREENWOOD.

WHEN troubled in spirit, when weary of life,
  When I faint 'neath its burdens, and shrink from its
    strife ;
When its fruits, turned to ashes, are mocking my taste,
And its fairest scenes seem but a desolate waste,
Then come ye not near me, my sad heart to cheer,
With friendship's soft accents, or sympathy's tear, —
No pity I ask, and no counsel I need.
But bring me, O bring me, my gallant young steed,
With his high-archéd neck, and his nostrils spread wide,
His eyes full of fire, and his step full of pride !
As I spring to his back, as I seize the strong rein,
The strength of my spirit returneth again !
The bonds are all broken that fettered my mind,
And my cares borne away on the wings of the wind ;
My pride lifts its head, for a moment bowed down,
And the queen in my nature now puts on her crown !

Now we 're off, like the winds to the plains whence they came,
And the rapture of motion is thrilling my frame !
On, on speeds my courser, scarce printing the sod,
Scarce crushing a daisy to mark where he trod !
On, on like a deer, when the hound's early bay
Awakes the wild echoes, away and away !
Still faster, still farther, he leaps at my cheer,
Till the rush of the startled air whirs in my ear !
Now 'long a clear rivulet lieth his track, —
See his glancing hoofs tossing the white pebbles back !
Now a glen, dark as midnight, — what matter ? — we 'll down,
Though shadows are round us, and rocks o'er us frown !
The thick branches shake as we 're hurrying through,
And deck us with spangles of silvery dew !

What a wild thought of triumph, that this girlish hand
Such a steed in the might of his strength may command !

E

What a glorious creature! Ah! glance at him now,
As I check him awhile on this green hillock's brow!
How he tosses his mane, with a shrill, joyous neigh,
And paws the firm earth in his proud, stately play!
Hurrah! off again, dashing on as in ire,
Till the long, flinty pathway is flashing with fire!
Ho! a ditch!— Shall we pause? No; the bold leap we dare,
Like a swift-wingéd arrow we rush through the air!
O, not all the pleasures that poets may praise,
Not the wildering waltz in the ball-room's blaze,
Nor the chivalrous joust, nor the daring race,
Nor the swift regatta, nor merry chase,
Nor the sail high heaving the waters o'er,
Nor the rural dance on the moonlight shore,
Can the wild and thrilling joy exceed
Of a fearless leap on a fiery steed.

THE VEILED PICTURE.

TWO artist lovers sought the hand of a noted painter's daughter. The question which of the two should possess himself of the prize so earnestly coveted by both having come, finally, to the father, he promised to give his child to the one that could paint best. So each strove for the maiden with the highest skill his genius could command.

One painted a picture of fruit, and displayed it to the father's inspection in a beautiful grove, where gay birds sang sweetly among the foliage, and all nature rejoiced in the luxuriance of bountiful life. Presently the birds came down to the canvas of the young painter, and attempted to eat the fruit he had pictured there. In his surprise and joy at the young artist's skill, the father declared that no one could triumph over that.

Soon, however, the second lover came with his picture, and it was veiled. "Take the veil from your painting," said the old man. " I leave that to you," said the young artist, with simple modesty. The father of the young and lovely maiden then approached the veiled picture and attempted to uncover it. But imagine his astonishment when, as he attempted to take off the veil, he found the veil itself to be a picture ! We need not say who was the lucky lover ; for, if the artist who deceived the birds by skill in fruit manifested great powers of art, he who could so veil his canvas with the pencil as to deceive a skilful master was surely the greater artist.

————◆————

THE SHIP ON FIRE. — Henry Bateman.

MORNING ! all speedeth well ; the bright sun
    Lights up the deep blue wave, and favoring breeze
Fills the white sails, while o'er that Southern sea
The ship, with all the busy life within,
Holds on her ocean course, alone, but glad !
For all is yet, as all has been the while
Since the white cliffs were left, without or fear
Or danger to those hundreds grouping now
Upon the sunny deck.

Fire ! — Fire ! — Fire ! — Fire !
  .   .   .   .   .

Scorching smoke in many a wreath,
    Sulphurous blast of heated air,
Grim presentment of quick death,
    Crouching fear and stern despair,
Hist, to what the Master saith, —
    " Steady, steersman, steady there ! " — Ay ! ay !

To the deck the women led,
    Children helped by stalwart men,
Calmly, firmly mustered
    All the crew assemble then,

And to orders briefly said,
    Comes the sharp response again, — Ay ! ay !

" To the mast-head ! " — it is done, —
    " Look to leeward," — scores obey, —
" And to windward," — many a one
    Turns, and never turns away ;
Steadfast is the word and tone,
    " Man the boats, and clear away ! " — Ay ! ay !

Hotter ! hotter ! — heave and strain ; —
    In the hollow, on the wave, —
Pump ! and flood the deck again, —
    Work ! no danger daunts the brave, —
Hope and trust are not in vain,
    God looks on, and he can save. — Ay ! ay !

Desolate ! all desolate !
    Nothing, nothing to be seen, —
Wait and watch, and hope and wait,
    Hope has never hopeless been, —
" Men, ye know that God is great,
    Would he — he can intervene. " — Ay ! ay !

" What above ? " — nor sail, nor sound, —
    " Leeward ? " — nothing, far or near, —
" What to windward ? " — to the bound
    Of the horizon all is clear ; —
Yet again the words go round,
    " Work, men, work ; we dare not fear ! " — Ay ! ay !

From a heavy lurch abeam,
    Struggling, shivering, reeling back, —
Crash ! — with rush and shout and scream
    Comes the foreyard, with its wrack
Crushing hope as it might seem, —
    " Steady ! — keep the sun-line track ! " — Ay ! ay !

All is order! — ready all! —
   Watching in appointed place
Underneath the smoky pall,
   Firm of foot, with tranquil face,
Resolute, whate'er befall,
   Holds the Captain's measured pace. — Ay! ay!

Hotter! hotter! hotter still!
   Backward driven every one ;
All in vain the various skill,
   All that man may do is done ;
" Brave hearts! strive yet with a will,
   Never deem that hope is gone! " — Ay! ay!

Hist! — as if a sudden thought
   Dare not utter what it knew, —
Falls a trembling whisper, fraught
   As of hope, to frightened few ;
With a doubting heart-ache caught,
   And a choking " Is it true? " — Ay! ay!

Then it comes, — " A sail! a sail! " —
   Up from prostrate misery,
Up from heart-break woe and wail,
   Up to shuddering ecstasy ; —
" Can so strange a promise fail? "
   " Call the Master, let him see! " — Ay! ay!

Silence!   Silence!   Silence! — Pray!
   .   .   .   .   .

Every moment is an hour,
   Minutes long as weary years,
While with concentrated power,
   Through the haze that clear eye peers, —
" No," — " Yes," — " No," — the strong men cower,
   Till he sighs, — faith conquering fears, — " Ay! ay! "

Riseth now the throbbing cry,
  Born of hope and hopelessness ;
Iron men weep bitterly,
  Unused hands and cheeks caress, —
Feeling's wild variety ; —
  Strange and heartless were it less. — Ay ! ay !

Through the sunlight's glittering gleam
  On old Ocean's rugged breast,
As a fantasy in dream,
  Yet beyond all doubt confest,
Comes the ship, — God's gift, they deem,
  Ah, " He overruleth best ! " — Ay ! ay !

Coming ! — Come ! — that foremost man
  Shouts as only true heart may,
" Ship on fire ! " — " You will ? " — " You can ? " —
  " Near us, for the rescue, stay ! "
Almost as the words began,
  Answering words are on their way, — " Ay ! ay ! "

" Ay ! ay ! " — words of little worth
  But as imaging the soul ; —
See, the boats are struggling forth, —
  Marvel ! how they pitch and roll
On the dark wave, through the froth, —
  God can bring them safe and whole. — Ay! ay !

Have a care, men ! have a care !
  Steady, — steady, to the stern, —
Now, my brave hearts, handy there, —
  See, the deck begins to burn !
Child and woman, soft and fair,
  Go, — thank God, — be quick, — return. — Ay ! ay !

Blistering smoke all dim and red,
  Writhing flakes of lurid flame, —

Decks that scorch the hasty tread, —
    Shuddering sounds, as if they came
Wailing from a tortured bed, —
    "Boatswain, call each man by name!" — Ay! ay!

Strong, sad now, one by one,
    At the voice which all obey,
Silently, till all are gone,
    Fill the boats, and pass away,
And the Captain stands alone ; —
    Has he not done well the day ? — Ay! ay!

O that boat-load! — anxious eyes,
    Hearts, where painful throbbings swell,
Watch and wait, with sympathies
    Far too deep for tongue to tell ;
All suppressed are words and cries, —
    Surely it will all go well! — Ay! ay!

All is well! that man so true
    Stands upon the stranger's deck,
And a thrilling pulse runs through
    Those glad hearts, which none may check, —
Listen to the wild halloo !
    Rainbow joy, in fortune's wreck : — Ay! ay!

Pah ! — a rush of smothered light
    Bursts the staggering ship asunder, —
Lightning flashes, fierce and bright, —
    Blasting sounds, as if of thunder, —
Dread destruction wins the fight
    Round about, above, and under. — Ay! ay!

Come away ! we may not stay ;
    All is done that man can do ;
Let us take our onward way,
    Life has claims and duties new ;

God is a strong help and stay,
  He can guide all sorrow through ! — Ay ! ay !

Thanks unceasing ! thanks and praise !
  For his great deliverance shown,
Let the remnant of our days
  Testify what he has done ;
Marvellous his loving ways !
  Merciful, as we have known ! — Ay ! ay !

And so the good ship Merchantman sailed on,
With double freight of life, and God's kind care,
Till at the Cape, the rescued voyagers left
To other kindness of the dwellers there,
She spread her sails again, and went her way.

SONG OF THE RIVER.

CLEAR and cool, clear and cool,
    By laughing shadow and dreaming pool ;
Cool and clear, cool and clear,
    By shining shingle and foaming weir ;
Under the crag where the ouzel sings,
And the ivied wall where the church-bell rings ;
        Undefiled for the undefiled,
Play by me, bathe in me, mother and child.

Dank and foul, dank and foul,
    By the smoke-grimed town in its murky cowl ;
Foul and dank, foul and dank,
    By wharf, and sewer, and slimy bank ;
Darker and darker the farther I go,
Baser and baser the richer I grow ; —
        Who dare sport with the sin-defiled ?
Shrink from me, turn from me, mother and child.

Strong and free, strong and free,
 The flood-gates are open ; away to the sea !
Free and strong, free and strong,
 Cleansing my stream as I hurry along,
To the golden sands and the leaping bar,
And the taintless tide that awaits me afar,
As I lose myself in the infinite main,
Like a soul that has sinned and is pardoned again.
 Undefiled for the undefiled,
Play by me, bathe in me, mother and child.

THE FATE OF MACGREGOR. — James Hogg.

"MACGREGOR, Macgregor, remember our foeman ;
 The moon rises broad from the brow of Ben-Lomond ;
The clans are impatient, and chide thy delay ;
Arise ! let us bound to Glen-Lyon away."
 Stern scowled the Macgregor ; then, silent and sullen,
He turned his red eye to the braes of Strathfillan :
 " Go, Malcolm, to sleep, let the clans be dismissed ;
The Campbells this night for Macgregor must rest."

" Macgregor, Macgregor, our scouts have been flying
Three days round the hills of M'Nab and Glen-Lyon ;
Of riding and running such tidings they bear,
We must meet them at home, else they 'll quickly be here."
 " The Campbell may come, as his promises bind him,
And haughty M'Nab, with his giants behind him ;
This night I am bound to relinquish the fray,
And do what it freezes my vitals to say.

" Forgive me, dear brother, this horror of mind ;
Thou knowest in the strife I was never behind,
Nor ever receded a foot from the van,
Or blenched at the ire or the prowess of man ;

4

But I 've sworn, by the cross, by my God, and my all !
An oath which I cannot, and dare not recall, —
Ere the shadows of midnight fall east from the pile,
To meet with a spirit this night in Glen-Gyle.

" Last night, in my chamber, all thoughtful and lone,
I called to remembrance some deeds I had done,
When entered a lady, with visage so wan,
And looks such as never were fastened on man.
I knew her, O brother ! I knew her too well !
Of that once fair dame such a tale I could tell
As would thrill thy bold heart ; but how long she remained,
So racked was my spirit, my bosom so pained,
I knew not, — but ages seemed short to the while,
Though, proffer the Highlands, nay, all the green isle,
With length of existence no man can enjoy,
The same to endure, the dread proffer I 'd fly !
The thrice-threatened pangs of last night to forego,
Macgregor would dive to the mansions below.
Despairing and mad, to futurity blind,
The present to shun, and some respite to find,
I swore, ere the shadow fell east from the pile,
To meet her alone by the brook of Glen-Gyle.

" She told me, and turned my chilled heart to a stone,
The glory and name of Macgregor were gone ;
That the pine which for ages had shed a bright halo
Afar on the mountains of Highland Glen-Falo,
Should wither and fall ere the turn of yon moon
Smit through by the canker of hated Colquhoun ;
That a feast on Macgregors each day should be common,
For years, to the eagles of Lennox and Lomond.

" A parting embrace in one moment she gave ;
Her breath was a furnace, her bosom the grave !
Then flitting illusive, she said, with a frown,
  ' The mighty Macgregor shall yet be my own ! ' "

" Macgregor, thy fancies are wild as the wind ;
The dreams of the night have disordered thy mind,
Come, buckle thy panoply, — march to the field, —
See, brother, how hacked are thy helmet and shield !
Ay, that was M'Nab, in the height of his pride,
When the lions of Dochart stood firm by his side.
This night the proud chief his presumption shall rue ;
Rise, brother, these chinks in his heart-blood will glue ;
Thy fantasies frightful shall flit on the wing,
When loud with thy bugle Glen-Lyon shall ring."

Like glimpse of the moon through the storm of the night,
Macgregor's red eye shed one sparkle of light ;
It faded, — it darkened, — he shuddered, — he sighed, —
" No ! not for the universe ! " low he replied.
    Away went Macgregor, but went not alone :
To watch the dread rendezvous, Malcolm has gone.
They oared the broad Lomond, so still and serene,
And deep in her bosom, how awful the scene !
O'er mountains inverted the blue waters curled,
And rocked them on skies of a far nether world.

All silent they went, for the time was approaching ;
The moon the blue zenith already was touching ;
No foot was abroad on the forest or hill,
No sound but the lullaby sung by the rill :
Young Malcolm, at distance crouched, trembling the while, —
Macgregor stood lone by the brook of Glen-Gyle.

Few minutes had passed, ere they spied on the stream
A skiff sailing light, where a lady did seem ;
Her sail was the web of the gossamer's loom ;
The glow-worm her wake-light, the rainbow her boom ;
A dim rayless beam was her prow and her mast,
Like wold-fire at midnight, that glares on the waste.
Though rough was the river with rock and cascade,
No torrent, no rock, her velocity stayed ;

She wimpled the water to weather and lee,
And heaved as if borne on the waves of the sea.
Mute Nature was roused in the bounds of the glen;
The wild deer of Gairtney abandoned his den,
Fled panting away, over river and isle,
Nor once turned his eye to the brook of Glen-Gyle.

The fox fled in terror; the eagle awoke
As slumbering he dozed on the shelve of the rock;
Astonished, to hide in the moonbeam he flew,
And screwed the night-heaven till lost in the blue.
　Young Malcolm beheld the pale lady approach,
The chieftain salute her, and shrink from her touch.
He saw the Macgregor kneel down on the plain,
As begging for something he could not obtain;
She raised him indignant, derided his stay,
Then bore him on board, set her sail and away.

Though fast the red bark down the river did glide,
Yet faster ran Malcolm adown by its side;
"Macgregor! Macgregor!" he bitterly cried;
"Macgregor! Macgregor!" the echoes replied.
He struck at the lady, but, strange though it seem,
His sword only fell on the rocks and the stream;
But the groans from the boat, that ascended amain,
Were groans from a bosom in horror and pain.
They reached the dark lake, and bore lightly away, —
Macgregor is vanished forever and aye!

SCENE IN AN IRISH SCHOOL. — Gerald Griffin.

THE school-house at Glendalough was situated near the romantic river which flows between the wild scenery of Drumgoff and the Seven Church. It was a low stone building, indifferently thatched; the whole interior consisting of one oblong room, floored with clay, and lighted by two or three windows, the panes of which were patched with old copy-books, or altogether supplanted by school slates. The walls had once been plastered and whitewashed, but now partook of that appearance of dilapidation which characterized the whole building. Along each wall was placed a row of large stones, — the one intended for the boys, the other for the girls ; the decorum of Mr. Lenigan's establishment requiring that they should be kept apart on ordinary occasions, for Mr. Lenigan, it should be understood, had not been furnished with any Pestalozzian light. The only chair in the whole establishment was that which was usually occupied by Mr. Lenigan himself ; and a table appeared to be a luxury of which they were either ignorant or wholly regardless.

One morning Mr. Lenigan was rather later than his usual hour in taking possession of the chair above alluded to. The sun was mounting swiftly up the heavens. The row of stones before described were already occupied, and the babble of a hundred voices like the sound of a beehive filled the house. Now and then a school-boy in frieze coat and corduroy trousers, with an ink-bottle dangling at his breast, copy-book, slate, Voster, and reading-book under one arm, and a turf under the other, dropped in and took his place on the next unoccupied stone. A great boy, with a huge slate in his arms, stood in the centre of the apartment, making a list of all those who were guilty of any indecorum in the absence of the 'Masther.' Near the door was a blazing turf fire, which the sharp autumnal winds already rendered agreeable. In a corner behind the door lay a heap of fuel formed by the contributions of all the scholars ; each being obliged to bring one sod of turf every day, and each having the privilege of sitting by the fire while his own sod was burning. Those who failed to pay their tribute of fuel sat cold and shivering the whole day long at the farther end of the room, huddling together their bare and frost-bitten toes, and casting a longing, envious eye toward the peristyle of well-marbled shins that surrounded the fire.

Full in the influence of the cherishing flame was placed the hay-bottomed chair that supported the person of Mr. Henry Lenigan, when that great man presided in person in his rural academy. On his right lay a close bush of hazel of astounding size, the emblem of his authority and the implement of castigation. Near this was a wooden sthroker, that is to say, a large rule of smooth and polished deal, used for sthroking lines in the copy-book, and also for sthroking the palms of refractory pupils. On the other side lay a lofty heap of copy-books, which were left by the boys and girls for the purpose of having their copies 'sot' by the 'Masther!'

About noon a sudden hush was produced by the appearance at the open door of a young man, dressed in rusty black, and with something clerical in his costume and demeanor. This was Mr. Lenigan's classical assistant; for to himself the volumes of ancient literature were a fountain sealed. Five or six stout young men, all of whom were intended for learned professions, were the only portion of Mr. Lenigan's scholars that aspired to those lofty sources of information. At the sound of the word "Virgil!" from the lips of the assistant the whole class started from their seats, and crowded around him, each brandishing a smoky volume of the great Augustan poet, who, could he have looked into this Irish academy from that part of the infernal regions in which he had been placed by his pupil Dante, might have been tempted to exclaim, in the pathetic words of his hero: —

> "Sunt hic etiam sua præmia laudi,
> Sunt lachryma rerum et mentem mortalia tangunt."

"Who's head?" was the first question proposed by the assistant, after he had thrown open the volume at that part marked as the day's lesson.

"Jim Naughtin, sir."

"Well, Naughtin, begin. Consther,* consther now, an' be quick!

> "At puer Ascanius mediis in vallibus acri
> Gaudet equo; jamque hos cursu, jam præterit illos:
> Spumantemque dari —"

* Consther, — translate.

"Go on, sir. Why don't you consther?"

"*At puer Ascanius,*" the person so addressed began, "but the boy Ascanius; *mediis in vallibus,* in the middle of the valley; *gaudet,* rejoices."

"Exults, aragal, exults is a better word."

"*Gaudet,* exults; *acri equo,* upon his bitther horse."

"O, murther alive! his bitther horse, inagh? Erra, what would make a horse be bitther, Jim? Sure, 't is not of sour beer he's talking! Rejoicin' upon a bitther horse! Dear knows what a show he was, what raison he had for it! *Acri equo,* upon his mettlesome steed; that's the construction."

Jim proceeded: —

Acri equo, upon his mettlesome steed; *jamque,* and now; *præterit,* he goes beyond — "

"Outstrips, achree!"

"*Præterit,* he outstrips; *hos,* these; *jamque illos,* and now those; *cursu,* in his course; *que,* and; *optat,* he longs — "

"Very good, Jim; 'longs' is a very good word there; I thought you were going to say 'wishes.' Did anybody tell you that?"

"Dickens a one, sir!"

"That's a good boy. Well?"

"*Optat,* he longs; *spumantem aprum,* that a foaming boar; *dari,* shall be given; *votis,* to his desires; *aut fulvum leonum,* or that a tawny lion — "

"That's a good word again. 'Tawny''s a good word; betther than 'yellow.'"

"*Descendere,* shall descend; *monte,* from the mountain."

"Now, boys, observe the beauty of the poet. There's great nature in the picture of the boy Ascanius. Just the same way as we see young Misther Keiley of the Grove, at the fox-chase the other day, leadin' the whole of 'em right and left, *jamque hos, jamque illos,* an' now Misther Cleary, an' now Captain Davis, he outsthripped in his course. A beautiful picture, boys, there is in them four lines, of a fine high-blooded youth. Yes, people are always the same; times an' manners change, but the heart o' man is the same now as

it was in the days of Augustus. But consther your task,
Jim, an' then I 'll give you an' the boys a little commentary
upon its beauties."

The boy obeyed, and read as far as *prœtexit nomine culpam*,
after which the assistant proceeded to pronounce his little
commentary : —

"Now, boys, for what I told ye. Them seventeen lines
that Jim Naughtin consthered this minute contains as much
as fifty in a modern book. I pointed out to ye before the
picture of Ascanius, an' I 'll back it again the world for nature. Then there 's the incipient storm, —

> ' Interea magno misceri murmure cœlum
> Incipit.'

Erra! don't be talkin', but listen to that! There 's a rumbling in the language like the sound of comin' thundher, —

> '. . . . insequitur commixta grandine nimbus.'

D' ye hear the change? D' ye hear all the s's? D' ye hear 'em
whistlin'? D' ye hear the black squall comin' up the hillside, brushin' up the dust and dry leaves off the road, and
hissin' through the threes and bushes? An' d' ye hear the
hail dhriven afther, an' spattherin' the laves, and whitenin' the
face o' the counthry? *Commixta grandine nimbus!* That I
might n't sin, but when I read them words, I gather my head
down between my shouldhers, as if it was hailin' atop o' me.
An' then the sighth of all the huntin' party! Dido, an' the
Throjans, an' all the great court ladies and the Tyrian companions scatthered like cracked people about the place, lookin' for shelther, and peltin' about right and left, hether and
thether in all directions for the bare life, an' the floods swellin' an' coming, an' thundherin' down in rivers from the mountains, an' all in three lines : —

> ' Et Tyrii comites passim, et Trojana juventus
> Dardaniusque nepos Veneris, diversa per agros
> Tecta metû petiere : ruunt de montibus amnes.'

An' see the beauty of the poet, followin' up the character of Ascanius ; he makes him the last to quit the field. First the Tyrian comrades, an effeminate race, that ran at the sighth of a shower, as if they were made o' salt, that they 'd melt under it ; and then the Throjan youth, lads that were used to it in the first book ; and last of all the spirited boy Ascanius himself. (Silence near the doore !)

> 'Speluncam Dido, dux et Trojanus eandem,
> Deveniunt.'

Observe, boys, he no longer, as of old, calls him the *pius* Æneas, only Dux Trojanus, the Throjan laidher, an' 't is he that was the laidher and the lad ; see the taste of the poet not to call him the pious Æneas now, nor even mention his name, as if he were half ashamed of him, knowin' well what a lad he had to dale with. There 's where Virgil took the crust out o' Homer's mouth in the nateness of his language, that you 'd gather a part o' the feelin' from the very shape o' the line an' turn o' the prosidy. As formerly, when Dido was askin' Æneas concernin' where he come from, an' where he was born, he makes answer : —

> 'Est locus Hesperiam Graii cognomine dicunt,
> Terra antiqua, potens armis atque ubere glebæ.
> Huc cursus fuit.'

An' there the line stops short, as much as to say, just as I cut this line short in spakin' to you, just so our coorse was cut in going to Italy. The same way, when Juno is vexed in talkin' o' the Throjans, he makes her spake bad Latin to show how mad she is : — (Silence !)

> 'Mene incepto desistere victam
> Nec posse Italia Teucrorum avertere regem ?
> Quippe vetor fatis ! Pallasne exurere classem
> Argivûm, atque ipsos potuit submergere ponto.'

So he laves you to guess what a passion she is in, when he makes her lave an' infinitive mood without anything to govern it. You can't attribute it ignorance, for it would be a dhroll

4 *   F

thing in airnest, if Juno, the queen of all the gods, did n't know a common rule in syntax, so that you have nothing for it but to say that she must be the very moral of a jury. Such, boys, is the art o' poets an' the janius o' languages.

"But I kept ye long enough. Go along to yer Greek now, as fast as ye can, an' reharse. An' as for ye," continued the learned commentator, turning to the mass of English scholars, "I see one comin' over the river that 'll taich ye how to behave yerselves, as it is a thing ye won't do for me. Put up yer Virgils now, boys, an' out with the Greek, an' remember the beauties I pointed out to ye, for they 're things that few can explain to ye, if ye have n't the luck to think of 'em yerselves."

The class separated, and a hundred anxious eyes were directed toward the open door. It afforded a glimpse of a sunny green, and a bubbling river, over which Mr. Lenigan, followed by his brother David, was now observed in the act of picking his cautious way. At this apparition a sudden change took place in the entire condition of the school. Stragglers flew to their places; the impatient burst of laughter was cut short; the growing bit of rage was quelled; the uplifted hand dropped harmless by the side of its owner; merry faces grew serious, and angry ones peaceable; the eyes of all seemed poring on their books; and the extravagant uproar of the last half-hour was hushed on a sudden into a diligent murmur. Those who were most proficient in the study of the 'Masther's' physiognomy detected in the expression of his eyes, as he entered and greeted his assistant, something of a troubled and uneasy character. He took the list with a severe countenance from the hands of the boy above-mentioned, sent all those whose names he found upon the fatal record to kneel down in a corner until he should find leisure to 'haire' them, and then prepared to enter upon his daily functions.

For the present, however, the delinquents are saved by the entrance of a fresh character upon the scene.

The new-comer was a handsome young woman, who carried

a pet child in her arms and held another by the hand. The sensation of pleasure which ran among the young culprits at her appearance showed her to be their 'great Captain's Captain," the beloved and loving helpmate of Mr. Lenigan. Casting, unperceived by her lord, an encouraging smile toward the kneeling culprits, she took an opportunity while engaged in a wheedling conversation with her husband, to purloin his deal rule and to blot out the list of the proscribed from the slate, after which she stole out, calling David to dig the potatoes for dinner.

And so we, too, will leave the school.

SHIPS AT SEA. — BARRY GRAY.

I HAVE ships that went to sea
  More than fifty years ago ;
None have yet come home to me,
  But are sailing to and fro.
I have seen them in my sleep,
Plunging through the shoreless deep,
With tattered sails, and battered hulls,
While around them screamed the gulls,
  Flying low, — flying low.

I have wondered why they stayed
  From me, sailing round the world ;
And I 've said, "I 'm half afraid
  That their sails will ne'er be furled."
Great the treasure that they hold, —
Silks, and plumes, and bars of gold ;
While the spices that they bear
Fill with fragrance all the air,
  As they sail, — as they sail.

Ah ! each sailor in the port
  Knows that I have ships at sea,

Of the waves and winds the sport ;
　And the sailors pity me.
Oft they come and with me walk,
Cheering me with hopeful talk,
Till I put my fears aside,
And, contented, watch the tide
　Rise and fall, — rise and fall.

I have waited on the piers,
　Gazing for them down the bay,
Days and nights, for many years,
　Till I 've turned, heart-sick, away.
But the pilots, when they land,
Stop and take me by the hand,
Saying you will like to see
Your proud ships come home from sea,
　One and all, — one and all.

So I never quite despair,
　Nor let hope nor courage fail ;
And some day, when skies are fair,
　Up the bay my ships will sail.
I shall buy then all I need, —
Prints to look at, books to read,
Horses, wines, and works of art,
Everything, — except a heart.
　That is lost, — that is lost !

Once when I was pure and young,
　Richer too than I am now,
Ere a cloud was o'er me flung,
　Or a wrinkle crossed my brow,
There was one whose heart was mine ;
But she 's something now divine,
And though come my ships from sea,
They can bring no heart to me
　Evermore, — evermore.

OLD CHUMS. — ALICE CARY.

IS it you, Jack? Old boy, is it really you?
   I should n't have known you but that I was told
You might be expected ; — pray, how do you do?
   But what, under heaven, has made you so old?

Your hair! why, you 've only a little gray fuzz!
   And your beard 's white! but that can be beautifully dyed;
And your legs are n't but just half as long as they was ;
   And then — stars and garters! your vest is so wide!

Is this your hand? Lord, how I envied you that
   In the time of our courting, — so soft, and so small,
And now it is callous inside, and so fat, —
   Well, you beat the very old deuce, that is all.

Turn round! let me look at you! is n't it odd
   How strange in a few years a fellow's chum grows!
Your eye is shrunk up like a bean in a pod,
   And what are these lines branching out from your nose?

Your back has gone up and your shoulders gone down,
   And all the old roses are under the plough ;
Why, Jack, if we 'd happened to meet about town,
   I would n't have known you from Adam, I vow!

You 've had trouble, have you? I 'm sorry ; but, John,
   All trouble sits lightly at your time of life.
How 's Billy, my namesake? You don't say he 's gone
   To the war, John, and that you have buried your wife?

Poor Katherine! so she has left you, — ah me!
   I thought she would live to be fifty, or more.
What is it you tell me? She *was* fifty-three!
   O no, Jack! she was n't so much by a score!

Well, there's little Katy, — was that her name, John?
  She'll rule your house one of these days like a queen.
That baby! good Lord! is she married and gone?
  With a Jack ten years old! and a Katy fourteen!

Then I give it up! Why, you're younger than I
  By ten or twelve years, and to think you've come back
A sober old graybeard, just ready to die!
  I don't understand how it is, — do you, Jack?

I've got all my faculties yet, sound and bright;
  Slight failure my eyes are beginning to hint;
But still, with my spectacles on, and a light
  'Twixt them and the page, I can read any print.

My hearing *is* dull, and my leg is more spare,
  Perhaps, than it was when I beat you at ball;
My breath gives out, too, if I go up a stair, —
  But nothing worth mentioning, nothing at all!

My hair is just turning a little, you see,
  And lately I've put on a broader-brimmed hat
Than I wore at your wedding, but you will agree,
  Old fellow, I look all the better for that.

I'm sometimes a little rheumatic, 't is true,
  And my nose is n't quite on a straight line, they say;
For all that, I don't think I've changed much, do you?
  And I don't feel a day older, Jack, not a day.

———◆———

THE OLD MAN'S PRAYER. — JEAN INGELOW.

THERE was a poor old man
  Who sat and listened to the raging sea,
And heard it thunder, lunging at the cliffs
As like to tear them down. He lay at night;
And "Lord have mercy on the lads," said he,

" That sailed at noon, though they be none of mine !
For when the gale gets up, and when the wind
Flings at the window, when it beats the roof,
And lulls and stops and rouses up again,
And cuts the crest clean off the plunging wave,
And scatters it like feathers up the field,
Why then I think of my two lads, — my lads
That would have worked and never let me want,
And never let me take the parish pay.
No, none of mine ; my lads were drowned at sea
My two — before the most of these were born.
I know how sharp that cuts, since my poor wife
Walked up and down, and still walked up and down,
And I walked after, and one could not hear
A word the other said, for wind and sea
That raged and beat and thundered in the night, —
The awfullest, the longest, lightest night
That ever parents had to spend, — a moon
That shone like daylight on the breaking wave.
Ah me ! and other men have lost their lads,
And other women wiped their poor dead mouths,
And got them home and dried them in the house,
And seen the drift-wood lie along the coast,
That was a tidy boat but one day back,
And seen next tide the neighbors gather it
To lay it on their fires.
     Ay, I was strong
And able-bodied, — loved my work ; — but now
I am a useless hull ; 't is time I sunk ;
I am in all men's way ; I trouble them ;
I am a trouble to myself : but yet
I feel for mariners of stormy nights,
And feel for wives that watch ashore.   Ay, ay !
If I had learning I would pray the Lord
To bring them in : but I 'm no scholar, no ;
Book-learning is a world too hard for me :
But I make bold to say, ' O Lord, good Lord,

I am a broken-down poor man, a fool
To speak to thee : but in the Book 't is writ,
As I hear from others that can read,
How, when thou camest, thou didst love the sea,
And live with fisherfolk, whereby 't is sure
Thou knowest all the peril they go through,
And all their trouble.

           As for me, good Lord,
I have no boat ; I am too old, too old, —
My lads are drowned ; I buried my poor wife ;
My little lassies died so long ago
That mostly I forget what they were like.
Thou knowest, Lord ; they were such little ones
I know they went to thee, but I forget
Their faces, though I missed them sore.

                      O Lord,
I was a strong man ; I have drawn good food
And made good money out of thy great sea :
But yet I cried for them at nights ; and now,
Although I be so old, I miss my lads,
And there be many folk this stormy night
Heavy with fear for theirs.   Merciful Lord,
Comfort them ; save their honest boys, their pride,
And let them hear next ebb the blessedest,
Best sound, — their boat-keels grating on the sand.

I cannot pray with finer words : I know
Nothing ; I have no learning, cannot learn, —
Too old, too old.   They say I want for naught,
I have the parish pay ; but I am dull
Of hearing, and the fire scarce warms me through.
God save me, I have been a sinful man, —
And save the lives of them that still can work,
For they are good to me ; ay, good to me.
But, Lord, I am a trouble ! and I sit,
And I am lonesome, and the nights are few
That any think to come and draw a chair,

And sit in my poor place and talk awhile.
Why should they come, forsooth? Only the wind
Knocks at my door, O, long and loud it knocks,
The only thing God made that has a mind
To enter in."
       Yea, thus the old man spake :
These were the last words of his aged mouth, —
BUT ONE DID KNOCK. One came to sup with him,
That humble, weak old man ; knocked at his door,
In the rough pauses of the laboring wind.
I tell you that One knocked while it was dark,
Save where their foaming passion had made white
Those livid seething billows. What he said
In that poor place where he did talk awhile,
I cannot tell; but this I am assured,
That when the neighbors came the morrow morn,
What time the wind had bated, and the sun
Shone on the old man's floor, they saw the smile
He passed away in, and they said, " He looks
As he had woke and seen the face of Christ,
And with that rapturous smile held out his arms
To come to Him ! "

————◆————

WAR'S END. — A. MELVILLE BELL.

AH ! what inventive skill has man displayed,
    To maim and slay his brother of the sod, —
Slaughter his pastime, horrid War a trade ! —
Yet mark how, ordered by a righteous God,
His skill becomes at once his chastisement and healing rod !

     A steel-tipped dart drawn back
      And released with a spring,
    And you trace its fluttering track —
      Like a bird on the wing —
        Whizz !

How it staggers when its targe is won !
Whizz ! whizz !
Feathered mischief that it is.

A curling puff of smoke,
And a quick little flash,
Then the viewless bullet spoke
Its message with a rash
Ping !
And the vicious thing its work has done.
Ping ! ping !
Cruel little leaden thing.

A rolling coil of smoke
And scathing gush of fire,
Then the cannon's roar outbroke
In a howl of death-desire —
Bang !
And the bloody cleaving ball speeds on.
Bang ! bang !
How the mowing iron sang !

A shrouding pall of smoke,
A winding-sheet of flame,
Then the splitting thunder-stroke
That stops the deadly game —
Boom !
And the thing whate'er opposed is gone.

Granite, iron ramparts, all,
Swept as cobwebs from the wall ;
Defence's utmost strength
O'ermatched by Power at length, —
Even War has met its doom,
In that Boom !
Whizz ! Ping ! Bang ! Boom !
First units fall, then sheaves, then all 's a tomb.

Thanks for that tomb, for from it shall arise
　　The spirit of a Universal Peace !
To bid just Reason her true place assume,
　　Right from brute Might's supremacy release,
And by the deadliness of war, make war itself to cease !

----·----

THE PILGRIMS. — J. G. Whittier.

A WORTHY New England deacon once described a brother in the church as a very good man Godward, but rather hard manward. It cannot be denied that some very satisfactory steps have been taken in the latter direction, at least, since the days of the Pilgrims. Our age is tolerant of creed and dogma, broader in its sympathies, more keenly sensitive to temporal need, and practically recognizing the brotherhood of the race ; wherever a cry of suffering is heard, its response is quick and generous. It has abolished slavery, and is lifting woman from world-old degradation to equality with man before the law. Our criminal codes no longer embody the maxim of barbarism, " An eye for an eye, and a tooth for a tooth," but have regard not only for the safety of the community, but to the reform and well-being of the criminal. All the more, however, for this amiable tenderness do we need the counterpoise of a strong sense of justice. With our sympathy for the wrong-doer we need the old Puritan and Quaker hatred of wrong-doing ; with our just tolerance of men and opinions a righteous abhorrence of sin. All the more for the sweet humanities and Christian liberalism which, in drawing men nearer to each other, are increasing the sum of social influences for good or evil, we need the bracing atmosphere, healthful, if austere, of the old moralities. Individual and social duties are quite as imperative now as when they were minutely specified in statute-books and enforced by penalties no longer admissible. It is well that stocks, whipping-post, and ducking-stool are now only matters of tradition ; but the honest reprobation of vice and crime which they symbolized should by no means perish with them. The true life of a nation is in its personal morality, and no excellence of constitution and laws can avail much if the people lack purity and integrity. Culture, art, refinement, care for our own comfort and that of others, are all well; but truth, honor, reverence, and fidelity to duty are indispensable.

The Pilgrims were right in affirming the paramount authority of the law of God. If they erred in seeking that authoritative law, and passed over the Sermon on the Mount for the stern Hebraisms of Moses; if they hesitated in view of the largeness of Christian liberty; if they seemed unwilling to accept the sweetness and light of the good tidings, — let us not forget that it was the mistake of men who feared more than they dared to hope, whose estimate of the exceeding awfulness of sin caused them to dwell upon God's vengeance rather than his compassion; and whose dread of evil was so great that, in shutting their hearts against it, they sometimes shut out the good. It is well for us if we have learned to listen to the sweet persuasion of the Beatitudes; but there are crises in all lives which require also the emphatic "Thou shalt not" of the Decalogue which the founders wrote on the gate-posts of their commonwealth.

Let us, then, be thankful for the assurances which the last few years have afforded us that

> "The Pilgrim spirit is not dead,
> But walks in noon's broad light."

We have seen it in the faith and trust which no circumstances could shake, in heroic self-sacrifice, in entire consecration to duty. The fathers have lived in their sons. Have we not all known the Winthrops and Brewsters, the Saltonstalls and Sewalls, of old times, in gubernatorial chairs, in legislative halls, around winter camp-fires, in the slow martyrdoms of prison and hospital? The great struggle through which we have passed has taught us how much we owe to the men and women of the Plymouth Colony, — the noblest ancestry that ever a people looked back to with love and reverence. Honor, then, to the Pilgrims! Let their memory be green forever!

KNOCKED ABOUT. — Daniel Connolly.

WHY don't I work ?   Well, sir, will you,
    Right here on the spot, give me suthin' to do ?
Work !   Why, sir, I don't want no more
'N a chance in any man's shop or store ;
That 's what I 'm lookin' for every day,
But thar ain't no jobs ; well, what d' ye say ?
Hain't got nothin' at present !   Just so ;
That 's how it always is, I know !

Fellers like me ain't wanted much ;
Folks are gen'rally jealous of such ;
Thinks they ain't the right sort o' stuff, —
Blessed if it is n't a kind o' rough
On a man to have folks hintin' belief
That he ain't to be trusted more 'n a thief,
When p'r'aps his fingers are cleaner far
'N them o' chaps that talk so are !

Got a look o' the sea ?   Well, I 'xpect that 's so ;
Had a hankerin' that way some years ago,
And run off ; I shipped in a whaler fust,
And got cast away ; but that warn't the wust ;
Took fire, sir, next time, we did, and — well,
We blazed up till everything standin' fell,
And then me and Tom — my mate — and some more,
Got off, with a notion of goin' ashore.

But thar warn't no shore to see round thar,
So we drifted and drifted everywhar
For a week, and then all but Tom and me
Was food for the sharks or down in the sea.
But we prayed — me and Tom — the best we could,
For a sail.   It come, and at last we stood
On old arth once more, and the captain told
Us we was ashore in the land o' gold.

Gold! We did n't get much. But we struck
For the mines, of course, and tried our luck.
'T warn't bad at the start, but things went wrong
Pooty soon, for one night thar come along,
While we was asleep, some redskin chaps,
And they made things lively round thar — perhaps!
Anyhow we left mighty quick — Tom and me,
And we did n't go back, — kind o' risky, yer see!

By'm-by, sir, the war come on, and then
We 'listed. Poor Tom! I was nigh him when
It all happened. He looked up and sez, sez he,
" Bill, it 's come to partin' 'twixt you and me,
Old chap. I hain't much to leave — here, this knife —
Stand to your colors, Bill, while you have life!"
That was all. — Yes, got wounded myself, sir, here,
And — I 'm pensioned on water and air a year!

It ain't much to thank for that I 'm alive,
Knockin' about like this — What, a five!
That 's suthin' han'some, now, that is. I 'm blest
If things don't quite frequent turn out for the best
Arter all! A V! Hi! Luck! It 's far more!
Mister, I kind o' liked the looks o' your store.
You 're a trump, sir, a reg — Eh? O, all right!
I 'm off, — but you are, sir, a trump, honor bright!

———— ◆ ————

THE LABORER. — WILLIAM D. GALLAGHER.

STAND up — erect! Thou hast the form
And likeness of thy God! — who more?
A soul as dauntless 'mid the storm
Of daily life, a heart as warm
    And pure, as breast e'er wore.

What then? — Thou art as true a man
    As moves the human mass among;

THE LABORER.

As much a part of the great plan
That with Creation's dawn began,
   As any of the throng.

Who is thine enemy ? the high
   In station, or in wealth the chief ?
The great, who coldly pass thee by,
With proud step and averted eye ?
   Nay ! Nurse not such belief.

If true unto thyself thou wast,
   What were the proud one's scorn to thee ?
A feather, which thou mightest cast
Aside, as idly as the blast
   The light leaf from the tree.

No ; — uncurbed passions, low desires,
   Absence of noble self-respect,
Death, in the breast's consuming fires
To that high nature which aspires
   Forever, till thus checked, —

These are thy enemies, — thy worst ;
   They chain thee to thy lowly lot,
Thy labor and thy life accursed :
O, stand erect ! and from them burst,
   And longer suffer not !

Thou art thyself thine enemy !
The great ! — what better they than thou ?
As theirs is not thy will as free ?
Has God with equal favors thee
   Neglected to endow ?

True, wealth thou hast not, — 't is but dust !
   Nor place, — uncertain as the wind !
But that thou hast which, with thy crust

And water, may despise the lust
  Of both, — a noble mind.

With this, and passions under ban,
  True faith, and holy trust in God,
Thou art the peer of any man.
Look up, then ; that thy little span
  Of life may well be trod.

THE GRAY FOREST EAGLE. — A. B. Street.

WITH storm-daring pinion, and sun-gazing eye,
  The Gray Forest Eagle is King of the sky !
O, little he loves the green valley of flowers,
Where sunshine and song cheer the bright summer hours,
But the dark, gloomy gorge, where down plunges the foam
Of the fierce, rocky torrent, he claims as his home ;
There he blends his keen shriek with the roar of the flood,
And the many-voiced sounds of the blast-smitten wood.

A fitful red glaring, a low, rumbling jar,
Proclaim the Storm-Demon, yet raging afar ;
The black cloud strides upward, the lightning more red,
And the roll of the thunder, more deep and more dread :
The Gray Forest Eagle, where, where has he sped ?
Does he shrink to his eyry, and shiver with dread ?
Does the glare blind his eyes ?   Has the terrible blast
On the wing of the Sky-King a fear-fetter cast ?

O no, the brave Eagle ! he thinks not of fright ;
The wrath of the tempest but rouses delight ;
To the flash of the lightning his eye casts a gleam,
To the shriek of the wild blast he echoes his scream,
And with front like a warrior that speeds to the fray,
And a clapping of pinions, he 's up and away !
Away, O away, soars the fearless and free !

What recks he the sky's strife ? — its monarch is he !
The lightning darts round him, — undaunted his sight ;
The blast sweeps against him, — unwavered his flight ;
High upward, still upward he wheels, till his form
Is lost in the dark scowling gloom of the storm.

The tempest glides o'er with its terrible train,
And the splendor of sunshine is glowing again ;
And full on the form of the tempest in flight,
The rainbow's magnificence gladdens the sight !
The Gray Forest Eagle ! O, where is he now,
While the sky wears the smile of its God on its brow ?
There 's a dark floating spot by yon cloud's pearly wreath,
With the speed of the arrow 't is shooting beneath ;
Down, nearer and nearer, it draws to the gaze, —
Now over the rainbow, — now blent with its blaze ;
'T is the Eagle, — the Gray Forest Eagle ! — once more
He sweeps to his eyry, — his journey is o'er !

Time whirls round his circle, his years roll away,
But the Gray Forest Eagle minds little his sway ;
The child spurns its buds for youth's thorn-hidden bloom
Seeks manhood's bright phantoms, finds age and a tomb ;
But the Eagle's eye dims not, his wing is unbowed,
Still drinks he the sunshine, still scales he the cloud.

An emblem of Freedom, stern, haughty, and high,
Is the Gray Forest Eagle, that King of the sky !
When his shadows steal black o'er the empires of kings,
Deep terror, — deep heart-shaking terror, — he brings ;
Where wicked oppression is armed for the weak,
There rustles his pinion, there echoes his shriek ;
His eye flames with vengeance, he sweeps on his way,
And his talons are bathed in the blood of his prey.

O that Eagle of Freedom ! when cloud upon cloud
Swathed the sky of my own native land with a shroud,

5   G

When lightnings gleamed fiercely, and thunderbolts rung,
How proud to the tempest those pinions were flung !
Though the wild blast of battle rushed fierce through the air
With darkness and dread, still the Eagle was there ;
Unquailing, still speeding, his swift flight was on,
Till the rainbow of Peace crowned the victory won.

O, that Eagle of Freedom ! age dims not his eye,
He has seen earth's mortality spring, bloom, and die !
He has seen the strong nations rise, flourish, and fall ;
He mocks at time's changes, he triumphs o'er all ;
He has seen our own land with wild forests o'erspread,
He sees it with sunshine and joy on its head ;
And his presence will bless this his own chosen clime,
Till the Archangel's fiat is set upon Time.

WHEN MARY WAS A LASSIE.

THE maple-trees are tinged with red,
   The birch with golden yellow ;
And high above the orchard wall
   Hang apples, rich and mellow ;
And that 's the way, through yonder lane
   That looks so still and grassy, —
The way I took one Sunday eve,
   When Mary was a lassie.

You 'd hardly think that patient face,
   That looks so thin and faded,
Was once the very sweetest one
   That ever bonnet shaded ;
But when I went through yonder lane,
   That looks so still and grassy,
Those eyes were bright, those cheeks were fair,
   When Mary was a lassie.

But many a tender sorrow,
　　And many a patient care,
Have made those furrows on the face
　　That used to be so fair.
Four times to yonder churchyard,
　　Through the lane, so still and grassy,
We 've borne and laid away our dead,
　　Since Mary was a lassie.

And, as you see, I 've grown to love
　　The wrinkles more than roses ;
Earth's winter flowers are sweeter far
　　Than all spring's dewy posies :
They 'll carry us through yonder lane
　　That looks so still and grassy,
Adown the lane I used to go
　　When Mary was a lassie.

THE PIANO MANIA. — JENNIE JUNE.

THERE is no social disease so widespread, so virulent, and so fatal in its attack as the piano mania. Before a girl is born, nowadays, she is predestined to sit and exact dreadful screechings and wailings from some unhappy instrument for at least ten years of her natural life. No question as to whether she possesses an ear, and no consideration for the ears of other people, is permitted to interfere with the decree, which is irrevocable as the laws of the Medes and Persians, that " Katy " or " Lucindy," as the case may be, "must play the piano." The poor thing may be a natural-born house-keeper, with a genius for sweeping and dusting, washing and baking, but with no more perception of chords and cadences than of the music of the spheres. Still she will not be per-mitted to follow her natural bent because it is so horribly vul-gar. She will be wept over, scolded, and fretted at, and any lazy, fine lady, sister, or cousin held up as an example of gentility.

To be able to play the piano in company is the *sine qua non* of many foolish, fond mothers' hopes, who look back with regret on their own limited chances for education, and are therefore apt sadly to overrate the value of what are called accomplishments. Playing the piano is undoubtedly a very good thing when it is well done, and by a person who possesses musical taste; but otherwise it is only a torture for a sensitive ear to listen to it. Jingle, jingle, jingle! thump, thump, thump! Who has not shivered and winced, and tried to appear amiable through the interminable hours of a small evening-party, while some youthful tormentor, harassed into the display by stupid friends, was vigorously pounding out a miscellaneous assortment of battles and marches, songs and quadrilles, waltzes and opera, without the slightest notion concerning them, except that certain keys in the piano correspond to certain notes in the book.

Excepting for evening parlor dances, the piano should never be played without accompaniment of a voice, unless by a Thalberg, and even then only a few will be found to care enthusiastically for the mere science or grace of execution; and if this is true of the professor in the art, how much pleasure is it supposed can be obtained from hearing the monotonous or spasmodic thrumming of a girl, whose entire capacity for music has been scolded or cajoled into her, and who would much rather be employed in doing something else, even though it were sweeping or washing dishes!

If the knowledge of the piano were easily acquired and retained, the objections against this universal passion would lose much of their force; but the truth is, that it wastes so much of the valuable time in many young girls' lives that could be turned to good account, that it becomes absolute sin; and what real use do they make of it after all? How many young women who were supposed to possess musical talents have made the remark, " O, I have never touched the piano since I was married ! " — an exaggerated statement, which soon becomes a literal truth.

The truth is, that "playing the piano" don't pay, unless a certain amount of musical genius is developed, and a voice. Any quantity of girls could perfect themselves in other and quite as attractive branches of a "polite education" for which they have a taste, and prepare to become good wives and mothers in the time which is uselessly spent in endeavoring to make them "play the piano."

But there is little hope that it will be so. Fathers will continue to gratify their pride and vanity by buying second-hand pianos instead of sewing-machines, and mothers will urge slipshod daughters to sit down to them, instead of teaching them to mend stockings. The signor's bill will be preferred to the grocer's, because "the girls" must have the advantage of the best, — that is to say, the most expensive masters, — and so they are taught lessons in music, extravagance, dishonesty, and personal neglect, all at the same time. Surely a cheap way of acquiring so much that is made available in after life, besides learning to play on the piano.

FONTENOY. — Thomas Davis.

THRICE, at the huts of Fontenoy, the English column failed,
And twice the lines of St. Antoine the Dutch in vain assailed;
For town and slope were filled with fort and flanking battery,
And well they swept the English ranks, and Dutch auxiliary.
As, vainly, through De Barri's wood the British soldiers burst,
The French artillery drove them back, diminished and dispersed.
The bloody Duke of Cumberland beheld with anxious eye,
And ordered up his last reserve his latest chance to try.
On Fontenoy, on Fontenoy, how fast his generals ride,
And mustering come his chosen troops, like clouds at eventide.

Six thousand English veterans in stately column tread,
Their cannon blaze in front and flank, — Lord Hay is at their
head ;
Steady they step adown the slope, — steady they climb the
hill ;
Steady they load, — steady they fire, moving right onward
still,
Betwixt the wood and Fontenoy, as through a furnace blast,
Through rampart, trench, and palisade, and bullets showering
fast ;
And on the open plain above they rose, and kept their course,
With ready fire and grim resolve, that mocked at hostile
force ;
Past Fontenoy, past Fontenoy, while thinner grow their ranks,
They break, as broke the Zuyder Zee through Holland's ocean
banks.

More idly than the summer flies, French tirailleurs rush
round ;
As stubble to the lava tide, French squadrons strew the
ground ;
Bomb-shell, and grape, and round-shot tore, still on they
marched and fired, —
Fast from each volley grenadier and voltigeur retired.
" Push on, my household cavalry ! " King Louis madly cried ;
To death they rush, but rude their shock, — not unavenged
they died.
On through the camp the column trod, — King Louis turns
his rein :
" Not yet, my liege," Saxe interposed, "the Irish troops re-
main " ;
And Fontenoy, famed Fontenoy, had been a Waterloo,
Were not these exiles ready then, fresh, vehement, and true.

" Lord Clare," he says, " you have your wish, there are your
Saxon foes ! "
The Marshal almost smiles to see how furiously he goes !

How fierce the look those exiles wear, who 're won't to be so
 gay,
The treasured wrongs of fifty years are in their hearts to-
 day, —
The treaty broken, ere the ink wherewith 'twas writ could
 dry,
Their plundered homes, their ruined shrines, their women's
 parting cry,
Their priesthood hunted down like wolves, their country over-
 thrown,
Each looks as if revenge for all were staked on him alone.
On Fontenoy, on Fontenoy, nor ever yet elsewhere,
Rushed on to fight a nobler band than these proud exiles
 were.

O'Brien's voice is hoarse with joy, as, halting, he commands,
" Fix bayonets — charge ! " Like mountain storm rush on
 these fiery bands.
Thin is the English column now, and faint their volleys grow,
Yet, mustering all the strength they have, they make a gal-
 lant show.
They dress their ranks upon the hill to face that battle-wind,
Their bayonets the breaker's foam ; like rocks, the men be-
 hind !
One volley crashes from their line, when, through the surging
 smoke,
With empty guns clutched in their hands, the headlong Irish
 broke.
On Fontenoy, on Fontenoy, hark to that fierce huzza !
" Revenge ! remember Limerick ! dash down the Sacsanach ! "

Like lions leaping at a fold, when mad with hunger's pang,
Right up against the English line the Irish exiles sprang ;
Bright was their steel, 't is bloody now, their guns are filled
 with gore ;
Through shattered ranks, and severed files, and trampled flags
 they tore :

The English strove with desperate strength, paused, rallied,
    staggered, fled —
The green hillside is matted close with dying and with dead.
Across the plain and far away passed on that hideous wrack,
While cavalier and fantassin dash in upon their track.
On Fontenoy, on Fontenoy, like eagles in the sun,
With bloody plumes the Irish stand, — the field is fought and
    won !

BEAUTIFUL SNOW. — J. W. Watson.

O THE snow, the beautiful snow,
    Filling the sky and earth below ;
Over the house-tops, over the street,
Over the heads of the people you meet,
        Dancing,
            Flirting,
                Skimming along ;
Beautiful snow ; it can do no wrong.
Flying to kiss a fair lady's cheek ;
Clinging to lips in a frolicsome freak.
Beautiful snow from the heavens above,
Pure as an angel, gentle as love !

O the snow, the beautiful snow !
How the flakes gather and laugh as they go !
Whirling about in the maddening fun,
It plays in its glee with every one.
        Chasing,
            Laughing,
                Hurrying by ;
It lights on the face and it sparkles the eye !
And even the dogs, with a bark and a bound,
Snap at the crystals that eddy around.
The town is alive, and its heart in a glow,
To welcome the coming of beautiful snow !

How the wild crowd goes swaying along,
Hailing each other with humor and song !
How the gay sledges, like meteors, flash by,
Bright for the moment, then lost to the eye.
                    Ringing,
                        Swinging,
                            Dashing they go,
Over the crust of the beautiful snow ;
Snow so pure when it falls from the sky,
To be trampled in mud by the crowd rushing by,
To be trampled and tracked by the thousands of feet,
Till it blends with the horrible filth in the street.

Once I was pure as the snow — but I fell :
Fell like the snow-flakes from heaven — to hell ;
Fell to be trampled as filth of the street ;
Fell to be scoffed, to be spit on and beat.
                    Pleading,
                        Cursing,
                            Dreading to die,
Selling my soul to whoever would buy,
Dealing in shame for a morsel of bread,
Hating the living and fearing the dead.
Merciful God ! have I fallen so low ?
And yet I was once like the beautiful snow.

Once I was fair as the beautiful snow,
With an eye like its crystal, a heart like its glow ;
Once I was loved for my innocent grace, —
Flattered and sought for the charms of my face !
                    Father,
                        Mother,
                            Sisters all,
God, and myself, I have lost by my fall.
The veriest wretch that goes shivering by
Will take a wide sweep lest I wander too nigh ;
For of all that is on or about me, I know
There is nothing that 's pure but the beautiful snow.

5 *

How strange it should be that this beautiful snow
Should fall on a sinner with nowhere to go !
How strange it would be, when the night comes again,
If the snow and the ice struck my desperate brain!
Fainting,
Freezing,
Dying alone,
Too wicked for a prayer, too weak for a moan,
To be heard in the crash of the crazy town,
Gone mad in its joy at the snow's coming down,
To lie, and so die in my terrible woe,
With a bed and a shroud of the beautiful snow.

LOVE LIGHTENS LABOR.

A GOOD wife rose from her bed one morn,
    And thought with a nervous dread
Of the piles of clothes to be washed, and more
    Than a dozen mouths to be fed.
There 's the meals to get for the men in the field,
    And the children to fix away
To school, and the milk to be skimmed and churned;
    And all to be done this day.

It had rained in the night, and all the wood
    Was wet as it could be ;
There were puddings and pies to bake, besides
    A loaf of cake for tea.
And the day was hot, and her aching head
    Throbbed wearily as she said :
" If maidens but knew what good wives know,
    They would be in no haste to wed !"

" Jennie, what do you think I told Ben Brown ?"
    Called the farmer from the well ;

And a flush crept up to his bronzéd brow,
   And his eyes half bashfully fell.
" It was this," he said, and, coming near,
   He smiled, and, stooping down,
Kissed her cheek, — " 'T was this : that you were the best
   And the dearest wife in town ! "

The farmer went back to the field, and the wife,
   In a smiling and absent way,
Sang snatches of tender little songs
   She 'd not sung for many a day.
And the pain in her head was gone, and the clothes
   Were white as the foam of the sea ;
Her bread was light, and her butter was sweet
   And as golden as it could be.

' Just think," the children all called in a breath,
   " Tom Wood has run off to sea !
He would n't, I know, if he only had
   As happy a home as we."
The night came down, and the good wife smiled
   To herself, as she softly said :
" 'T is so sweet to labor for those we love,
   It 's not strange that maids will wed ! "

THE RING. — G. E. Lessing.

Translated by Miss Frothingham.

IN gray antiquity there lived a man
   In Eastern lands, who had received a ring
Of priceless worth from a beloved hand.
Its stone, an opal, flashed a hundred colors,
And had the secret power of giving favor,
In sight of God and man, to him who wore it
With a believing heart. What wonder, then,

This Eastern man would never put the ring
From off his finger, and should so provide
That to his house it be preserved forever?
Such was the case.   Unto the best-beloved
Among his sons he left the ring, enjoining
That he in turn bequeath it to the son
Who should be dearest ; and the dearest ever,
In virtue of the ring, without regard
To birth, be of the house the prince and head.

From son to son the ring, descending, came
To one, the sire of three ; of whom all three
Were equally obedient ; whom all three
He therefore must with equal love regard.
And yet, from time to time, now this, now that,
And now the third, — as each alone was by,
The others not dividing his fond heart, —
Appeared to him the worthiest of the ring ;
Which then, with loving weakness, he would promise
To each in turn.   Thus it continued long.
But he must die ; and then the loving father
Was sore perplexed.   It grieved him thus to wound
Two faithful sons who trusted in his word ;
But what to do ?   In secrecy he calls
An artist to him, and commands of him
Two other rings, the pattern of his own ;
And bids him neither cost nor pains to spare
To make them like, precisely like to that.
The artist's skill succeeds.   He brings the rings,
And e'en the father cannot tell his own.
Relieved and joyful summons he his sons,
Each by himself ; to each one by himself
He gives his blessing, and his ring, — and dies.
But bring your story to an end.   'T is ended,
For what remains would tell itself.   The father
Was scarcely dead, when each brings forth his ring,
And claims the headship.   Questioning ensues,

Strife, and appeal to law; but all in vain.
The genuine ring was not to be distinguished, —
As undistinguishable as with us
The true religion.

           As I have said
The sons appealed to law, and each took oath
Before the judge, that from his father's hand
He had the ring, — as was indeed the truth, —
And had received his promise long before,
One day the ring, with all its privileges,
Should be his own, — as was not less the truth.
The father could not have been false to him,
Each one maintained; and rather than allow
Upon the memory of so dear a father
Such stain to rest, he must against his brothers,
Though gladly he would nothing but the best
Believe of them, bring charge of treachery;
Means would he find the traitors to expose,
And be revenged on them.

              Thus spoke the judge : Produce your father
At once before me, else from my tribunal
Do I dismiss you.   Think you I am here
To guess your riddles ?   Either would you wait
Until the genuine ring shall speak ? — But hold!
A magic power in the true ring resides,
As I am told, to make its wearer loved,
Pleasing to God and man.   Let that decide,
For in the false can no such virtue lie.
Which one among you, then, do two love best ?
Speak!   Are you silent?   Work the rings but backward,
Not outward?   Loves each one himself the best ?
Then cheated cheats are all of you!   The rings,
All three, are false.   The genuine ring was lost;
And to conceal, supply the loss, the father
Made three in place of one.

Go, therefore, said the judge, unless my counsel
You 'd have in place of sentence.   It were this :
Accept the case exactly as it stands.
Had each his ring directly from his father,
Let each believe his own is genuine.
'T is possible your father would no longer
His house to one ring's tyranny subject ;
And certain that all three of you he loved,
Loved equally, since two he would not humble
That one might be exalted.   Let each one
To his unbought, impartial love aspire ;
Each with the others vie to bring to light
The virtue of the stone within his ring ;
Let gentleness, a hearty love of peace,
Beneficence, and perfect trust in God,
Come to its help.   Then, if the jewel's power
Among your children's children be revealed,
I bid you, in a thousand thousand years,
Again before this bar.   A wiser man
Than I shall occupy this seat, and speak.
Go !   Thus the modest judge dismissed them.

THE MERRY SOAP–BOILER.

A STEADY and a skilful toiler,
   John got his bread as a soap-boiler ;
Earned all he wished, — his heart was light,
He worked and sang from morn till night.
E'en during meals his notes were heard,
And to his beer were oft preferred ;
At breakfast, and at supper too,
His throat had double work to do.
He oftener sang than said his prayers,
And dropped asleep while humming airs ;
Until his every next-door neighbor

Had learned the tunes that cheered his labor,
And every passer-by could tell
Where merry John was wont to dwell.
At reading he was rather slack,
Studied at most the almanac,
To know when holidays were nigh,
And put his little savings by ;
But sang the more on vacant days,
To waste the less his means and ways.

'T is always well to live and learn.
The owner of the soap concern —
A fat and wealthy burgomaster,
Who drank his hock and smoked his knaster,
At marketing was always apter
Than any prelate in the chapter,
And thought a pheasant in sour-krout
Superior to a turkey-poult ;
But woke at times before daybreak
With heartburn, gout, or liver-ache —
Oft heard our skylark of the garret
Sing to his slumber, but to mar it.

He sent for John one day, and said,
" What 's your year's income from your trade ? "
" Master, I never thought of counting
To what my earnings are amounting
At the year's end ; if every Monday
I 've paid my meat and drink for Sunday,
And something in the box unspent
Remains for fuel, clothes, and rent,
I 've husbanded the needful scot,
And feel quite easy with my lot.
The maker of the almanac
Must, like your lordship, know no lack,
Else a red-letter, earnless day
Would oftener be struck away."

" John, you 've been long a faithful fellow,
Though always merry, seldom mellow.
Take this rouleau of fifty dollars, —
My purses glibly slip their collars, —
But before breakfast let this singing
No longer in my ears be ringing ;
When once your lips and eyes unclose,
I must forego my morning doze."

John blushes, bows, and stammers thanks,
And steals away on bended shanks,
Hiding and hugging his new treasure,
As had it been a stolen seizure.
At home he bolts his chamber-door,
Views, counts, and weighs his tinkling store,
Nor trusts it to the savings-box
Till he has screwed on double locks.
His dog and he play tricks no more,
They 're rival watchmen of the door.
Small wish has he to sing a word,
Lest thieves should climb his stair unheard.
At length he finds, the more he saves,
The more he frets, the more he craves ;
That his old freedom was a blessing
Ill sold for all he 's now possessing.

One day, he to his master went
And carried back his hoard unspent.
" Master," says he, " I 've heard of old,
Unblest is he who watches gold.
Take back your present, and restore
The cheerfulness I knew before.
I 'll take a room not quite so near,
Out of your worship's reach of ear,
Sing at my pleasure, laugh at sorrow,
Enjoy to-day, nor dread to-morrow,
Be still the steady, honest toiler,
The merry John, the old soap-boiler."

DEATH OF POÓR JO. — Dickens.

JO is very glad to see his old friend, and says, when they are left alone, that he takes it uncommon kind as Mr. Sangsby should come so far out of his way on accounts of sich as him. Mr. Snagsby, touched by the spectacle before him, immediately lays upon the table half a crown, — that magic balm of his for all kinds of wounds.

"And how do you find yourself, my poor lad?" inquires the stationer, with his cough of sympathy.

"I am in luck, Mr. Sangsby, I am," returns Jo, "and don't want for nothink. I 'm more cumfbler nor you can't think. Mr. Sangsby! I 'm wery sorry that I done it, but I did n't go fur to do it, sir."

The stationer softly lays down another half-crown, and asks him what it is that he is so sorry for having done.

"Mr. Sangsby," says Jo, "I went and give a illness to the lady as wos and yit as warn't the t'other lady, and none of 'em never says nothink to me for having done it, on accounts of their being ser good and my having been s' unfortnet. The lady come herself and see me yesday, and she ses, ' Ah, Jo!' she ses. 'We thought we 'd lost you, Jo!' she ses. And she sits down a smilin' so quiet, and don't pass a word nor yit a look upon me for having done it, she don't, and I turns agin the wall, I doos, Mr. Sangsby. And Mr. Jarnders, I see him forced to turn away his own self. And Mr. Woodcot, he come fur to giv me somethink for to ease me, wot he 's allus a doin' on day and night, and wen he come a bendin' over me and a speakin' up so bold, I see his tears a fallin', Mr. Sangsby."

The softened stationer deposits another half-crown on the table. Nothing less than a repetition of that infallible remedy will relieve his feelings.

"Wot I wos a thinkin' on, Mr. Sangsby," proceeds Jo, "wos, as you wos able to write wery large, p'r'aps?"

"Yes, Jo, please God," returns the stationer.

"Uncommon precious large, p'r'aps?" says Jo, with eagerness.   H

"Yes, my poor boy."

Jo laughs with pleasure. " Wot I was thinkin' on then, Mr. Sangsby, wos, that wen I was moved on as fur as ever I could go and could n't be moved no furder, whether you might be so good, p'r'aps, as to write out, wery large so that any one could see it anywheres, as that I wos wery truly hearty sorry that I done it and that I never went fur to do it; and that though I did n't know nothink at all, I knowd as Mr. Woodcot once cried over it and wos allus grieved over it, and that I hoped as he 'd be able to forgiv me in his mind. If the writin' could be made to say it wery large, he might."

" It shall say it, Jo. Very large."

Jo laughs again. " Thank'ee, Mr. Sangsby. It 's wery kind of you, sir, and it makes me more cumfbler nor I was afore."

The meek little stationer, with a broken and unfinished cough, slips down his fourth half-crown, — he has never been so close to a case requiring so many, — and is fain to depart. And Jo and he upon this little earth shall meet no more. No more.

For the cart, so hard to draw, is near its journey's end, and drags over stony ground. All round the clock, it labors up the broken steeps, shattered and worn. Not many times can the sun rise, and behold it still upon its weary road.

Jo is in a sleep or stupor to-day, and Allan Woodcourt, newly arrived, stands by him, looking down upon his wasted form. After a while, he softly seats himself upon the bedside with his face toward him, and touches his chest and heart. The cart had very nearly given up, but labors on a little more.

" Well, Jo ! What is the matter ? Don't be frightened."

" I thought," says Jo, who has started, and is looking round, — " I thought I was in Tom-all-Alone's agin. An't there nobody here but you, Mr. Woodcot ?"

" Nobody."

" And I an't took back to Tom-all-Alone's. Am I, sir ? "

" No." Jo closes his eyes, muttering, " I 'm wery thankful."

After watching him closely a little while, Allan puts his mouth very near his ear, and says to him in a low, distinct voice, —

"Jo! Did you ever know a prayer?"

"Never knowd nothink, sir."

"Not so much as one short prayer?"

"No, sir. Nothink at all. Mr. Chadbands he wos a prayin' wunst at Mr. Sangsby's, and I heerd him, but he sounded as if he wos speakin' to hisself, and not to me. He prayed a lot, but *I* could n't make out nothink on it. Different times there wos other genlmen come down Tom-all-Alone's a prayin', but they all mostly sed as the t' other wuns prayed wrong, and all mostly sounded to be a talking to theirselves, or a passing blame on the t' others, and not a talkin' to us. *We* never knowd nothink. *I* never knowd what it wos all about."

It takes him a long time to say this; and few but an experienced and attentive listener could hear, or, hearing, understand him. After a short relapse into sleep or stupor, he makes, of a sudden, a strong effort to get out of bed.

"Stay, Jo, stay! What now?"

"It 's time for me to go to that there berryin-ground, sir," he returns, with a wild look.

"Lie down, and tell me. What burying-ground, Jo?"

"Where they laid him as wos very good to me; very good to me indeed, he wos. It 's time fur me to go down to that there berryin-ground, sir, and ask to be put along with him. I wants to go there and be berried. He used fur to say to me, ' I am as poor as you to-day, Jo,' he ses. I wants to tell him that I am as poor as him now, and have come there to be laid along with him."

"By and by, Jo. By and by."

"Ah! P'r'aps they would n't do it if I wos to go myself. But will you promise to have me took there, sir, and have me laid along with him?"

"I will, indeed."

"Thank'ee, sir! Thank'ee, sir! They 'll have to get the key of the gate afore they can take me in, for it 's allus locked.

And there 's a step there, as I used fur to clean with my broom. It 's turned wery dark, sir. Is there any light a comin' ? "

" It is coming fast, Jo."

Fast. The cart is shaken all to pieces, and the rugged road is very near its end.

" Jo, my poor fellow ! "

" I hear you, sir, in the dark, but I 'm a gropin', — a gropin', — let me catch hold of your hand."

" Jo, can you say what I say ? "

" I 'll say anythink as you say, sir, for I knows it 's good."

" OUR FATHER."

" Our Father ! — yes, that 's wery good, sir."

" WHICH ART IN HEAVEN."

" Art in Heaven — is the light a comin', sir ? "

" It is close at hand. HALLOWED BE THY NAME ! "

" Hallowed be — thy — name ! "

The light is come upon the dark benighted way. Dead !

Dead, your Majesty. Dead, my lords and gentlemen. Dead, Right Reverends and Wrong Reverends of every order. Dead, men and women, born with heavenly compassion in your hearts. And dying thus around us every day !

————◆————

ADDRESS OF LEONIDAS. — RICHARD GLOVER.

HE alone
Remains unshaken. Rising, he displays
His godlike presence. Dignity and grace
Adorn his frame, and manly beauty, joined
With strength herculean. On his aspect shines
Sublimest virtue and desire of fame,
Where justice gives the laurel ; in his eye
The inextinguishable spark, which fires
The souls of patriots ; while his brow supports
Undaunted valor and contempt of death.

Serene he rose, and thus addressed the throng :
" Why this astonishment on every face,
Ye men of Sparta ?   Does the name of death
Create this fear and wonder ?   O my friends !
Why do we labor through the arduous paths
Which lead to virtue ?   Fruitless were the toil,
Above the reach of human feet were placed
The distant summit, if the fear of death
Could intercept our passage.   But in vain
His blackest frowns and terrors he assumes
To shake the firmness of the mind which knows
That, wanting virtue, life is pain and woe ;
That, wanting liberty, even virtue mourns,
And looks around for happiness in vain.
Then speak, O Sparta ! and demand my life ;
My heart, exulting, answers to thy call,
And smiles on glorious fate.   To live with fame
The gods allow to many ; but to die
With equal lustre is a blessing Heaven
Selects from all the choicest boons of fate,
And with a sparing hand on few bestows."
Salvation thus to Sparta he proclaimed.
Joy, wrapped awhile in admiration, paused
Suspending praise ; nor praise at last resounds
In high acclaim to rend the arch of Heaven ;
A reverential murmur breathes applause.

ANNABEL LEE. — EDGAR A. POE.

IT was many and many a year ago,
   In a kingdom by the sea,
That a maiden there lived whom you may know
   By the name of Annabel Lee.
And this maiden she lived with no other thought
   Than to love and be loved by me.

I was a child and *she* was a child,
  In this kingdom by the sea ;
But we loved with a love that was more than love,
  I and my Annabel Lee ;
With a love that the winged seraphs of heaven
  Coveted her and me.

And this was the reason that, long ago,
  In this kingdom by the sea,
A wind blew out of a cloud, chilling
  My beautiful Annabel Lee ;
So that her high-born kinsmen came
  And bore her away from me,
To shut her up in a sepulchre
  In this kingdom by the sea.

Our love it was stronger by far than the love
  Of those who were older than we,
  Of many far wiser than we ;
And neither the angels in heaven above,
  Nor the demons down under the sea,
Can ever dissever my soul from the soul
  Of the beautiful Annabel Lee.

For the moon never beams without bringing me dreams
  Of this beautiful Annabel Lee ;
And the stars never rise but I feel the bright eyes
  Of the beautiful Annabel Lee :
And so all the night-tide I lie down by the side
Of my darling, my darling, my life and my bride,
  In the sepulchre there by the sea,
  In her tomb by the sounding sea.

BOY LOST.

HE had black eyes, with long lashes, red cheeks, and hair almost black and almost curly. He wore a crimson plaid jacket, with full trousers buttoned on; had a habit of whistling, and liked to ask questions; was accompanied by a small black dog. It is a long while now since he disappeared. I have a very pleasant house and much company. My guests say, "Ah! it is pleasant here! Everything has such an orderly, put-away look, — nothing about under foot, no dirt!"

But my eyes are aching for the sight of whittlings and cut paper upon the floor, of tumble-down card-houses, of wooden sheep and cattle, of pop-guns, bows and arrows, whips, tops, go-carts, blocks, and trumpery. I want to see boats a-rigging, and kites a-making, crumbles on the carpet, and paste spilt on the kitchen-table. I want to see the chairs and tables turned the wrong way about. I want to see candy-making and corn-popping, and to find jack-knives and fish-hooks among my muslins. Yet these things used to fret me once.

They say, "How quiet you are here! Ah! one here may settle his brains and be at peace." But my ears are aching for the pattering of little feet, for a hearty shout, a shrill whistle, a gay tra-la-la, for the crack of little whips, for the noise of drums, fifes, and tin trumpets; yet these things made me nervous once.

They say, "Ah! you have leisure, — nothing to disturb you; what heaps of sewing you have time for!" But I long to be asked for a bit of string or an old newspaper, for a cent to buy a slate-pencil or peanuts. I want to be coaxed for a piece of new cloth for jibs or main-sails, and then to hem the same. I want to make little flags, and bags to hold marbles. I want to be followed by little feet all over the house, teasing for a bit of dough, for a little cake, or to bake a pie in a sau. cer. Yet these things used to fidget me once.

They say, "Ah! you are not tied at home! How delightful to be always at liberty to go to concerts, lectures, and parties ! No confinement for you."

But I want confinement. I want to listen for the school-bell mornings, to give the last hasty wash and brush, and then to watch from the window nimble feet bounding to school. I want frequent rents to mend, and to replace lost buttons. I want to obliterate mud-stains, fruit-stains, molasses-stains, and paints of all colors. I want to be sitting by a little crib of evenings, when weary feet are at rest, and prattling voices are hushed that mothers may sing their lulla-bys, and tell over the oft-repeated stories. They don't know their happiness then, — those mothers. I did n't. All these things I called confinement once.

A manly figure stands before me now. He is taller than I, has thick black whiskers, and wears a frock-coat, bosomed shirt, and cravat. He has just come from college. He brings Latin and Greek in his countenance, and busts of the old philosophers for the sitting-room. He calls me mother, but I am rather unwilling to own him.

He stoutly declares that he is my boy, and says that he will prove it. He brings me a small pair of white trousers, with gay stripes at the sides, and asks if I did n't make them for him when he joined the boys' militia. He says he is the very boy, too, that made the bonfire near the barn, so that we came very near having a fire in earnest. I see it all. My little boy is lost. O, I wish he were a little tired boy, in a long white nightgown, lying in his crib, with me sitting by, holding his hand in mine, pushing the curls back from his forehead, watching his eyelids droop, and listening to his deep breathing !

If I only had my little boy again, how patient I would be ! How much I would bear, and how little I would fret and scold ! I can never have him back again ; but there are still many mothers who have n't yet lost their little boys. I won-der if they know they are living their very best days ; that now is the time to really enjoy their children.

BORRIOBOOLA GHA. — O. Goodrich.

A STRANGER preached last Sunday,
  And crowds of people came
To hear a two hours' sermon
  On a theme I scarce can name ;
'T was all about some heathen,
  Thousands of miles afar,
Who live in a land of darkness,
  Called Borrioboola Gha.

So well their wants he pictured,
  That when the box was passed,
Each listener felt his pocket,
  And goodly sums were cast ;
For all must lend a shoulder
  To push the rolling car
That carries light and comfort
  To Borrioboola Gha.

That night their wants and sorrows
  Lay heavy on my soul,
And deep in meditation,
  I took my morning stroll,
When something caught my mantle
  With eager grasp and wild ;
And, looking down in wonder,
  I saw a little child, —

A pale and puny creature,
  In rags and dirt forlorn :
" What do you want ? " I asked her,
  Impatient to be gone ;
With trembling voice she answered,
  " We live just down the street,
And mamma, she 's a-dying,
  And we 've nothing left to eat."

6

Down in a dark, damp cellar,
  With mould o'er all the walls,
Through whose half-buried windows
  God's sunlight never falls;
Where cold and want and hunger
  Crouched near her as she lay,
I found that poor child's mother,
  Gasping her life away.

A chair, a broken table,
  A bed of mouldy straw,
A hearth all dark and fireless;
  But these I scarcely saw,
For the mournful sight before me,
  So sad and sickening, — O,
I had never, never pictured
  A scene so full of woe!

The famished and the naked,
  The babe that pined for bread,
The squalid group that huddled
  Around that dying bed;
All this distress and sorrow
  Should be in lands afar;
Was I suddenly transported
  To Borrioboola Gha?

Ah no! the poor and wretched
  Were close beside my door,
And I had passed them heedless
  A thousand times before:
Alas, for the cold and hungry
  That met me every day,
While all my tears were given
  To the suffering far away!

There's work enough for Christians,
  In distant lands, we know,

Our Lord commands his servants
  Through all the world to go,
Not only to the heathen ;
  This was his command to them :
" Go, preach the Word, beginning
  Here, at Jerusalem."

O Christian, God has promised
  Whoe'er to such has given
A cup of pure, cold water
  Shall find reward in heaven.
Would you secure this blessing ?
  You need not seek it far ;
Go find in yonder hovel
  A Borrioboola Gha.

THE OLD APPLE-WOMAN.

ONCE she was fair as thou ;
  Had ringlets on her brow ;
Do not despise her now, —
    Not now.

She sitteth in the cold ;
She seemeth very old ;
Be not to her too bold, —
    Too bold.

She sitteth in the heat ;
In the hot and jostling street ;
She never seems to eat, —
    To eat.

From earliest morning light
To the dim shades of the night,
A patient, weary sight, —
    Weary sight.

No one e'er comes to greet,
As she sits on the street;
Sits ever o'er her feet, —
　　　Her feet.

Yet all do pass that way, —
The young, old, grave, and gay;
Yet no one goes to say
　　　Good day.

She looketh on her stand;
She wipes it with her hand, —
Wipes apples, dust, and sand
　　　With her hand.

You stop and ask the way:
" One cent," you hear her say;
Naught else she saith all day, —
　　　All day.

The crowd it ebbs and flows,
Each season comes and goes;
The only " change " she knows,
　　　One cent.

No one e'er calls the name
Of that aged, crooning dame;
None knoweth whence she came, —
　　　She came.

Yet she hath been a bride;
Stood by a mother's side;
Was once a husband's pride, —
　　　His pride.

She had a home as thou;
Gone are both fruit and bough;

Deal gently with her now, —
　　Gently now.

One home ye both shall have ;
One hope beyond the grave ;
One faith ye both shall save, —
　　Shall save.

———◆———

THE VAGABONDS. — J. T. Trowbridge.

WE are two travellers, Roger and I.
　　Roger 's my dog. — Come here, you scamp !
Jump for the gentlemen, — mind your eye !
　　Over the table, — look out for the lamp ! —
The rogue is growing a little old ;
　　Five years we 've tramped through wind and weather,
And slept out doors when nights were cold,
　　And ate and drank — and starved — together.

We 've learned what comfort is, I tell you !
　　A bed on the floor, a bit of rosin,
A fire to thaw our thumbs, (poor fellow !
　　The paw he holds up there 's been frozen,)
Plenty of catgut for my fiddle,
　　(This out-door business is bad for strings,)
Then a few nice buckwheats hot from the griddle,
　　And Roger and I set up for kings !

No, thank ye, sir, — I never drink ;
　　Roger and I are exceedingly moral, —
Are n't we, Roger ? — See him wink ! —
　　Well, something hot, then, — we won't quarrel.
He 's thirsty, too, — see him nod his head ?
　　What a pity, sir, that dogs can't talk !
He understands every word that 's said, —
　　And he knows good milk from water-and-chalk.

The truth is, sir, now I reflect,
  I 've been so sadly given to grog,
I wonder I 've not lost the respect
  (Here 's to you, sir !) even of my dog.
But he sticks by, through thick and thin ;
  And this old coat, with its empty pockets,
And rags that smell of tobacco and gin,
  He 'll follow while he has eyes in his sockets.

There is n't another creature living
  Would do it, and prove, through every disaster,
So fond, so faithful, and so forgiving,
  To such a miserable thankless master !
No, sir ! — see him wag his tail and grin !
  By George ! it makes my old eyes water !
That is, there 's something in this gin
  That chokes a fellow.   But no matter !

We 'll have some music, if you 're willing,
  And Roger (hem ! what a plague a cough is, sir !)
Shall march a little. — Start, you villain !
  Stand straight !   'Bout face !   Salute your officer !
Put up that paw !   Dress !   Take your rifle !
  (Some dogs have arms, you see !)   Now hold your
Cap while the gentleman gives a trifle,
  To aid a poor old patriot soldier !

March !   Halt !   Now show how the rebel shakes,
  When he stands up to hear his sentence.
Now tell us how many drams it takes
  To honor a jolly new acquaintance.
Five yelps, — that 's five ; he 's mighty knowing !
  The night 's before us, fill the glasses ! —
Quick, sir !   I 'm ill, — my brain is going ! —
  Some brandy, — thank you, — there ! — it passes !

Why not reform ?   That 's easily said ;
  But I 've gone through such wretched treatment,

Sometimes forgetting the taste of bread,
   And scarce remembering what meat meant,
That my poor stomach 's past reform ;
   And there are times when, mad with thinking,
I 'd sell out heaven for something warm
   To prop a horrible inward sinking.

Is there a way to forget to think ?
   At your age, sir, home, fortune, friends,
A dear girl's love, — but I took to drink ; —
   The same old story ; you know how it ends.
If you could have seen these classic features, —
   You need n't laugh, sir ; they were not then
Such a burning libel on God's creatures :
   I was one of your handsome men !

If you had seen HER, so fair and young,
   Whose head was happy on this breast !
If you could have heard the songs I sung
   When the wine went round, you would n't have guessed
That ever I, sir, should be straying
   From door to door, with fiddle and dog,
Ragged and penniless, and playing
   To you to-night for a glass of grog !

She 's married since, — a parson's wife :
   'T was better for her that we should part, —
Better the soberest, prosiest life
   Than a blasted home and a broken heart.
I have seen her ?   Once : I was weak and spent
   On the dusty road : a carriage stopped :
But little she dreamed, as on she went,
   Who kissed the coin that her fingers dropped !

You 've set me talking, sir ; I 'm sorry ;
   It makes me wild to think of the change !
What do you care for a beggar's story ?
   Is it amusing ? you find it strange ?

I had a mother so proud of me !
   'T was well she died before —   Do you know
If the happy spirits in heaven can see
   The ruin and wretchedness here below ?

Another glass, and strong, to deaden
   This pain ; then Roger and I will start.
I wonder, has he such a lumpish, leaden,
   Aching thing, in place of a heart ?
He is sad sometimes, and would weep, if he could,
   No doubt, remembering things that were, —
A virtuous kennel, with plenty of food,
   And himself a sober, respectable cur.

I 'm better now ; that glass was warming. —
   You rascal ! limber your lazy feet !
We must be fiddling and performing
   For supper and bed, or starve in the street. —
Not a very gay life to lead, you think ?
   But soon we shall go where lodgings are free,
And the sleepers need neither victuals nor drink ;—
   The sooner, the better for Roger and me !

————◆————

OUTWARD BOUND. — William Allingham.

CLINK — clink — clink ! goes our windlass.
   " Ahoy ! " — " Haul in ! " — ": Let go ! "
Yards braced and sails set, —
   Flags uncurl and flow.
Some eyes that watch from shore are wet,
   (How bright their welcome shone !)
While, bending softly to the breeze,
And rushing through the parted seas,
   Our gallant ship glides on.

Though one has left a sweetheart,
  And one has left a wife,
'T will never do to mope and fret,
  Or curse a sailor's life.
See, far away they signal yet, —
  They dwindle, — fade, — they 're gone !
For, dashing outwards, bold and brave,
And springing light from wave to wave,
  Our merry ship flies on.

Gay spreads the sparkling ocean ;
  But many a gloomy night
And stormy morrow must be met
  Ere next we heave in sight.
The parting look we 'll ne'er forget,
  The kiss, the benison,
As round the rolling world we go.
God bless you all ! — Blow, breezes, blow ! —
  Sail on, good ship, sail on !

DIGGING FOR HIDDEN TREASURE. — Charles Reade.

"MY lad, I should like to tell you a story, but I suppose I shall make a bungle of it; sha' n't cut the furrow clean, I 'm doubtful."

"Never mind; try ! "

"Well then. Once upon a time there was an old chap that had heard or read about treasures being found in odd places, — a pot full of guineas, or something, — and it took root in his heart, till nothing would serve him but he must find a pot of guineas too. He used to poke about all the old ruins, grubbing away, and would have taken up the floor of the church, but the church-wardens would not have it. One morning he comes down and says to his wife, ' It is all right, old woman ; I 've found the treasure.'

6 *   I

" ' No ! have you though ? ' says she.

" ' Yes ! ' says he ; ' leastways it is as good as found ; it is only waiting till I 've had my breakfast, and then I 'll go out and fetch it in.'

" ' La, John, but how did you find it ? '

" ' It was revealed to me in a dream,' says he, as grave as a judge.

" ' And where is it ? ' asks the old woman.

" ' Under a tree in our own orchard, — no farther,' says he.

" ' O John ! how long you are at breakfast to-day ! '

" Up they both got, and into the orchard.

" ' Now, which tree is it under ? '

" John, he scratches his head. ' Blest if I know.'

" ' Why, you old ninny,' says the mistress, ' did n't you take the trouble to notice ? '

" ' That I did,' said he ; ' I saw plain enough which tree it was in my dream, but now they muddle it all, there are so many of 'em.'

" ' Drat your stupid old head ! ' says she ; ' why did n't you put a nick on the right one at the time ? '

" ' Well,' says he, ' I must dig till I find the right one.'

" The wife she loses heart at this ; for there were eighty apple-trees and a score of cherry-trees. ' Mind you don't cut the roots,' says she, and she heaves a sigh.

" John, he gives them bad language, root and branch. ' What signifies cut or not cut ! the old fagots, they don't bear me a bushel of fruit, the whole lot. They used to bear two sacks apiece in father's time. Drat 'em ! '

" ' Well, John,' says the old woman, smoothing him down, ' father used to give them a deal of attention.'

" ' 'T ain't that ! 't ain't that ! ' says he, quick and spiteful-like ; ' they have got old like ourselves, and good for fire wood.'

" Out pickaxe and spade, and digs three feet deep round one, and, finding nothing but mould, goes at another, makes a little mound all round him too, — no guinea-pot.

" Well, the village let him dig three or four quiet enough ;

but after that curiosity was awakened, and while John was digging, and that was all day, there was mostly seven or eight watching through the fence and passing their jests. After a bit, a fashion came up of flinging a stone or two at John ; then John, he brought out his gun loaded with dust-shot along with his pick and spade, and the first stone came he fired sharp in that direction, and then loaded again. So they took that hint, and John dug on in peace till about the fourth Sunday, and then the parson had a slap at him in church. 'Folks were not to heap up to themselves treasures on earth,' was all his discourse.

"But it seemed he was only heaping up mould; for when he had dug the five-score holes, no pot of gold came to light. Then the neighbors called the orchard Jacobs's Folly ; his name was Jacobs, — John Jacobs.

"'Now then, wife,' says he, 'suppose you and I look out for another village to live in, for their gibes are more than I can bear.'

"Old woman begins to cry. 'Been here so long, — brought me home here, John, when we were first married, John, and I was a comely lass, and you the smartest young man I ever saw, to my fancy anyway ; could n't sleep or eat my victuals in any house but this.'

"'Oh! could n't ye ? Well, then, we must stay ; perhaps it will blow over.'

"'Like everything else, John; but, dear John, do ye fill in those holes ; the young folk come far and wide on Sundays to see them.'

"'Wife, I have n't the heart,' says he. 'You see, when I was digging for the treasure I was always a going to find, it kept my heart up ; but take out a shovel and fill them in, — I 'd as lief dine off white of egg on a Sunday.'

"So for six blessed months the heaps were out in the heat and frost till the end of February, and then when the weather broke, the old man takes heart and fills them in, and the village soon forgot 'Jacobs's Folly' because it was out of sight.

"Comes April, and out burst the trees. 'Wife,' says he, 'our bloom is richer than I 've known it this many a year; it is richer than our neighbors'.' Bloom dies, and then out come about a million little green things quite hard.

"Michaelmas Day the old trees were staggering, and the branches down to the ground with the crop; thirty shillings on every tree one with another; and so on for the next year, and the next; sometimes more, sometimes less, according to the year. Trees were old and wanted a change. His letting in the air to them and turning the subsoil up to the frost and sun had renewed their youth. So by that he learned that tillage is the way to get treasure from the earth. Men are ungrateful at times, but the soil is never ungrateful; it always makes a return for the pains we give it."

THE OLD SERGEANT. — Forceythe Willson.

January 1, 1863.

THE carrier cannot sing to-day the ballads
    With which he used to go,
Rhyming the glad rounds of the happy New Years
    That are now beneath the snow.

For the same awful and portentous shadow
    That overcast the earth,
And smote the land last year with desolation,
    Still darkens every hearth.

And the carrier hears Beethoven's mighty death-march
    Come up from every mart;
And he hears and feels it breathing in his bosom,
    And beating in his heart.

And to-day, a scarred and weather-beaten veteran,
    Again he comes along,

To tell the story of the Old Year's struggles
    In another New Year's song.

And the song is his, but not so with the story,
    For the story, you must know,
Was told in prose to Assistant Surgeon Austin,
    By a soldier of Shiloh.

By Robert Burton, who was brought up on the Adams,
    With his death-wound in his side ;
And who told the story to the assistant surgeon
    On the same night that he died.

But the singer feels it will better suit the ballad,
    If all should deem it right,
To tell the story as if what it speaks of
    Had happened but last night.

"Come a little nearer, doctor, — thank you, — let me take
    the cup ;
Draw your chair up, — draw it closer, — just another little
    sup !
Maybe you may think I 'm better ; but I 'm pretty well
    used up, —
Doctor, you 've done all you could do, but I 'm just a going up !

"Feel my pulse, sir, if you want to, but it ain't much use to
    try — "
"Never say that," said the surgeon, as he smothered down a
    sigh ;
"It will never do, old comrade, for a soldier to say die ! "
"What you *say* will make no difference, doctor, when you
    come to die."

"Doctor, what has been the matter ? " "You were very
    faint, they say ;
You must try to get some sleep now." "Doctor, have I
    been away ? "

"Not that anybody knows of!"   "Doctor, — doctor, please
  to stay!
There is something I must tell you, and you won't have long
  to stay!

"I have got my marching orders, and I 'm ready now to go;
Doctor, did you say I fainted? — but it could n't ha' been
  so, —
For as sure as I 'm a sergeant, and was wounded at Shiloh,
I 've this very night been back there, on the old field of
  Shiloh!

"This is all that I remember!   The last time the lighter
  came,
And the lights had all been lowered, and the noises much the
  same,
He had not been gone five minutes before something called
  my name:
'ORDERLY SERGEANT — ROBERT BURTON!' just that way it
  called my name.

"And I wondered who could call me so distinctly and so
  slow,
Knew it could n't be the lighter, — he could not have spoken
  so, —
And I tried to answer, 'Here, sir!' but I could n't make it go!
For I could n't move a muscle, and I could n't make it go!

"Then I thought: 'It 's all a nightmare, all a humbug and
  a bore;
Just another foolish *grape-vine*, — and it won't come any
  more';
But it came, sir, notwithstanding, just the same way as
  before:
'ORDERLY SERGEANT — ROBERT BURTON!' even plainer than
  before.

" That is all that I remember, till a sudden burst of light,
And I stood beside the river, where we stood that Sunday
          night,
Waiting to be ferried over to the dark bluffs opposite,
When the river was perdition and all hell was opposite !

" And the same old palpitation came again in all its power,
And I heard a bugle sounding, as from some celestial tower ;
And the same mysterious voice said : ' It is the eleventh
          hour !
Orderly Sergeant — Robert Burton, — it is the eleventh
          hour ! '

" Doctor Austin ! what *day* is this ? "   " It is Wednesday
          night, you know."
" Yes, — to-morrow will be New Year's, and a right good
          time below !
What *time* is it, Doctor Austin ? "   " Nearly twelve."   " Then
          don't you go !
Can it be that all this happened — all this — not an hour
          ago ?

" There was where the gunboats opened on the dark rebel-
          lious host ;
And where Webster semicircled his last guns upon the coast ;
There were still the two log-houses, just the same, or else
          their ghost, —
Aud the same old transport came and took me over, — or its
          ghost !

" And the old field lay before me all deserted far and wide ;
There was where they fell on Prentiss, — there McClernand
          met the tide ;
There was where stern Sherman rallied, and where Hurlbut's
          heroes died, —
Lower down where Wallace charged them, and kept charging
          till he died.

" There was where Lew Wallace showed them he was of the
    canny kin,
There was where old Nelson thundered, and where Rousseau
    waded in ;
There McCook sent 'em to breakfast, and we all began to win, —
There was where the grape-shot took me, just as we began to
    win.

" Now a shroud of snow and silence over everything was
    spread ;
And but for this old blue mantle and the old hat on my head,
I should not have even doubted, to this moment, I was dead, —
For my footsteps were as silent as the snow upon the dead !

" Death and silence ! — death and silence ! all around me as
    I sped !
And behold a mighty tower, as if builded to the dead,
To the heaven of the heavens, lifted up its mighty head,
Till the stars and stripes of heaven all seemed waving from
    its head !

" Round and mighty-based it towered, — up into the infi-
    nite, —
And I knew no mortal mason could have built a shaft so
    bright ;
For it shone like solid sunshine ; and a winding stair of
    light
Wound around it and around it till it wound clear out of
    sight !

" And, behold, as I approached it, with a rapt and dazzled
    stare, —
Thinking that I saw old comrades just ascending the great
    stair, —
Suddenly the solemn challenge broke of — ' Halt, and who
    goes there ? '
' I 'm a friend,' I said, ' if you are.' ' Then advance, sir, to
    the stair ! '

"I advanced ! — That sentry, doctor, was Elijah Ballantyne ! —

First of all to fall on Monday, after we had formed the line ! —

'Welcome, my old sergeant, welcome ! Welcome by that countersign ! '

And he pointed to the scar there, under this old cloak of mine !

"As he grasped my hand, I shuddered, thinking only of the grave ;

But he smiled and pointed upward with a bright and bloodless glaive ;

'That 's the way, sir, to head-quarters.' 'What head-quarters ?' 'Of the brave.'

'But the great tower ?' 'That,' he answered, 'is the way, sir, of the brave !'

"Then a sudden shame came o'er me at his uniform of light ;

At my own so old and tattered, and at his so new and bright.

'Ah ! said he, 'you have forgotten the new uniform to-night, —

Hurry back, for you must be here at just twelve o'clock to-night !'

"And the next thing I remember, you were sitting *there*, and I —

Doctor, — did you hear a footstep ? Hark ! — God bless you all ! Good by !

Doctor, please to give my musket and my knapsack, when I die,

To my son — my son that 's coming, — he won't get here till I die !

"Tell him his old father blessed him as he never did before, —

And to carry that old musket — " Hark ! a knock is at the door —

" Till the Union — " 	See ! it opens ! — 	" Father ! Father !
    speak once more ! " —
" Bless you ! " gasped the old gray sergeant, and he lay and
    said no more !

———◆———

LITTLE GOLDENHAIR.

GOLDENHAIR climbed up on grandpapa's knee ;
  Dear little Goldenhair, tired was she,
All the day busy as busy could be.

Up in the morning as soon as 't was light,
Out with the birds and butterflies bright,
Skipping about till the coming of night.

Grandpapa toyed with the curls on her head.
" What has my darling been doing," he said,
"Since she rose with the sun from her bed ? "

" Pitty much," answered the sweet little one.
" I cannot tell so much things I have done,
Played with my dolly and feeded my bun.

" And then I jumped with my little jump-rope,
And I made out of some water and soap
Bootiful worlds, mamma's castles of hope.

" Then I have readed in my picture-book,
And Bella and I, we went to look
For the smooth little stones by the side of the brook.

" And then I comed home and eated my tea,
And I climbed up on grandpapa's knee,
And I jes as tired as tired can be."

Lower and lower the little head pressed,
Until it had dropped upon grandpapa's breast;
Dear little Goldenhair, sweet be thy rest!

We are but children; things that we do
Are as sports of a babe to the Infinite view,
That marks all our weakness, and pities it too.

God grant that when night overshadows our way,
And we shall be called to account for our day,
He shall find us as guileless as Goldenhair's lay.

And O, when aweary, may we be so blest,
And sink like the innocent child to our rest,
And feel ourselves clasped to the Infinite breast!

———◆———

HOW 'S MY BOY ? — S. DOBELL.

HO, sailor of the sea!
  How 's my boy — my boy?
" What 's your boy's name, good wife,
And in what good ship sailed he?"

My boy John, —
He that went to sea, —
What care I for the ship, sailor?
My boy 's my boy to me.

You come back from sea,
And not know my John?
I might as well have asked some landsman
Yonder down in the town.
There 's not a dolt in all the parish
But he knows my John.

How 's my boy — my boy ?
And unless you let me know,
I 'll swear you are no sailor,
 Blue jacket or no,
Brass button or no, sailor,
Anchor and crown or no !
Sure his ship was the Jolly Briton —
"Speak low, woman, speak low ! "

And why should I speak low, sailor,
About my own boy John ?
If I was loud as I am proud
I'd sing him over the town !
Why should I speak low, sailor,
" That good ship went down."

How 's my boy — my boy ?
What care I for the ship, sailor,
I never was aboard her.
Be she afloat, or be she aground,
Sinking or swimming, I 'll be bound
Her owners can afford her !
I say how 's my John ?
" Every man on board went down,
Every man aboard her."

How 's my boy — my boy ?
What care I for the men, sailor ?
I 'm not their mother, —
How 's my boy — my boy ?
Tell me of him and no other !
How 's my boy — my boy ?

JOHN VALJOHN AND THE SAVOYARD.
VICTOR HUGO.

A S the sun was sinking towards the horizon, John Valjohn, a convict lately released from the galleys, was
seated behind a thicket in a large barren plain. There was
no horizon but the Alps. Not even the steeple of a village
church. It might have been three leagues from the city. A
by-path, which crossed the plain, passed a few steps from the
thicket.

In the midst of his meditation, which would have height-
ened not a little the frightful effect of his rags to any one
who might have met him, he heard a joyous sound. He
turned his head, and saw coming along the path a little
Savoyard, a dozen years old, singing, with his hurdy-gurdy at
his side, and his marmot on his back ; — one of those pleasant
and gay youngsters who go from place to place, with their
knees sticking through their trousers.

Always singing, the boy stopped from time to time, and
played at tossing up some pieces of money that he had
in his hand, probably his whole fortune. Among them there
was one forty-sous piece.

The boy stopped by the side of the thicket without seeing
John Valjohn, and tossed up his handful of sous. Until this
time he had skilfully caught the whole of them upon the back
of his hand. This time the forty-sous piece escaped him, and
rolled towards the thicket near John Valjohn.

John Valjohn put his foot upon it.

The boy, however, had followed the piece with his eye,
and had seen where it went. He was not frightened, and
walked straight to the man.

It was an entirely solitary place. Far as the eye could
reach, there was no one on the plain or in the path. Nothing could be heard but the faint cries of a flock of birds
of passage, that were flying across the sky at an immense
height. The child turned his back to the sun, which made

his hair like threads of gold, and flushed the savage face of John Valjohn with a lurid glow.

"Mister," said the little Savoyard, with that childish confidence which is made up of ignorance and innocence, "my piece?"

"What is your name?" said John Valjohn.

"Little Gervais, mister."

"Get out!" said John Valjohn.

"Mister," continued the boy, "give me my piece."

John Valjohn dropped his head and did not answer.

The child began again : "My piece, mister!"

John Valjohn's eye remained fixed on the ground.

"My piece!" exclaimed the boy, "my white piece! my silver!"

John Valjohn did not appear to understand. The boy took him by the collar of his blouse and shook him. And at the same time he made an effort to move the big, iron-soled shoe which was placed upon his treasure.

"I want my piece! my forty-sous piece!"

The child began to cry. John Valjohn raised his head. He still kept his seat. His look was troubled. He looked upon the boy with an air of wonder, then reached out his hand towards his stick, and exclaimed in a terrible voice, "Who is there?"

"Me, mister," answered the boy. "Little Gervais! me! me! give me my forty-sous, if you please! Take away your foot, mister, if you please!" Then becoming angry, small as he was, and almost threatening, —

"Come, now, will you take away your foot? Why don't you take away your foot?"

"Ah! you here yet!" said John Valjohn; and, rising hastily to his feet, without releasing the piece of money, he added, "You'd better take care of yourself!"

The boy looked at him in terror, then began to tremble from head to foot, and after a few seconds of stupor, took to flight and ran with all his might, without daring to turn his head, or to utter a cry.

At a little distance, however, he stopped for want of breath, and John Valjohn, in his revery, heard him sobbing.

In a few minutes the boy was gone.

The sun had gone down.

The shadows were deepening around John Valjohn. He had not eaten during the day ; probably he had some fever.

He had remained standing, and had not changed his attitude since the child fled. His breathing was at long and unequal intervals. His eyes were fixed on a spot ten or twelve steps before him, and seemed to be studying with profound attention the form of an old piece of blue crockery that was lying in the grass. All at once he shivered ; he began to feel the cold night air.

He pulled his cap down over his forehead, sought mechanically to fold and button his blouse around him, stepped forward and stooped to pick up his stick.

At that instant he perceived the forty-sous piece which his foot had half buried in the ground, and which glistened among the pebbles. It was like an electric shock. " What is that ?" said he, between his teeth. He drew back a step or two, then stopped, without the power to withdraw his gaze from this point which his foot had covered the instant before, as if the thing that glistened there in the obscurity had been an open eye fixed upon him.

After a few minutes he sprang convulsively towards the piece of money, seized it, and, rising, looked away over the plain, straining his eyes towards all points of the horizon, standing and trembling like a frightened deer which is seeking a place of refuge.

He saw nothing. Night was falling, the plain was cold and bare, thick purple mists were rising in the glimmering twilight.

He said, " Oh !" and began to walk rapidly in the direction in which the child had gone. After some thirty steps he stopped, looked about, and saw nothing.

Then he called with all his might, " Little Gervais! Little Gervais !" He listened. There was no answer.

The country was desolate and gloomy. On all sides was

space. There was nothing about him but a shadow in which his gaze was lost, and a silence in which his voice was lost.

A biting norther was blowing, which gave a kind of dismal life to everything about him. The bushes shook their little thin arms with an incredible fury. One would have said that they were threatening and pursuing somebody.

He began to walk again, then quickened his pace to a run, and from time to time stopped and called out in that solitude, in a most desolate and terrible voice: "Little Gervais! Little Gervais!"

Surely, if the child had heard him, he would have been frightened, and would have hid himself. But doubtless the boy was already far away.

He met a priest on horseback. He went up to him and said: "Mr. Curate, have you seen a child go by?"

"No," said the priest.

"Little Gervais was his name?"

"I have seen nobody."

He took two five-franc pieces from his bag and gave them to the priest.

"Mr. Curate, this is for your poor. Mr. Curate, he is a little fellow, about ten years old, with a marmot, I think, and a hurdy-gurdy. He went this way. One of these Savoyards, you know?"

"I have not seen him."

"Little Gervais? Is his village near here? Can you tell me?"

"If it be as you say, my friend, the little fellow is a foreigner. They roam about this country. Nobody knows them."

John Valjohn hastily took out two more five-franc pieces, and gave them to the priest. "For your poor," said he.

Then he added wildly: "Mr. Abbé, have me arrested; I am a robber."

The priest put spurs to his horse, and fled in great fear.

John Valjohn began to run again in the direction which he had first taken.

He went on in this wise for a considerable distance, looking around, calling and shouting, but met nobody else. Two or three times he left the path to look at what seemed to be somebody lying down or crouching ; it was only low bushes or rocks.

Finally, at a place where three paths met, he stopped. The moon had risen. He strained his eyes in the distance, and called out once more, " Little Gervais ! Little Gervais ! Little Gervais ! " His cries died away into the mist, without even awakening an echo. Again he murmured, " Little Gervais ! " but with a feeble and almost inarticulate voice.

That was his last effort ; his knees suddenly bent under him, as if an invisible power overwhelmed him at a blow, with the weight of his conscience. He fell exhausted upon a great stone, his hands clenched in his hair, and his face on his knees, and exclaimed, " What a wretch I am ! "

Then his heart swelled, and he burst into tears. It was the first time he had wept for nineteen years.

How long did he weep thus ? What did he do after weeping ? Where did he go ? Nobody ever knew. It is known simply that, on that very night, the stage-driver who drove at that time on the Grenoble route, and arrived at the city about three o'clock in the morning, saw, as he passed through a certain street, a man in the attitude of prayer, kneeling upon the pavement in the shadow, before the door of the Bishop's residence.

SHAMUS O'BRIEN. — J. S. LE FANU.

JIST afther the war, in the year '98,
  As soon as the boys wor all scattered and bate,
'T was the custom, whenever a pisant was got,
To hang him by thrial — barrin' sich as was shot.
There was trial by jury goin' on by daylight,
And the martial-law hangin' the lavins by night.

7   J

It 's them was hard times for an honest gossoon :
If he missed in the judges — he 'd meet a dragoon ;
An' whether the sodgers or judges gev sentence,
The divil a much time they allowed for repentance.
An' it 's many 's the fine boy was then on his keepin'
Wid small share iv restin', or atin', or sleepin',
An' because they loved Erin, an' scorned to sell it,
A prey for the bloodhound, a mark for the bullet, —
Unsheltered by night, and unrested by day,
With the heath for their barrack, revenge for their pay ;
An' the bravest an' hardiest boy iv them all
Was Shamus O'Brien, from the town iv. Glingall.
His limbs were well set, an' his body was light,
An' the keen-fanged hound had not teeth half so white ;
But his face was as pale as the face of the dead,
And his cheek never warmed with the blush of the red ;
An' for all that he was n't an ugly young bye,
For the divil himself could n't blaze with his eye,
So droll an' so wicked, so dark and so bright,
Like a fire-flash that crosses the depth of the night !
An' he was the best mower that ever has been,
An' the illigantest hurler that ever was seen.
An' his dancin' was sich that the men used to stare,
An' the women turn crazy, he done it so quare ;
An', by gorra, the whole world gev it into him there.
An' it 's he was the boy that was hard to be caught,
An' it 's often he run, an' it 's often he fought,
An' it 's many the one can remember right well
The quare things he done : an' it 's often I heerd tell
How he lathered the yeomen, himself agin' four,
An' stretched the two strongest on old Galtimore.
But the fox must sleep sometimes, the wild deer must rest,
An' treachery prey on the blood iv the best ;
Afther many a brave action of power and pride,
An' many a hard night on the mountain's bleak side,
An' a thousand great dangers and toils overpast,
In the darkness of night he was taken at last.

Now, Shamus, look back on the beautiful moon,
For the door of the prison must close on you soon,
An' take your last look at her dim lovely light,
That falls on the mountain and valley this night;
One look at the village, one look at the flood,
An' one at the sheltheriug, far-distant wood ;
Farewell to the forest, farewell to the hill,
An' farewell to the friends that will think of you still;
Farewell to the pathern, the hurlin' an' wake,
And farewell to the girl that would die for your sake.
An' twelve sodgers brought him to Maryborough jail,
An' the turnkey resaved him, refusin' all bail ;
The fleet limbs wor chained, an' the sthrong hands wor bound,
An' he laid down his length on the cowld prison ground,
An' the dreams of his childhood kem over him there
As gentle an' soft as the sweet summer air ;
An' happy remembrances crowding on ever,
As fast as the foam-flakes dhrift down on the river,
Bringing fresh to his heart merry days long gone by,
Till the tears gathered heavy and thick in his eye.
But the tears did n't fall, for the pride of his heart
Would not suffer one drop down his pale cheek to start ;
An' he sprang to his feet in the dark prison cave,
An' he swore with the fierceness that misery gave,
By the hopes of the good, an' the cause of the brave,
That when he was mouldering in the cold grave
His enemies never should have it to boast
His scorn of their vengeance one moment was lost ;
His bosom might bleed, but his cheek should be dhry,
For undaunted he lived, and undaunted he 'd die.

Well, as soon as a few weeks was over and gone,
The terrible day iv the thrial kem on ;
There was sich a crowd there was scarce room to stand,
An' sodgers on guard, an' dhragoons sword in hand ;
An' the court-house so full that the people were bothered,
An' attorneys an' criers on the point iv bein' smothered ;

An' counsellors almost gev over for dead,
An' the jury sittin' up in their box overhead ;
An' the judge settled out so detarmined an' big,
With his gown on his back, and an illegant new wig ;
An' silence was called, an' the minute it was said
The court was as still as the heart of the dead,
An' they heard but the openin' of one prison lock,
An' Shamus O'Brien kem into the dock.
For one minute he turned his eye round on the throng,
An' he looked at the bars, so firm and so strong,
An' he saw that he had not a hope nor a friend,
A chance to escape, nor a word to defend ;
An' he folded his arms as he stood there alone,
As calm and as cold as a statue of stone ;
And they read a big writin', a yard long at laste,
An' Jim did n't understand it, nor mind it a taste ;
An' the judge took a big pinch iv snuff, and he says,
" Are you guilty or not, Jim O'Brien, av you plase ? "

An' all held their breath in the silence of dhread,
An' Shamus O'Brien made answer and said :
" My lord, if you ask me, if in my life-time
I thought any treason, or did any crime
That should call to my cheek, as I stand alone here,
The hot blush of shame, or the coldness of fear,
Though I stood by the grave to receive my death-blow,
Before God and the world I would answer you, no !
But if you would ask me, as I think it like,
If in the rebellion I carried a pike,
An' fought for ould Ireland from the first to the close,
An' shed the heart's blood of her bitterest foes,
I answer you, yes ; and I tell you again,
Though I stand here to perish, it 's my glory that then
In her cause I was willing my veins should run dhry,
An' that now for her sake I am ready to die."

Then the silence was great, and the jury smiled bright,
An' the judge was n't sorry the job was made light ;

By my sowl, it 's himself was the crabbed ould chap !
In a twinklin' he pulled on his ugly black cap.
Then Shamus' mother in the crowd standin' by,
Called out to the judge with a pitiful cry :
" O judge ! darlin', don't, O, don't say the word !
The crathur is young, have mercy, my lord ;
He was foolish, he did n't know what he was doin' ;
You don't know him, my lord, — O, don't give him to ruin !
He 's the kindliest crathur, the tendherest-hearted ;
Don't part us forever, we that 's so long parted.
Judge, mavourneen, forgive him, forgive him, my lord,
An' God will forgive you — O, don't say the word ! "
That was the first minute that O'Brien was shaken,
When he saw that he was not quite forgot or forsaken ;
An' down his pale cheeks, at the word of his mother,
The big tears wor runnin' fast, one after th' other ;
An' two or three times he endeavored to spake,
But the sthrong, manly voice used to falther and break ;
But at last, by the strength of his high-mounting pride,
He conquered and masthered his grief's swelling tide,
" An', " says he, " mother, darlin', don't break your poor heart
For, sooner or later, the dearest must part ;
And God knows it 's betther than wandering in fear
On the bleak, trackless mountain, among the wild deer,
To lie in the grave, where the head, heart, and breast,
From thought, labor, and sorrow forever shall rest.
Then, mother, my darlin', don't cry any more,
Don't make me seem broken, in this, my last hour ;
For I wish, when my head 's lyin' undher the raven,
No thrue man can say that I died like a craven ! "
Then towards the judge Shamus bent down his head,
An' that minute the solemn death-sentince was said.

The mornin' was bright, an' the mists rose on high,
An' the lark whistled merrily in the clear sky ;
But why are the men standin' idle so late ?
An' why do the crowds gather fast in the street ?

What come they to talk of ? what come they to see ?
An' why does the long rope hang from the cross-tree ?
O Shamus O'Brien ! pray fervent and fast,
May the saints take your soul, for this day is your last ;
Pray fast an' pray sthrong, for the moment is nigh,
When, sthrong, proud, an' great as you are, you must die.
An' fasther an' fasther the crowd gathered there,
Boys, horses, and gingerbread, just like a fair ;
An' whiskey was sellin', an' cussamuck too,
An' ould men and young women enjoying the view.
An' ould Tim Mulvany, he med the remark,
There was n't sich a sight since the time of Noah's ark,
An' be gorry, 't was thrue for him, for divil sich a scruge,
Sich divarshin and crowds, was known since the deluge,
For thousands were gathered there, if there was one,
Waitin' till such time as the hangin' id come on.

At last they threw open the big prison gate,
An' out came the sheriffs and sodgers in state,
An' a cart in the middle, an' Shamus was in it,
Not paler, but prouder than ever, that minute.
An' as soon as the people saw Shamus O'Brien,
Wid prayin' and blessin', and all the girls cryin',
A wild wailin' sound kem on by degrees,
Like the sound of the lonesome wind blowin' through trees.
On, on to the gallows the sheriffs are gone,
An' the cart an' the sodgers go steadily on ;
An' at every side swellin' around of the cart,
A wild, sorrowful sound, that id open your heart.
Now under the gallows the cart takes its stand,
An' the hangman gets up with the rope in his hand ;
An' the priest, havin' blest him, goes down on the ground,
An' Shamus O'Brien throws one last look round.
Then the hangman dhrew near, an' the people grew still,
Young faces turned sickly, and warm hearts turned chill ;
An' the rope bein' ready, his neck was made bare,
For the gripe iv the life-strangling cord to prepare ;

An' the good priest has left him, havin' said his last prayer.
But the good priest done more, for his hands he unbound,
And with one daring spring Jim has leaped on the ground ;
Bang ! bang ! goes the carbines, and clash goes the sabres ;
He 's not down ! he 's alive still ! now stand to him, neighbors !
Through the smoke and the horses he 's into the crowd, —
By the heavens, he 's free ! — than thunder more loud,
By one shout from the people the heavens were shaken, —
One shout that the dead of the world might awaken.
The sodgers ran this way, the sheriffs ran that,
An' Father Malone lost his new Sunday hat ;
To-night he 'll be sleepin' in Aherloe Glin,
An' the divil 's in the dice if you catch him ag'in.
Your swords they may glitter, your carbines go bang,
But if you want hangin', it 's yourself you must hang.

He has mounted his horse, and soon he will be
In America, darlint, the land of the free.

COME UP FROM THE FIELDS, FATHER!
WALT WHITMAN.

COME up from the fields, father ; here 's a letter from
    our Pete,
And come to the front door, mother ; here 's a letter from thy
    dear son.
Lo, 't is autumn ;
Lo, where the fields, deeper green, yellower and redder,
Cool and sweeten Ohio's villages, with leaves fluttering in the
    moderate wind ;
Where apples ripe in the orchards hang, and grapes on the
    trellised vines.
(Smell you the smell of the grapes on the vines ?
Smell you the buckwheat, where the bees were lately
    buzzing ?)

Above all, lo ! the sky so calm, so transparent after the rain,
and with wondrous clouds ;
Below, too, all calm, all vital and beautiful, — and the farm
prospers well.

Down in the fields all prospers well ;
But now from the fields come, father, — come at the daughter's
call ;
And come to the entry, mother, — to the front door come,
right away.

Fast as she can she hurries, — something ominous, — her steps
trembling ;
She does not tarry to smooth her white hair, nor adjust her
cap.

Open the envelope quickly ;
O, this is not our son's writing, yet his name is signed !
O, a strange hand writes for our dear son — O stricken
mother's soul !
All swims before her eyes, — flashes with black, — she catches
the main words only ;
Sentences broken, — *gunshot wound in the breast — cavalry
skirmish, taken to hospital,*
At present low, but will soon be better.

Ah ! now the single figure to me
Amid all teeming and wealthy Ohio, with all its cities and
farms,
Sickly white in the face and dull in the head, very faint,
By the jamb of a door leans.

Grieve not so, dear mother (the just grown daughter speaks
through her sobs ;
The little sisters huddle around, speechless and dismayed).
See, dearest mother, the letter says Pete will soon be better.

Alas, poor boy ! he will never be better (nor, maybe, needs to
be better, that brave and simple soul).
While they stand at home at the door he is dead already,
The only son is dead.

But the mother needs to be better ;
She, with thin form, presently dressed in black ;
By day her meals untouched, — then at night fitfully sleep-
ing, often waking,
In the midnight waking, weeping, longing with one deep long-
ing,
O that she might withdraw unnoticed, silent from life, escape
and withdraw,
To follow, to seek, to be with her dear dead son !

———◆———

JUPITER AND TEN. — J. T. FIELDS.

MRS. CHUB was rich and portly,
Mrs. Chub was very grand,
Mrs. Chub was always reckoned
A lady in the land.

You shall see her marble mansion
In a very stately square, —
Mr. C. knows what it cost him,
But that 's neither here nor there.

Mrs. Chub was so sagacious,
Such a patron of the arts,
And she gave such foreign orders,
That she won all foreign hearts.

Mrs. Chub was always talking,
When she went away from home,
7 *

Of a most prodigious painting
  Which had just arrived from Rome.

"Such a treasure," she insisted,
  "One might never see again!"
"What's the subject?" we inquired.
  "*It is Jupiter and Ten!*"

"Ten *what?*" we blandly asked her,
  For the knowledge we did lack.
"Ah! that I cannot tell you,
  But the name is on the back.

"There it stands in printed letters, —
  Come to-morrow, gentlemen, —
Come and see our splendid painting,
  Our fine *Jupiter and Ten.*"

When Mrs. Chub departed,
  Our brains began to rack, —
She could not be mistaken,
  For the name was on the back.

So we begged a great Professor
  To lay aside his pen,
And give some information
  Touching "Jupiter and Ten."

And we pondered well the subject,
  And our Lemprière we turned,
To find out who the *Ten* were;
  But we could not, though we burned!

But when we saw the picture, —
  O Mrs. Chub! O, fie! O!
We perused the printed label,
  And 't was *Jupiter and Io!*

JEANIE DEANS AND QUEEN CAROLINE.
WALTER SCOTT.

THE Duke of Argyle made a signal for Jeanie to advance from the spot where she had hitherto remained, watching countenances which were too long accustomed to suppress all apparent signs of emotion to convey to her any interesting intelligence. Her Majesty could not help smiling at the awe-struck manner in which the quiet, demure figure of the little Scotchwoman advanced towards her, and yet more at the first sound of her broad Northern accent. But Jeanie had a voice low and sweetly toned, — an admirable thing in woman, — and she besought " her leddyship to have pity on a poor, misguided young creature," in tones so affecting that, like the notes of some of her native songs, provincial vulgarity was lost in pathos.

The queen asked Jeanie how she travelled up from Scotland.

" On foot mostly, madam," was the reply.

" What! all that immense way on foot! How far can you walk in a day ? "

" Five-and-twenty miles, and a bittock."

" And a what ? " said the queen, looking towards the Duke of Argyle.

" And about five miles more," replied the duke.

" I thought I was a good walker," said the queen; " but this shames me sadly. "

" May your leddyship never hae sae weary a heart that ye canna be sensible of the weariness of the limbs ! " said Jeanie. " And I didna, just a' thegether, walk the hail way neither ; for I had whiles the cast of a cart, and I had the cast of a horse from Ferrybridge, and divers other easements," said Jeanie, cutting short her story ; for she observed the duke made the sign he had fixed upon.

" With all these accommodations," answered the queen, " you must have had a very fatiguing journey, and I fear to little purpose ; since, if the king were to pardon your sister, in all probability it would do her. little good; for I suppose **your** people of Edinburgh would hang her out of spite."

"She will sink herself now outright," thought the duke. But he was wrong. This rock was above water, and she avoided it.

"She was confident," she said, "that baith town and country wad rejoice to see his Majesty taking compassion on a poor unfriended creature."

"His Majesty has not found it so in a late instance," said the queen; "but I suppose my lord duke would advise him to be guided by the votes of the rabble themselves, who should be hanged and who spared."

"No, madam," said the duke; "but I would advise his Majesty to be guided by his own feelings and those of his royal consort; and then I am sure punishment will only attach itself to guilt, and even then with cautious reluctance."

"Well, my lord," said her Majesty, "all these fine speeches do not convince me of the propriety of so soon showing favor to your — I suppose I must not say rebellious — but, at least, your very disaffected and intractable metropolis. Why, the whole nation is in a league to screen the savage and abominable murderers of that unhappy man; otherwise, how is it possible but that, of so many perpetrators, and engaged in so public an action for such a length of time, one, at least, must have been recognized? Even this wench, for aught I can tell, may be a depositary of the secret. Hark ye, young woman, had you any friends engaged in the Porteous mob?"

"No, madam," answered Jeanie; happy that the question was so framed that she could, with a good conscience, answer it in the negative.

"But I suppose," continued the queen, "if you were possessed of such a secret, you would hold it matter of conscience to keep it to yourself."

"I would pray to be directed and guided in the line of duty, madam," answered Jeanie.

"Yes, and take that which suited your own inclinations," replied her Majesty.

"If it like you, madam," said Jeanie, "I would hae' gaen to the end o' the earth to save the life of John Porteous, or of any other unhappy man in his condition; but I might lawfully doubt how far I am called upon to be the avenger of his blood, though it may become the civil magistrate to do so. He is dead and gane to his place; and they that have slain him must answer for their ain act. But my sister — my puir sister, Effie — still lives, though her days and hours are numbered. She still lives, and a word of the king's mouth might restore her to a broken-hearted auld man, that never, in his daily and nightly exercise, forgot to pray that his Majesty might be blessed with a long and a prosperous reign; and that his throne, and the throne of his posterity, might be established in righteousness. O madam, if ever ye kenned what it was to sorrow for and with a sinning and suffering creature, whose mind is sae tossed that she can be neither ca'd fit to live or die, — have some compassion on our misery! Save an honest house from dishonor, and an unhappy girl, not eighteen years of age, from an early and dreadful death. Alas! it is not when we sleep soft, and wake merrily ourselves, that we think on other people's sufferings. Our hearts are waxed light within us then; and we are for righting our ain wrongs, and fighting our ain battles. But when the hour of trouble comes to the mind, or to the body, — and seldom may it visit your leddyship, — and when the hour of death comes, that comes to high and low, — long and late may it be yours, — O my leddy, then, it is na what we have dune for oursels, but what we have dune for others, that we think on maist pleasantly. And the thoughts, that ye hae intervened to spare the puir thing's life will be sweeter in that hour, come when it may, than if a word of your mouth could hang the hail Porteous mob at the tail of ae tow."

Tear followed tear down Jeanie's cheek, as, with features glowing and quivering with emotion, she pleaded her sister's cause, with a pathos which was at once simple and solemn.

"This is eloquence," said her Majesty to the Duke of

Argyle. "Young woman," she continued, addressing herself to Jeanie, "I cannot grant a pardon to your sister, but you shall not want my warm intercession with his Majesty. Take this housewife case," she continued, putting a small embroidered needle-case into Jeanie's hands; "do not open it now, but at your leisure; you will find something in it which will remind you that you have had an interview with Queen Caroline."

Jeanie, having her suspicions thus confirmed, dropped on her knees, and would have expanded herself in gratitude; but the duke, who was upon thorns lest she should say more or less than just enough, touched his chin once more.

"Our business is, I think, ended for the present, my lord duke," said the queen, "and, I trust, to your satisfaction. Hereafter I hope to see your Grace more frequently, both at Richmond and St. James's. Come, Lady Suffolk, we must wish his Grace good morning."

They exchanged their parting reverences, and the duke, so soon as the ladies had turned their backs, assisted Jeanie to rise from the ground, and conducted her back through the avenue, — which she trod with the feeling of one who walks in her sleep.

OUR SISTER. — *Household Words.*

UP many flights of crazy stairs,
    Where oft one's head knocks unawares;
With a rickety table and without chairs,
And only a stool to kneel to prayers,
                  Dwells our sister.

There is no carpet upon the floor,
The wind whistles in through the cracks of the door;
One might reckon her miseries now by the score,
But who feels interest in one so poor ?
                  Yet she is our sister !

She once was blooming and young and fair,
With bright blue eyes and auburn hair;
Now the rose is eaten with cankered care,
And her poor face is marked with a grim despair, —
                    Our poor sister.

When at early morning, to rest her head,
She throws herself on her weary bed,
Longing to sleep the sleep of the dead,
Since youth and health and love are fled, —
                    Pity our sister.

But the bright sun shines on her and me,
And on mine and hers, as on thine and thee,
And whatever our lot in life may be,
Whether of low or high degree, —
Still she's our sister! always our sister!
Pity her, succor her, pray for our sister!

THE BATTLE. — SCHILLER.

TRANSLATED BY BULWER LYTTON.

HEAVY and solemn,
    A cloudy column,
Through the green plain they marching come!
Measureless spread like a table dread,
For the wild grim dice of the iron game.
Looks are bent on the shaking ground,
Hearts beat loud with a knelling sound;
Swift by the breasts that must bear the brunt,
Gallops the Major along the front:
            "Halt!"
And fettered they stand at the stark command,
And the warriors, silent, halt!

Proud in the blush of morning glowing,
What on the hill-top shines in flowing?
"See you the foemen's banners waving?"

"We see the foeman's banners waving!"
"God be with ye, children and wife!"
Hark to the music, — the trump and the fife, —
How they ring through the ranks, which they rouse to the strife!
Thrilling they sound, with their glorious tone,
Thrilling they go through the marrow and bone!
Brothers, God grant, when this life is o'er,
In the life to come that we meet once more!

See the smoke how the lightning is cleaving asunder!
Hark! the guns, peal on peal, how they boom in their thunder!
From host to host, with kindling sound,
The shouted signal circles round ;
Ay, shout it forth to life or death, –
Freer already breathes the breath!
The war is waging, slaughter raging,
And heavy through the reeking pall
                    The iron death-dice fall!
Nearer they close, — foes upon foes, —
"Ready!" — from square to square it goes.

They kneel as one man from flank to flank,
The fire comes sharp from the foremost rank,
Many a soldier to the earth is sent,
Many a gap by balls is rent ;
O'er the corpse before springs the hinder man,
That the line may not fail to the fearless van.
To the right, to the left, and around and around,
Death whirls in its dance on the bloody ground.
God's sunlight is quenched in the fiery fight,
Over the hosts falls a brooding night!
Brothers, God grant, when this life is o'er,
In the life to come that we meet once more!

The dead men lie bathed in the weltering blood,
And the living are blent in the slippery flood,
And the feet, as they reeling and sliding go,
Stumble still on the corses that sleep below,
"What! Francis!"   "Give Charlotte my last farewell."

As the dying man murmurs the thunders swell, —
"I 'll 'give —   O God ! are their guns so near ?
Ho ! comrades ! — yon volley ! — look sharp to the rear !
I 'll give to thy Charlotte thy last farewell ;
Sleep soft ! where death thickest descendeth in rain,
The friend thou forsakest thy side may regain ! "
Hitherward, thitherward reels the fight ;
Dark and more darkly day glooms into night.
Brothers, God grant, when this life is o'er,
In the life to come that we meet once more !

> Hark to the hoofs that galloping go !
>   The adjutants flying, —
> The horsemen press hard on the panting foe,
>   Their thunder booms in dying, —
>   Victory !
> Terror has seized on the dastards all,
>   And their colors fall !
>   Victory !

Closed is the brunt of the glorious fight ;
And the day, like a conqueror, bursts on the night ;
Trumpet and fife swelling choral along,
The triumph already sweeps marching in song.
Farewell, fallen brothers ; though this life be o'er,
There 's another, in which we shall meet you once more !

———◆———

THE YOUNG GRAY HEAD. — *Blackwood's Magazine.*

" MOTHER," quoth Ambrose to his thrifty dame, —
    So oft our peasant's use his wife to name,
" Father," and " Master," to himself applied,
As life's grave duties matronize the bride, —
" Mother," quoth Ambrose, as he faced the north,
With hard-set teeth, before he issued forth
To his day labor, from the cottage door, —

"I 'm thinking that, to-night, if not before,
There 'll be wild work.   Dost hear Old Chewton* roar?
It 's brewing up down westward ; and look there,
One of those sea-gulls ! ay, there goes a pair ;
And such a sudden thaw !   If rain comes on,
As threats, the waters will be out anon.
That path by th' ford 's a nasty bit of way, —
Best let the young ones bide from school to-day."

" Do, mother, do ! " the quick-eared urchins cried, —
Two little lasses to the father's side
Close clinging as they looked from him, to spy
The answering language of the mother's eye.
There was denial, and she shook her head.
" Nay, nay, — no harm will come to them," she said,
" The mistress lets them off these short dark days
An hour the earlier ; and our Liz, she says,
May quite be trusted — and I know 't is true —
To take care of herself and Jenny too.
And so she ought, — she 's seven come first of May, —
Two years the oldest ; and they give away
The Christmas bounty at the school to-day."

The mother's will was law, (alas for her
That hapless day, poor soul !) *She* could not err,
Thought Ambrose ; and his little fair-haired Jane
(Her namesake) to his heart he hugged again,
When each had had her turn ; she clinging so
As if that day she could not let him go.
But Labor's sons must snatch a hasty bliss
In nature's tenderest mood.   One last fond kiss, —
" God bless my little maids ! " the father said,
And cheerly went his way to win their bread.

So to the mother's charge, with thoughtful brow,
The docile Lizzy stood attentive now ;

* A fresh-water spring rushing into the sea, called Chewton Bunny.

Proud of her years and of imputed sense,
And prudence justifying confidence.
And little Jenny, more demurely still,
Beside her waited the maternal will.
So standing hand in hand, a lovelier twain
Gainsborough ne'er painted ; no, nor he of Spain,
Glorious Murillo ! — and by contrast shown
More beautiful, — the younger little one,
With large blue eyes, and silken ringlets fair,
By nut-brown Lizzy, with smooth parted hair
Sable and glossy as the raven's wing,
And lustrous eyes as dark.

                  " Now mind and bring
Jenny safe home," the mother said ; " don't stay
To pull a bough or berry by the way ;
And when you come to cross the ford, hold fast
Your little sister's hand, till you 're quite past, —
That plank 's so crazy, and so slippery
(If not o'erflowed) the stepping-stones will be.
But you 're good children, — steady as old folk,
I 'd trust ye anywhere." Then Lizzy's cloak,
A good gray duffle, lovingly she tied,
And amply little Jenny's lack supplied
With her own warmest shawl. " Be sure," said she,
" To wrap it round and knot it carefully
(Like this) when you come home ; just leaving free
One hand to hold by. Now, make haste away, —
Good will to school, and then good right to play."

Was there no sinking at the mother's heart,
When all equipt, they turned them to depart ?
When down the lane, she watched them as they went
Till out of sight, was no foreboding sent
Of coming ill ? In truth I cannot tell ;
Such warnings *have been sent*, we know full well,
And must believe — believing that they are —

In mercy then, — to rouse — restrain — prepare.
And, now I mind me, something of the kind
Did surely haunt that day the mother's mind,
Making it irksome to bide all alone
By her own quiet hearth.   Though never known
For idle gossipry was Jenny Gray,
Yet so it was, that morn she could not stay
At home with her own thoughts, but took her way
To her next neighbor's, half a loaf to borrow, —
Yet might her store have lasted out the morrow, —
And with the loan obtained, she lingered still.
Said she : " My master, if he 'd had his will,
Would have kept back our little ones from school
This dreadful morning ; and I 'm such a fool,
Since they 've been gone, I 've wished them back.   But then
It won't do in such things to humor men, —
Our Ambrose specially.   If let alone,
He 'd spoil those children.   But it 's coming on, —
That storm he said was brewing, — sure enough —
Well ! what of that ? — To think what idle stuff
Will come into one's head ! and here with you
I stop, as if I 'd nothing else to do.
And they 'll come home drowned rats.   I must be gone
To get dry things, and set the kettle on."

His day's work done, three mortal miles and more
Lay between Ambrose and his cottage door.
A weary way, God wot ! for weary wight !
But yet far off, the curling smoke in sight
From his own chimney, and his heart felt light.

.   .   .   .   .

With what a thankful gladness in his face,
(Silent heart-homage, — plant of special grace !)
At the lane's entrance, slackening oft his pace,
Would Ambrose send a loving look before ;
Conceiting the caged blackbird at the door,
The very blackbird strained its little throat

In welcome, with a more rejoicing note ;
And honest Tinker ! dog of doubtful breed,
All bristle, back, and tail, but "good at need,"
Pleasant his greeting to the accustomed ear ;
But of all welcomes pleasantest, most dear,
The ringing voices, like sweet silver bells,
Of his two little ones.   How fondly swells
The father's heart, as, dancing up the lane,
Each clasps a hand in her small hand again ;
And each must tell her tale, and " say her say,"
Impeding as she leads, with sweet delay,
(Childhood's blest thoughtlessness !) his onward way.

Such was the hour — hour sacred and apart —
Warmed in expectancy the poor man's heart.
Summer and winter, as his toil he plied,
To him and his the literal doom applied,
Pronounced on Adam.   But the bread was sweet
So earned, for such dear mouths.   The weary feet,
Hope-shod, stept lightly on the homeward way ;
So specially it fared with Ambrose Gray
That time I tell of.   He had worked all day
At a great clearing ; vigorous stroke on stroke
Striking, till, when he stopt, his back seemed broke
And the strong arm dropt nerveless.   What of that ?
There was a treasure hidden in his hat, —
A plaything for the young ones.   He had found
A dormouse-nest ; the living ball coiled round
For its long winter sleep ; and all his thought,
As he trudged stoutly homeward, was of naught
But the glad wonderment in Jenny's eyes,
And graver Lizzy's quieter surprise
When he should yield, by guess and kiss and prayer,
Hard won, the frozen captive to their care.

'T was a wild evening, — wild and rough.   "I knew,"
Thought Ambrose, "those unlucky gulls spoke true, —

And Gaffer Chewton never growls for naught, —
I should be mortal mazed now, if I thought
My little maids were not safe housed before
That blinding hail-storm, — ay, this hour and more, —
Unless by that old crazy bit of board,
They 've not passed dry-foot over Shallow Ford,
That I 'll be bound for, — swollen as it must be —
Well! if my mistress had been ruled by me — "
But, checking the half-thought as heresy,
He looked out for the Home-Star. There it shone,
And with a gladdened heart he hastened on.

He 's in the lane again, — and there below,
Streams from the door-way that red glow,
Which warms him but to look at. For his prize
Cautious he feels, — all safe and snug it lies, —
"Down, Tinker! — down, old boy! — not quite so free, —
The thing thou sniffest is no game for thee. —
But what 's the meaning? — no look-out to-night!
No living soul astir! — Pray God, all 's right!
Who 's flittering round the peat-stack in such weather?
Mother!" You might have felled him with a feather
When the short answer to his loud "Hillo!"
And the hurried question, "Are they come?" was "No!"

To throw his tools down, hastily unhook
The old cracked lantern from its dusty nook,
And while he lit it, speak a cheering word,
That almost choked him, and was scarcely heard,
Was but a moment's act, and he was gone
To where a fearful foresight led him on.
Passing a neighbor's cottage in his way, —
Mark Fenton's, — him he took with short delay
To bear him company, — for who could say
What need might be? They struck into the track
The children should have taken coming back
From school that day; and many a call and shout

Into the pitchy darkness they sent out,
And, by the lantern light, peered all about,
In every roadside thicket, hole, and nook,
Till suddenly — as nearing now the brook —
Something brushed past them.   That was Tinker's bark ;
Unheeded, he had followed in the dark,
Close at his master's heels, but, swift as light,
Darted before them now.   " Be sure he 's right, —
He 's on the track," cried Ambrose.   " Hold the light
Low down, — he 's making for the water.   Hark !
I know that whine, — the old dog 's found them, Mark."
So speaking, breathlessly he hurried on
Toward the old crazy foot-bridge.   It was gone !
And all his dull, contracted light could show
Was the black void and dark swollen stream below.
" Yet there 's life somewhere, more than Tinker's whine, —
That 's sure," said Mark.   " So let the lantern shine
Down yonder.   There 's the dog, — and, hark !"   " O dear !"
And a low sob came faintly on the ear,
Mocked by the sobbing gust.   Down, quick as thought,
Into the stream leapt Ambrose, where he caught
Fast hold of something, — a dark huddled heap, —
Half in the water, where 't was scarce knee-deep,
For a tall man ; and half above it, propped
By some old ragged side-piles, that had stopt
Endways the broken plank, when it gave way
With the two little ones that luckless day !
" My babes ! my lambkins !" was the father's cry.
One little voice made answer, " Here am I !"
'T was Lizzy's.   There she crouched, with face as white,
More ghastly, by the flickering lantern light,
Than sheeted corpse.   The pale blue lips, drawn tight,
Wide parted, showing all the pearly teeth,
And eyes on some dark object underneath,
Washed by the turbid water, fixed like stone, —
One arm and hand stretched out, and rigid grown,
Grasping, as in the death-gripe, — Jenny's frock.

There she lay drowned. Could he sustain that shock,
The doating father ? Where 's the unriven rock
Can bide such blasting in its flintiest part
As that soft sentient thing, the human heart ?
They lifted her from out her watery bed, —
Its covering gone, the lonely little head
Hung like a broken snow-drop all aside,
And one small hand. The mother's shawl was tied,
Leaving that free, about the child's small form,
As was her last injunction, — "*fast* and warm," —
Too well obeyed, — too fast ! A fatal hold
Affording to the scrag by a thick fold
That caught and pinned her in the river's bed,
While through the reckless water overhead
Her life-breath bubbled up.

        " She might have lived
Struggling like Lizzie," was the thought that rived
The wretched mother's heart when she knew all.
" But for my foolishness about that shawl, —
And Master would have kept them back the day ;
But I was wilful, — driving them away
In such wild weather ! "

        Thus the tortured heart
Unnaturally against itself takes part,
Driving the sharp edge deeper of a woe
Too deep already. They had raised her now,
And, parting the wet ringlets from her brow,
To that, and the cold cheek, and lips as cold,
The father glued his warm ones, ere they rolled
Once more the fatal shawl — her winding-sheet —
About the precious clay. One heart still beat,
Warmed by *his heart's* blood. To his *only child*
He turned him, but her piteous moaning mild
Pierced him afresh, — and now she knew him not.
" Mother ! " she murmured, " who says I forgot ?
Mother ! indeed, indeed, I kept fast hold,
And tied the shawl quite close, — she can't be cold, —

But she won't move, — we slipt, — I don't know how, —
But I held on, — and I 'm so weary now, —
And it 's so dark and cold ! O dear ! O dear ! —
And she won't move, — if daddy was but here ! "

. . . .

Poor lamb, she wandered in her mind, 't was clear ;
But soon the piteous murmur died away,
And quiet in her father's arms she lay, —
They their dead burden had resigned, to take
The living so near lost. For her dear sake,
And one at home, he armed himself to bear
His misery like a man, — with tender care,
Doffing his coat her shivering form to fold,
(His neighbor bearing *that* which felt no cold,)
He clasped her close ; and so, with little said,
Homeward they bore the living and the dead.

From Ambrose Gray's poor cottage, all that night,
Shone fitfully a little shifting light,
Above, below, — for all were watchers there
Save one sound sleeper. *Her*, parental care,
Parental watchfulness, availed not now.
But in the young survivor's throbbing brow,
And wandering eyes, delirious fever burned ;
And all night long from side to side she turned,
Piteously plaining like a wounded dove,
With now and then a murmur, — " She won't move,"
And lo ! when morning, as in mockery, bright
Shone on that pillow, — passing strange the sight, —
That young head's raven hair was streaked with white !
No idle fiction this. Such things have been,
We know. And *now I tell what I have seen.*

Life struggled long with death in that small frame,
But it was strong, and conquered. All became
As it had been with the poor family, —
All, saving that which nevermore might be, —
There was an empty place, — they were but three.

8

BOB CRATCHIT'S DINNER. — Dickens.

BUT soon the steeples called good people all to church and chapel, and away they came, flocking through the streets in their best clothes, and with their gayest faces. And at the same time there emerged from scores of by streets, lanes, and nameless turnings innumerable people carrying their dinners to the bakers' shops.

Up then rose Mrs. Cratchit, Cratchit's wife, dressed out but poorly in a twice-turned gown, but brave in ribbons, which are cheap and make a goodly show for sixpence ; and she laid the cloth, assisted by Belinda Cratchit, second of her daughters, also brave in ribbons ; while Master Peter Cratchit plunged a fork into the saucepan of potatoes, and, getting the corners of his monstrous shirt-collar (Bob's private property, conferred upon his son and heir in honor of the day) into his mouth, rejoiced to find himself so gallantly attired, and yearned to show his linen in the fashionable Parks. And now two smaller Cratchits, boy and girl, came tearing in, screaming that outside the baker's they had smelt the goose, and known it for their own ; and, basking in luxurious thoughts of sage and onion, these young Cratchits danced about the table, and exalted Master Peter Cratchit to the skies, while he (not proud, although his collars nearly choked him) blew the fire, until the slow potatoes, bubbling up, knocked loudly at the saucepan-lid to be let out and peeled.

"What has ever got your precious father then ? " said Mrs. Cratchit. "And your brother Tiny Tim ! and Martha warn't as late last Christmas day by half an hour ! "

"Here's Martha, mother ! " said a girl, appearing as she spoke.

"Here's Martha, mother ! " cried the two young Cratchits. "Hurrah ! There's *such* a goose, Martha ! "

"Why, bless your heart alive, my dear, how late you are ! " said Mrs. Cratchit, kissing her a dozen times, and taking off her shawl and bonnet for her.

" We 'd a deal of work to finish up last night," replied the girl, " and had to clear away this morning, mother ! "

" Well ! Never mind so long as you are come," said Mrs. Cratchit. " Sit ye down before the fire, my dear, and have a warm, Lord bless ye ! "

" No, no ! There 's father coming," cried the two young Cratchits, who were everywhere at once. " Hide, Martha, hide ! "

So Martha hid herself, and in came little Bob, the father, with at least three feet of comforter, exclusive of the fringe, hanging down before him ; and his threadbare clothes darned up and brushed, to look seasonable ; and Tiny Tim upon his shoulder. Alas for Tiny Tim, he bore a little crutch, and had his limbs supported by an iron frame !

" Why, where 's our Martha ? " cried Bob Cratchit, looking round.

" Not coming," said Mrs. Cratchit.

" Not coming ! " said Bob, with a sudden declension in his high spirits ; for he had been Tim's blood-horse all the way from church, and had come home rampant, — " not coming upon Christmas day ! "

Martha did n't like to see him disappointed, if it were only in joke ; so she came out prematurely from behind the closet door, and ran into his arms, while the two young Cratchits hustled Tiny Tim, and bore him off into the wash-house, that he might hear the pudding singing in the copper.

" And how did little Tim behave ? " asked Mrs. Cratchit, when she had rallied Bob on his credulity, and Bob had hugged his daughter to his heart's content.

" As good as gold," said Bob, " and better. Somehow he gets thoughtful, sitting by himself so much, and thinks the strangest things you ever heard. He told me, coming home, that he hoped the people saw him in the church, because he was a cripple, and it might be pleasant to them to remember, upon Christmas day, who made lame beggars walk and blind men see."

Bob's voice was tremulous when he told them this, and trembled more when he said that Tiny Tim was growing strong and hearty.

His active little crutch was heard upon the floor, and back came Tiny Tim before another word was spoken, escorted by his brother and sister, to his stool beside the fire ; and while Bob, turning up his cuffs, — as if, poor fellow, they were capable of being made more shabby, — compounded some hot mixture in a jug with gin and lemons, and stirred it round and round and put it on the hob to simmer, Master Peter and the two ubiquitous young Cratchits went to fetch the goose, with which they soon returned in high procession.

Mrs. Cratchit made the gravy (ready beforehand in a little saucepan) hissing hot; Master Peter mashed the potatoes with incredible vigor ; Miss Belinda sweetened up the apple-sauce; Martha dusted the hot plates ; Bob took Tiny Tim beside him in a tiny corner at the table ; the two young Cratchits set chairs for everybody, not forgetting themselves, and, mounting guard upon their posts, crammed spoons into their mouths, lest they should shriek for goose before their turn came to be helped. At last the dishes were set on, and grace was said. It was succeeded by a breathless pause, as Mrs. Cratchit, looking slowly all along the carving-knife, prepared to plunge it in the breast; but when she did, and when the long-expected gush of stuffing issued forth, one murmur of delight arose all round the board, and even Tiny Tim, excited by the two young Cratchits, beat on the table with the handle of his knife, and feebly cried, Hurrah !

There never was such a goose. Bob said he did n't believe there ever was such a goose cooked. Its tenderness and flavor, size and cheapness, were the themes of universal admiration. Eked out by apple-sauce and mashed potatoes, it was a sufficient dinner for the whole family ; indeed, as Mrs. Cratchit said with great delight (surveying one small atom of a bone upon the dish), they had n't ate it all at last ! Yet every one had had enough, and the youngest Cratchits in particular were steeped in sage and onion to the eyebrows !

But now, the plates being changed by Miss Belinda, Mrs. Cratchit left the room alone, — too nervous to bear witnesses — to take the pudding up, and bring it in.

Suppose it should not be done enough! Suppose it should break in turning out! Suppose somebody should have got over the wall of the back yard, and stolen it, while they were merry with the goose, — a supposition at which the two young Cratchits became livid! All sorts of horrors were supposed.

Hallo! A great deal of steam! The pudding was out of the copper. A smell like a washing-day! That was the cloth. A smell like an eating-house and a pastry-cook's next door to each other, with a laundress's next door to that! That was the pudding! In half a minute Mrs. Cratchit entered — flushed, but smiling proudly — with the pudding, like a speckled cannon-ball, so hard and firm, blazing in half of half a quartern of ignited brandy, and bedight with Christmas holly stuck into the top.

O, a wonderful pudding! Bob Cratchit said, and calmly too, that he regarded it as the greatest success achieved by Mrs. Cratchit since their marriage. Mrs. Cratchit said that now the weight was off her mind, she would confess she had had her doubts about the quantity of flour. Everybody had something to say about it, but nobody said or thought it was at all a small pudding for a large family. Any Cratchit would have blushed to hint at such a thing.

At last the dinner was all done, the cloth was cleared, the hearth swept, and the fire made up. The compound in the jug being tasted, and considered perfect, apples and oranges were put upon the table, and a shovelful of chestnuts on the fire.

Then all the Cratchit family drew round the hearth, in what Bob Cratchit called a circle, and at Bob Cratchit's elbow stood the family display of glass, — two tumblers, and a custard-cup without a handle.

These held the hot stuff from the jug, however, as well as golden goblets would have done; and Bob served it out with beaming looks, while the chestnuts on the fire sputtered and crackled noisily. Then Bob proposed : —

"A merry Christmas to us all, my dears. God bless us!" Which all the family re-echoed.

"God bless us every one!" said Tiny Tim, the last of all.

THE LITTLE BOY THAT DIED. — J. D. ROBINSON.

I AM all alone in my chamber now,
    And the midnight hour is near,
And the fagot's crack and the clock's dull tick
    Are the only sounds I hear ;
And over my soul, in its solitude,
    Sweet feelings of sadness glide ;
For my heart and my eyes are full, when I think
    Of the little boy that died.

I went one night to my father's house, —
    Went home to the dear ones all,
And softly I opened the garden gate,
    And softly the door of the hall ;
My mother came out to meet her son,
    She kissed me, and then she sighed,
And her head fell on my neck, and she wept
    For the little boy that died.

And when I gazed on his innocent face,
    As still and cold he lay,
And thought what a lovely child he had been,
    And how soon he must decay,
"O death, thou lovest the beautiful,"
    In the woe of my spirit I cried ;
For sparkled the eyes, and the forehead was fair,
    Of the little boy that died !

Again I will go to my father's house,
　　Go home to the dear ones all,
And sadly I 'll open the garden gate,
　　And sadly the door of the hall;
I shall meet my mother, but nevermore
　　With her darling by her side,
But she 'll kiss me and sigh and weep again
　　For the little boy that died.

I shall miss him when the flowers come
　　In the garden where he played;
I shall miss him more by the fireside,
　　When the flowers have all decayed;
I shall see his toys and his empty chair,
　　And the horse he used to ride;
And they will speak, with a silent speech,
　　Of the little boy that died.

I shall see his little sister again
　　With her playmates about the door,
And I 'll watch the children in their sports,
　　As I never did before;
And if in the group I see a child
　　That 's dimpled and laughing-eyed,
I 'll look to see if it may not be
　　The little boy that died.

We shall all go home to our Father's house, —
　　To our Father's house in the skies,
Where the hope of our souls shall have no blight,
　　And our love no broken ties;
We shall roam on the banks of the River of Peace,
　　And bathe in its blissful tide:
And one of the joys of our heaven shall be
　　The little boy that died!

KING CANUTE AND HIS NOBLES. — Dr. Wolcott.

CANUTE was by his nobles taught to fancy
　　That, by a kind of royal necromancy,
He had the power Old Ocean to control.
Down rushed the royal Dane upon the strand,
　　And issued, like a Solomon, command, — poor soul!

" Go back, ye waves, you blustering rogues," quoth he;
" Touch not your lord and master, Sea;
　　For by my power almighty, if you do — "
Then, staring vengeance, out he held a stick,
Vowing to drive Old Ocean to Old Nick,
　　Should he even wet the latchet of his shoe.

The sea retired, — the monarch fierce rushed on,
　　And looked as if he 'd drive him from the land;
But Sea, not caring to be put upon,
　　Made for a moment a bold stand.

Not only made a stand did Mr. Ocean,
But to his waves he made a motion,
　　And bid them give the king a hearty trimming.
The order seemed a deal the waves to tickle,
For soon they put his Majesty in pickle,
　　And set his royalties, like geese, a swimming.

All hands aloft, with one tremendous roar,
Sound did they make him wish himself on shore;
　　His head and ears most handsomely they doused, —
Just like a porpoise, with one general shout,
The waves so tumbled the poor king about, —
　　No anabaptist e'er was half so soused.

At length to land he crawled, a half-drowned thing,
Indeed more like a crab than like a king,
　　And found his courtiers making rueful faces;

But what said Canute to the lords and gentry,
Who hailed him from the water, on his entry,
   All trembling for their lives or places ?

" My lords and gentlemen, by your advice,
   I 've had with Mr. Sea a pretty bustle ;
My treatment from my foe, not over nice,
   Just made a jest for every shrimp and mussel.

" A pretty trick for one of my dominion ! —
My lords, I thank you for your great opinion.
You 'll tell me, p'r'aps, I 've only lost one game,
   And bid me try another, — for the rubber ;
Permit me to inform you all, with shame,
   That you 're a set of knaves and I 'm a lubber."

———◆———

HANNAH BINDING SHOES. — LUCY LARCOM.

POOR lone Hannah,
   .Sitting at the window binding shoes.
     Faded, wrinkled,
Sitting stitching in a mournful muse.
   Bright-eyed beauty once was she,
    When the bloom was on the tree ;
     Spring and winter
Hannah 's at the window binding shoes.

     Not a neighbor
Passing nod or answer will refuse,
     To her whisper,
" Is there from the fishers any news ? "
   O, her heart 's adrift with one
    On an endless voyage gone !
     Night and morning
Hannah 's at the window binding shoes.

8 *   L

Fair young Hannah
Ben, the sunburnt fisher, gayly woos ;
  Hale and clever,
For a willing heart and hand he sues.
  May-day skies are all aglow,
    And the waves are laughing so ?
    For her wedding
Hannah leaves her window and her shoes.

    May is passing ;
Mid the apple-boughs a pigeon coos.
    Hannah shudders,
For the mild southwester mischief brews.
  Round the rocks of Marblehead,
    Outward bound, a schooner sped ;
    Silent, lonesome,
Hannah 's at the window binding shoes.

    'T is November ;
Now no tear her wasted cheek bedews.
    From Newfoundland,
Not a sail returning will she lose,
  Whispering hoarsely, " Fishermen,
    Have you, have you heard of Ben ? "
    Old with watching,
Hannah 's at the window binding shoes.

    Twenty winters
Bleach and tear the ragged shore she views ;
    Twenty seasons, —
Never one has brought her any news.
  Still her dim eyes silently
    Chase the white sails o'er the sea ;
    Hopeless, faithful,
Hannah 's at the window binding shoes.

THE REGIMENT'S RETURN. — E. J. Cutler.

I.

HE is coming, he is coming, my true love comes home
to-day!
All the city throngs to meet him, as he lingers by the way.
He is coming from the battle with his knapsack and his gun, —
He, a hundred times my darling, for the dangers he hath run !

Twice they said that he was dead, but I would not believe the
lie ;
While my faithful heart kept loving him, I knew he could not
die.
All in white will I array me, with a rose-bud in my hair,
And his ring upon my finger, — he shall see it shining there !
He will kiss me, he will kiss me, with the kiss of long ago ;
He will fold his arms around me close, and I shall cry, I
know.
O the years that I have waited, rather lives they seemed to be,
For the dawning of the happy day that brings him back to me !
But the worthy cause has triumphed, O joy ! the war is over !
He is coming, he is coming, my gallant soldier lover !

II.

Men are shouting all around me, women weep and laugh for
joy,
Wives behold again their husbands, and the mother clasps
her boy ;
All the city throbs with passion ; 't is a day of jubilee :
But the happiness of thousands brings not happiness to me.
I remember, I remember, when the soldiers went away,
There was one among the noblest who is not returned to-day.
O, I loved him, how I loved him ! and I never can forget
That he kissed me as we parted, for the kiss is burning yet !

'T is his picture in my bosom, where his head will never lie ;
'T is his ring upon my finger, — I will wear it till I die.
O, his comrades say that, dying, he looked up and breathed
    my name ;
They have come to those that loved them, but my darling
    never came.
O, they say he died a hero, — but I knew how that would be,
And they say the cause has triumphed — Will that bring him
    back to me ?

ENLISTING AS ARMY NURSE. — LOUISA M. ALCOTT.

"I WANT something to do." — This remark being addressed to the world in general, no one in particular felt it his duty to reply ; so I repeated it to the smaller world about me, received the following suggestions, and settled the matter by answering my own inquiry, as people are apt to do when very much in earnest.

"Write a book," quoth my father.

"Don't know enough, sir.   First live, then write."

"Try teaching again," suggested my mother.

"No, thank you, ma'am ; ten years of that is enough."

"Take a husband like my Darby, and fulfil your mission," said Sister Jane, home on a visit.

"Can't afford expensive luxuries, Mrs. Coobiddy."

"Turn actress, and immortalize your name," said Sister Vashti, striking an attitude.

"I won't."

"Go nurse the soldiers," said my young neighbor, Tom, panting for "the tented field."

"I will ! "

Arriving at this satisfactory conclusion, the meeting adjourned ; and the fact that Miss Tribulation was available as army nurse went abroad on the wings of the wind.

In a few days a townswoman heard of my desire, approved of it, and brought about an interview with one of the sisterhood I wished to join, who was at home on a furlough, and able and willing to satisfy inquiries.

A morning chat with Miss General S. — we hear no end of Mrs. Generals, why not a Miss ? — produced three results : I felt that I could do the work, was offered a place, and accepted it, promising not to desert, but to stand ready to march on Washington at an hour's notice.

A few days were necessary for the letter containing my request and recommendation to reach head-quarters, and another, containing my commission, to return ; therefore no time was to be lost ; and, heartily thanking my pair of friends, I hurried home through the December slush, as if the Rebels were after me, and, like many another recruit, burst in upon my family with the announcement, — "I 've enlisted ! "

An impressive silence followed.   Tom, the irrepressible, broke it with a slap on the shoulder and the grateful compliment, — "Old Trib, you 're a trump ! "

"Thank you ; then I 'll *take* something," — which I did, in the shape of dinner, reeling off my news at the rate of three dozen words to a mouthful ; and as every one else talked equally fast, and all together, the scene was most inspiring.

As boys going to sea immediately become nautical in speech, walk as if they already had their sea-legs on, and shiver their timbers on all possible occasions, so I turned military at once, called my dinner my rations, saluted all new-comers, and ordered a dress-parade that very afternoon.

Having reviewed every rag I possessed, I detailed some pieces for picket duty while airing on the fence ; some to the sanitary influences of the wash-tub ; others to mount guard in the trunk ; while the weak and wounded went to the Work-basket Hospital, to be made ready for active service again.

To this squad I devoted myself for a week ; but all was done, and I had time to get powerfully impatient before the letter came.   It did arrive, however, and brought a disappointment along with its good-will and friendliness; for it told me that the place in the Armory Hospital that I supposed I was to take was already filled, and a much less desirable one at Hurly-burly House was offered instead.

"That's just your luck, Trib. I'll take your trunk up garret for you again; for of course you won't go," Tom remarked, with the disdainful pity which small boys affect when they get into their teens.

I was wavering in my secret soul; but that remark settled the matter, and I crushed him on the spot with martial brevity, — "It is now one; I shall march at six."

I have a confused recollection of spending the afternoon in pervading the house like an executive whirlwind, with my family swarming after me, — all working, talking, prophesying, and lamenting, while I packed such of my things as I was to take with me, tumbled the rest into two big boxes, danced on the lids till they shut, and gave them in charge, with the direction, — "If I never come back, make a bonfire of them."

Then I choked down a cup of tea, generously salted instead of sugared by some agitated relative, shouldered my knapsack, — it was only a travelling-bag, but do let me preserve the unities, — hugged my family three times all round without a vestige of unmanly emotion, till a certain dear old lady broke down upon my neck, with a despairing sort of wail, — "O my dear, my dear! how can I let you go?"

"I'll stay, if you say so, mother."

"But I don't; go, and the Lord will take care of you."

Much of the Roman matron's courage had gone into the Yankee matron's composition, and, in spite of her tears, she would have sent ten sons to the war, had she possessed them, as freely as she sent one daughter, smiling and flapping on the door-step till I vanished, though the eyes that followed me were very dim, and the handkerchief she waved was very wet.

My transit from The Gables to the village depot was a funny mixture of good wishes and good-bys, mud-puddles and shopping. A December twilight is not the most cheering time to enter upon a somewhat perilous enterprise; but I'd no thought of giving out, O bless you, no!

When the engine screeched "Here we are!" I clutched my escort in a fervent embrace, and skipped into the car with as blithe a farewell as if going on a bridal tour, — though I believe brides don't usually wear cavernous black bonnets and fuzzy brown coats, with a hair-brush, a pair of rubbers, two books, and a bag of gingerbread distorting the pockets.

If I thought that people would believe it, I'd boldly state that I slept from C. to B., which would simplify matters immensely; but as I know they would n't, I'll confess that the head under the funereal coal-hod fermented with all manner of high thoughts and heroic purposes "to do or die," — perhaps both; and the heart under the fuzzy brown coat felt very tender with the memory of the dear old lady, probably sobbing over her army socks and the loss of her topsy-turvy Trib.

At this juncture I took the veil, and what I did behind it is nobody's business; but I maintain that the soldier who cries when his mother says "Good by" is the boy to fight best, and die bravest, when the time comes, or go back to her better than he went.

MOTHER AND POET. — Mrs. Browning.

DEAD! one of them shot by the sea in the east,
     And one of them shot in the west by the sea.
Dead! both my boys! when you sit at the feast,
     And are wanting a great song for Italy free,
          Let none look at me!

Yet I was a poetess only last year,
     And good at my art, for a woman, men said;
But this woman, this, who is agonized here,
     The east sea and west sea rhyme on in her head
          Forever, instead!

What 's art for a woman ?   To hold on her knees
  Both darlings ! to feel all their arms round her throat
Cling, strangle a little ! to sew by degrees,
    And 'broider the long clothes and neat little coat ;
        To dream and to dote.

To teach them —   It stings there !   *I* made them, indeed,
  Speak plain the word " country," —*I* taught them, no doubt,
That a country 's a thing men should die for at need.
    I prated of liberty, rights, and about
        The tyrant cast out.

And when their eyes flashed ! O my beautiful eyes !
  I exulted !   Nay, let them go forth at the wheels
Of the guns, and denied not.   But then the surprise
    When one sits quite alone ! Then one weeps, then one kneels !
        — God ! how the house feels !

At first happy news came, in gay letters moiled
  With my kisses, of camp life and glory, and how
They both loved me, and soon, coming home to be spoiled,
    In return would fan off every fly from my brow
        With their green laurel-bough.

Then was triumph at Turin : " Ancona was free ! "
  And some one came out of the cheers in the street,
With a face pale as stone, to say something to me.
    My Guido was dead ! — I fell down at his feet
        While they cheered in the street.

I bore it ! friends soothed me ; my grief looked sublime
  As the ransom of Italy.   One boy remained
To be leant on, and walked with, recalling the time
    When the first grew immortal, while both of us strained
        To the height he had gained.

And letters still came, shorter, sadder, more strong,
  Writ now but in one hand : " I was not to faint.

One loved me for two ; would be with me erelong !
  And ' Viva l' Italia ! ' he died for, our saint,
     Who forbids our complaint."

My Nanni would add he " was safe, and aware
  Of a presence that turned off the balls, was imprest
It was Guido himself who knew what I could bear,
  And how 't was impossible, quite dispossessed,
     To live on for the rest."

On which, without pause, up the telegraph line
  Swept smoothly the next news from Gaeta :
" Shot.   Tell his mother." Ah ! ah ! " his," " their " mother ;
    not " mine."
  No voice says " my mother" again to me.   What !
     You think Guido forgot ?

Are souls straight so happy that, dizzy with heaven,
  They drop earth's affections, conceive not of woe ?
I think not.   Themselves were too lately forgiven
  Through THAT Love and that Sorrow which reconcile so
     The Above and Below.

O Christ of the seven wounds, who look'dst through the dark
  To the face of Thy mother ! consider, I pray,
How we common mothers stand desolate ; mark,
  Whose sons, not being Christs, die with eyes turned away,
     And no last word to say !

Both boys dead ! but that 's out of nature.   We all
  Have been patriots, yet each house must always keep one ;
'T were imbecile hewing out roads to a wall.
  And, when Italy 's made, for what end is it done,
     If we have not a son ?

Ah ! ah ! ah ! when Gaeta 's taken, what then ?
  When the fair wicked queen sits no more at her sport

Of the fire-balls of death, crashing souls out of men ?
　　When the guns of Cavalli, with final retort,
　　　　Have cut the game short ?

When Venice and Rome keep their new jubilee,
　　When your flag takes all heaven for its white, green, and red,
When *you* have your country, from mountain to sea,
　　When King Victor has Italy's crown on his head,
　　　　(And *I* have my dead) —

What then ?　Do not mock me.　Ah, ring your bells low
　　And burn your lights faintly !　*My* country is *there*,
Above the star pricked by the last peak of snow ;
　　My Italy 's THERE, — with my brave civic Pair,
　　　　To disfranchise despair !

Dead ! one of them shot by the sea in the east,
　　And one of them shot in the west by the sea.
Both ! both my boys !　If in keeping the feast,
　　You want a great song for Italy free,
　　　　Let none look at *me*.

———◆———

FETCHING WATER FROM THE WELL.

EARLY on a sunny morning, while the lark was singing
　　　sweet,
Came, beyond the ancient farm-house, sounds of lightly trip-
　　ping feet.
'T was a lowly cottage maiden going, — why, let young hearts
　　tell, —
With her homely pitcher laden, fetching water from the well.

Shadows lay athwart the pathway, all along the quiet
　　lane,
And the breezes of the morning moved them to and fro
　　again.

O'er the sunshine, o'er the shadow, passed the maiden of the
farm,
With a charméd heart within her, thinking of no ill nor harm.

Pleasant, surely, were her musings, for the nodding leaves
in vain
Sought to press their brightening image on her ever-busy
brain.
Leaves and joyous birds went by her, like a dim, half-waking
dream;
And her soul was only conscious of life's gladdest summer
gleam.

At the old lane's shady turning lay a well of water bright,
Singing soft its hallelujah to the gracious morning light.
Fern-leaves, broad and green, bent o'er it where its silvery
droplets fell,
And the fairies dwelt beside it, in the spotted foxglove bell.

Back she bent the shading fern-leaves, dipt the pitcher in
the tide, —
Drew it, with the dripping waters flowing o'er its glazéd side.
But before her arm could place it on her shiny, wavy hair,
By her side a youth was standing! — Love rejoiced to see the
pair!

Tones of tremulous emotion trailed upon the morning
breeze,
Gentle words of heart-devotion whispered 'neath the ancient
trees.
But the holy, blessed secrets it becomes me not to tell;
Life had met another meaning, fetching water from the well.

Down the rural lane they sauntered. He the burden-
pitcher bore;
She, with dewy eyes down looking, grew more beauteous than
before!

When they neared the silent homestead, up he raised the
    pitcher light ;
Like a fitting crown he placed it on her hair of wavelets
    bright :

Emblems of the coming burdens that for love of him she 'd
    bear,
Calling every burden blessed, if his love but lighted there.
Then, still waving benedictions, further, further off he drew,
While his shadow seemed a glory that across the pathway
    grew.

Now about her household duties silently the maiden went,
And an ever-radiant halo o'er her daily life was blent.
Little knew the aged matron, as her feet like music fell,
What abundant treasure found she, fetching water from the
    well !

THE PUMPKIN. — J. G. WHITTIER.

ON the banks of the Xenil a dark Spanish maiden
    Comes up with the fruit of the tangled vine laden ;
And the Creole of Cuba laughs out to behold
Through orange-leaves shining the broad spheres of gold ;
Yet with dearer delight from his home in the North,
On the fields of his harvest the Yankee looks forth,
Where crook-necks are coiling and yellow fruit shines,
And the sun of September melts down on his vines.

Ah ! on Thanksgiving Day, when from East and from West,
From North and from South come the pilgrim and guest,
When the gray-haired New-Englander sees round his board
The old broken links of affection restored,
When the care-wearied man seeks his mother once more,
And the worn matron smiles where the girl smiled before,
What moistens the lip, and what brightens the eye ?
What calls back the past like the rich pumpkin-pie ?

O, fruit loved of boyhood ! — the old days recalling,
When wood-grapes were purpling and brown nuts were falling !
When wild, ugly faces we carved in its skin,
Glaring out through the dark with a candle within !
When we laughed round the corn-heap, with hearts all in
      tune,
Our chair a broad pumpkin, our lantern the moon,
Telling tales of the fairy who travelled like steam
In a pumpkin-shell coach, with two rats for her team !

Then thanks for thy present ! — none sweeter or better
E'er smoked from an oven or circled a platter !
Fairer hands never wrought at a pastry more fine,
Brighter eyes never watched o'er its baking, than thine !
And the prayer, which my mouth is too full to express,
Swells my heart that thy shadow may never be less,
That the days of thy lot may be lengthened below,
And the fame of thy worth like a pumpkin-vine grow,
And thy life be as sweet, and its last sunset sky
Golden-tinted and fair as thy own pumpkin-pie !

CIVIL WAR. — CHARLES D. SHANLEY.

"RIFLEMAN, shoot me a fancy shot
    Straight at the heart of yon prowling vidette ;
Ring me a ball in the glittering spot
    That shines on his breast like an amulet !"

"Ah, captain ! here goes for a fine-drawn bead ;
    There 's music around when my barrel 's in tune !"
Crack ! went the rifle, the messenger sped,
    And dead from his horse fell the ringing dragoon.

" Now, rifleman, steal through the bushes, and snatch
    From your victim some trinket to handsel first blood ;

A button, a loop, or that luminous patch
　　That gleams in the moon like a diamond stud ! "

" O captain ! I staggered, and sunk on my track,
　　When I gazed on the face of that fallen vidette,
For he looked so like you, as he lay on his back,
　　That my heart rose upon me, and masters me yet.

" But I snatched off the trinket, — this locket of gold ;
　　An inch from the centre my lead broke its way,
Scarce grazing the picture, so fair to behold,
　　Of a beautiful lady in bridal array."

" Ha ! rifleman; fling me the locket ! — 't is she,
　　My brother's young bride, — and the fallen dragoon
Was her husband — Hush ! soldier, 't was Heaven's decree ;
　　We must bury him there, by the light of the moon !

" But, hark ! the far bugles their warnings unite ;
　　War is a virtue, — weakness, a sin ;
There 's a lurking and loping around us to-night ;
　　Load again, rifleman, keep your hand in ! "

PATIENT JOE.

HAVE you heard of a collier, of honest renown,
　　Who dwelt on the borders of Newcastle Town ?
His name it was Joseph, — you better may know
If I tell you he always was called Patient Joe.

Whatever betided, he thought it was right,
And Providence still he kept ever in sight ;
To those who love God, let things turn as they would,
He was certain that all worked together for good.

He praised his Creator, whatever befell !
How thankful was Joseph when matters went well !
How sincere were his carols of praise for good health,
And how grateful for any increase in his wealth !

In trouble he bowed him to God's holy will ;
How contented was Joseph when matters went ill !
When rich and when poor, he alike understood
That all things together were working for good.

If the land was afflicted with war, he declared
'T was a needful correction for sins, which he shared ;
And when merciful Heaven bid slaughter to cease,
How thankful was Joe for the blessings of peace !

When taxes ran high and provisions were dear,
Still Joseph declared he had nothing to fear ;
It was but a trial, he well understood,
From Him who made all work together for good.

Though his wife was but sickly, his gettings but small,
A mind so submissive prepared him for all ;
He lived on his gains, were they greater or less,
And the Giver he ceased not each moment to bless.

It was Joseph's ill fortune to work in a pit
With some who believed that profaneness was wit ;
When disasters befell him, much pleasure they showed,
And laughed and said, " Joseph, will this work for good ? "

But ever when these would profanely advance
That *this* happened by luck, and *that* happened by chance,
Still Joseph insisted no chance could be found,
Not a sparrow by accident falls to the ground.

Among his companions who worked in the pit,
And made him the butt of their profligate wit,

Was idle Tim Jenkins, who drank and who gamed,
Who mocked at his Bible and was not ashamed.

One day at the pit his old comrades he found,
And they chatted, preparing to go under ground ;
Tim Jenkins, as usual, was turning to jest
Joe's notion — that all things which happened were best.

As Joe on the ground had unthinkingly laid
His provision for dinner of bacon and bread,
A dog, on the watch, seized the bread and the meat,
And off with his prey ran with footsteps so fleet.

Now to see the delight that Tim Jenkins expressed !
" Is the loss of thy dinner too, Joe, for the best ? "
" No doubt on 't," said Joe, " but as I must eat,
'T is my duty to try to recover my meat."

So saying, he followed the dog a long round,
While Tim, laughing and swearing, went down under ground.
Poor Joe soon returned, though his bacon was lost,
For the dog a good dinner had made at his cost.

When Joseph came back, he expected a sneer ;
But the face of each collier spoke horror and fear.
" What a narrow escape hast thou had ! " they all said ;
" The pit has fallen in, and Tim Jenkins is dead."

How sincere was the gratitude Joseph expressed !
How warm the compassion which glowed in his breast !
Thus events, great and small, if aright understood,
Will be found to be working together for good.

" When my meat," Joseph cried, " was just now stolen away,
And I had no prospect of eating to-day,
How could it appear to a short-sighted sinner
That my life would be saved by the loss of my dinner ! "

THE CANAL-BOAT. — Harriet Beecher Stowe.

OF all the ways of travelling which obtain among our locomotive nation, this said vehicle, the canal-boat, is the most absolutely prosaic and inglorious. There is something picturesque, nay, almost sublime, in the lordly march of your well-built, high-bred steamboat. Go, take your stand on some overhanging bluff, where the Ohio winds its thread of silver, or the sturdy Mississippi tears its path through unbroken forests, and it will do your heart good to see the gallant boat walking the waters with powerful tread; and, like some fabled monster of the wave, breathing fire, and making the shores resound with its deep respirations. Then there is something mysterious, even awful, in the power of steam. But in a canal-boat there is no power, no mystery, no danger; one cannot blow up, one cannot be drowned, unless by some special effort. One sees all there is in the case, — a horse, a rope, and a muddy strip of water, — and that is all.

Did you ever try it? If not, take an imaginary trip with us, just for experiment.

"There's the boat!" exclaims a passenger in the omnibus, as we are rolling down from the Pittsburg Mansion House to the canal.

"Where?" exclaim a dozen voices, and forthwith a dozen heads go out of the window.

"Why, down there, under that bridge; don't you see those lights?"

"What, that little thing!" exclaims an inexperienced traveller; "dear me! we can't half of us get into it!"

"We! indeed," says some old hand in the business, "I think you'll find it will hold us and a dozen loads like us."

"Impossible!" say some.

"You'll see," say the initiated; and, as soon as you get out, you *do* see, and hear too, what seems like a general

9   M

breaking loose from the Tower of Babel, amid a perfect hailstorm of trunks, boxes, valises, carpet-bags, and every describable and indescribable form of what a Westerner calls "plunder."

"That's my trunk!" barks out a big round man.

"That's my bandbox!" screams a heart-stricken old lady, in terror for her immaculate Sunday caps.

"Where's my little red box? I had two carpet-bags and a ⸺ My trunk had a scarle ⸺ Halloo! where are you going with that portmanteau? ⸺ Husband! husband! do see after the large basket and the little hair trunk ⸺ O, and the baby's little chair!"

"Go below, for mercy's sake, my dear! I'll see to the baggage."

At last, the feminine part of creation, perceiving that, in this particular instance, they gain nothing by public speaking, are content to be led quietly under the hatches; and amusing is the look of dismay which each new-comer gives to the confined quarters that present themselves. Those who were so ignorant of the power of compression as to suppose the boat scarce large enough to contain them and theirs find, with dismay, a respectable colony of old ladies, babies, mothers, big baskets, and carpet-bags already established.

"Mercy on us!" says one, after surveying the little room, about ten feet long and six high, "where are we all to sleep to-night?"

"O me! what a sight of children!" says a young lady in a despairing tone.

"Poh!" says an initiated traveller; "children! scarce any here. Let's see: one; the woman in the corner, two; that child with the bread-and-butter, three; and then there's that other woman with two. Really it's quite moderate for a canal-boat. However, we can't tell till they have all come."

"All! for mercy's sake, you don't say there are any more coming!" exclaim two or three in a breath; "they *çan't* come; *there is not room!*"

Notwithstanding the impressive utterance of this sentence, the contrary is immediately demonstrated by the appearance of a very corpulent elderly lady, with three well-grown daughters, who come down looking about them most complacently, entirely regardless of the unchristian looks of the company. What a mercy it is that fat people are always good-natured!

After this follows an indiscriminate raining down of all shapes, sizes, sexes, and ages, — men, women, children, babies, and nurses. The state of feeling becomes perfectly desperate. Darkness gathers on all faces.

"We shall be smothered! we shall be crowded to death! we *can't stay* here!" are heard faintly from one and another; and yet, though the boat grows no wider, the walls no higher, they do live, and do stay there, in spite of repeated protestations to the contrary. Truly, as Sam Slick says, "there's a *sight of wear* in human natur'."

But, meanwhile, the children grow sleepy, and divers interesting little duets and trios arise from one part or another of the cabin.

"Hush, Johnny! be a good boy," says a pale, nursing mamma to a great, bristling, white-headed phenomenon, who is kicking very much at large in her lap.

"I won't be a good boy, neither," responds Johnny, with interesting explicitness; "I want to go to bed, and so-o-o-o!" and Johnny makes up a mouth as big as a teacup, and roars with good courage, and his mamma asks him "if he ever saw pa do so," and tells him that "he is mamma's dear, good little boy, and must not make a noise," with various observations of the kind, which are so strikingly efficacious in such cases. Meanwhile, the domestic concert in other quarters proceeds with vigor.

"Mamma, I'm tired!" bawls a child.

"Where's the baby's nightgown?" calls a nurse.

"Do take Peter up in your lap, and keep him still."

"Pray get some biscuits and stop their mouths."

Meanwhile sundry babies strike in "con spirito," as the

music-books have it, and execute various flourishes; the disconsolate mothers sigh, and look as if all was over with them; and the young ladies appear extremely disgusted, and wonder "what business women have to be travelling round with babies."

To these troubles succeeds the turning-out scene, when the whole caravan is ejected into the gentlemen's cabin, that the beds may be made. The red curtains are put down, and in solemn silence all the last mysterious preparations begin. At length it is announced that all is ready. Forthwith the whole company rush back, and find the walls embellished by a series of little shelves, about a foot wide, each furnished with a mattress and bedding, and hooked to the ceiling by a very suspiciously slender cord. Direful are the ruminations and exclamations of inexperienced travellers, particularly young ones, as they eye these very equivocal accommodations.

"What, sleep up there! *I* won't sleep on one of those top shelves, *I* know. The cords will certainly break."

The chambermaid here takes up the conversation, and solemnly assures them that such an accident is not to be thought of at all, that it is a natural impossibility, — a thing that could not happen without an actual miracle; and since it becomes increasingly evident that thirty ladies cannot all sleep on the lowest shelf, there is some effort made to exercise faith in this doctrine; nevertheless, all look on their neighbors with fear and trembling, and when the stout lady talks of taking a shelf, she is most urgently pressed to change places with her alarmed neighbor below. Points of location being after a while adjusted, comes the last struggle. Everybody wants to take off a bonnet, or look for a shawl, to find a cloak or get a carpet-bag, and all set about it with such zeal that nothing can be done.

"Ma'am, you 're on my foot!" says one.

"Will you please to move, ma'am?" says somebody who is gasping and struggling behind you.

"Move!" you echo. "Indeed, I should be very glad to, but I don't see much prospect of it."

"Chambermaid!" calls a lady, who is struggling among a heap of carpet-bags and children at one end of the cabin.

"Ma'am!" echoes the poor chambermaid, who is wedged fast, in a similar situation, at the other.

"Where's my cloak, chambermaid?"

"I'd find it, ma'am, if I could move."

"Chambermaid, my basket!"

"Chambermaid, my parasol!"

"Chambermaid, my carpet-bag!"

"Mamma, they push me so!"

"Hush, child; crawl under there, and lie still till I can undress you."

At last, however, the various distresses are over, the babies sink to sleep, and even that much-enduring being, the chambermaid, seeks out some corner for repose. Tired and drowsy, you are just sinking into a doze, when bang! goes the boat against the sides of a lock; ropes scrape, men run and shout, and up fly the heads of all the top shelfites, who are generally the more juvenile and airy part of the company.

"What's that! what's that!" flies from mouth to mouth; and forthwith they proceed to awaken their respective relations. "Mother! Aunt Hannah! do wake up; what is this awful noise?"

"O, only a lock! Pray be still!" groan out the sleepy members from below.

"A lock!" exclaim the vivacious creatures, ever on the alert for information; "and what *is* a lock, pray?"

"Don't you know what a lock is, you silly creatures? Do lie down and go to sleep."

"But say, there ain't any *danger* in a lock, is there?" respond the querists.

"Danger!" exclaims a deaf old lady, poking up her head. "What's the matter? There hain't nothin' burst, has there?"

"No, no, no!" exclaim the provoked and despairing opposition party, who find that there is no such thing as going to sleep till they have made the old lady below and the young ladies above understand exactly the philosophy of the lock. After a while the conversation again subsides; again all is still; you hear only the trampling of horses and the rippling of the rope in the water, and sleep again is stealing over you. You doze, you dream, and all of a sudden you are started by a cry, —

"Chambermaid! wake up the lady that wants to be set ashore."

Up jumps chambermaid, and up jump the lady and two children, and forthwith form a committee of inquiry as to ways and means.

"Where's my bonnet?" says the lady, half awake, and fumbling among the various articles of that name. "I thought I hung it up behind the door."

"Can't you find it?" says poor chambermaid, yawning and rubbing her eyes.

"O yes, here it is," says the lady; and then the cloak, the shawl, the gloves, the shoes, receive each a separate discussion. At last all seems ready, and they begin to move off, when, lo! Peter's cap is missing. "Now, where can it be?" soliloquizes the lady. "I put it right here by the table leg; maybe it got into some of the berths."

At this suggestion the chambermaid takes the candle, and goes round deliberately to every berth, poking the light directly in the face of every sleeper. "Here it is," she exclaims, pulling at something black under one pillow.

"No, indeed, those are my shoes," says the vexed sleeper.

"Maybe it's here," she resumes, darting upon something dark in another berth.

"No, that's my bag," responds the occupant.

The chambermaid then proceeds to turn over all the children on the floor, to see if it is not under them. In the course of which process they are most agreeably waked up and enlivened; and when everybody is broad awake, and most uncharitably wishing the cap, and Peter too, at the bottom of the canal, the good lady exclaims, "Well, if this isn't lucky; here I had it safe in my basket all the time!" And she departs amid the — what shall I say? — execrations? — of the whole company, ladies though they be.

Well, after this follows a hushing up and wiping up among the juvenile population; and a series of remarks commences from the various shelves, of a very edifying and instructive tendency. One says that the woman did not seem to know where anything was; another says that she has waked up all the children, too; and the elderly ladies make moral reflections on the importance of putting things where you can find them, — being always ready; which observations, being delivered in an exceedingly doleful and drowsy tone, form a sort of sub-bass to the lively chattering of the upper shelfites, who declare that they feel quite wide awake, — that they don't think they shall go to sleep again to-night, — and discourse over everything in creation, until you heartily wish you were enough related to them to give them a scolding.

At last, however, voice after voice drops off; you fall into a most refreshing slumber; it seems to you that you sleep about a quarter of an hour, when the chambermaid pulls you by the sleeve: "Will you please to get up, ma'am? We want to make the beds."

You start and stare. Sure enough the night is gone. So much for sleeping on board canal-boats.

Let us not enumerate the manifold perplexities of the morning toilet in a place where every lady realizes most forcibly the condition of the old lady who lived under a broom: "All she wanted was elbow room." Let us not tell how one glass is made to answer for thirty fair faces, one ewer and vase for thirty lavations, and — tell it not in Gath! — one towel for a company! Let us not intimate how ladies' shoes have, in a night, clandestinely slid into the gentlemen's cabin, and gentlemen's boots elbowed — or, rather, *toed* — their way among ladies' gear, nor recite the exclamations after runaway property that are heard.

"I can't find nothin' of Johnny's shoe!"

" Here 's a shoe in the water-pitcher, — is this it ? "

" My side-combs are gone ! " exclaims a nymph with dishevelled curls.

" Massy ! do look at my bonnet ! " exclaims an old lady, elevating an article crushed into as many angles as there are pieces in a mince-pie.

" I never did sleep *so much together* in my life," echoes a poor little French lady, whom despair has driven into talking English.

But we must not prolong our catalogue of distresses beyond reasonable bounds, and therefore we will close with advising all our friends, who intend to try this way of travelling for *pleasure,* to take a good stock both of patience and clean towels with them, for we think they will find abundant need for both.

THE LOSS OF THE HORNET.

CALL the watch ! call the watch !
    " Ho ! the starboard watch ahoy ! " Have you heard
How a noble ship so trim, like our own, my hearties, here,
    All scudding 'fore the gale, disappeared,
Where yon southern billows roll o'er their bed so green and
        clear ?
Hold the reel ! keep her full ! hold the reel !
How she flew athwart the spray, as, shipmates, we do now,
    Till her twice a hundred fearless hearts of steel
Felt the whirlwind lift its waters aft, and plunge her down-
        ward bow !
          Bear a hand !

Strike topgallants ! mind your helm ! jump aloft !
'T was such a night as this, my lads, a rakish bark was
        drowned,
    When demons foul, that whisper seamen oft,

Scooped a tomb amid the flashing surge that never shall be
      found.
  Square the yards ! a double reef !   Hark the blast !
O, fiercely has it fallen on the war-ship of the brave,
  When its tempest fury stretched the stately mast
All along her foamy sides, as they shouted on the wave,
      " Bear a hand ! "

  Call the watch ! call the watch !
  " Ho ! the larboard watch, ahoy ! "   Have you heard
How a vessel, gay and taut, on the mountains of the sea,
  Went below, with all her warlike crew on board,
They who battled for the happy, boys, and perished for the
      free ?
  Clew, clew up, fore and aft ! keep away !
How the vulture bird of death, in its black and viewless
  form,
  Hovered sure o'er the clamors of his prey,
While through all their dripping shrouds yelled the spirit of
  the storm !
      Bear a hand !

Now out reefs ! brace the yards ! lively there !
O, no more to homeward breeze shall her swelling bosom
  spread,
  But love's expectant eye bid Despair
Set her raven watch eternal o'er the wreck in ocean's bed.
  Board your tacks ! cheerly, boys !   But for them,
Their last evening gun is fired, their gales are overblown ;
  O'er their smoking deck no starry flag shall stream ;
They 'll sail no more, they 'll fight no more, for their gallant
  ship 's gone down.
      Bear a hand !

    9*

WOUNDED. — J. W. WATSON.

STEADY, boys, steady!
    Keep your arms ready,
God only knows whom we may meet here.
    Don't let me be taken;
    I 'd rather awaken,
To-morrow, in — no matter where,
Than lie in that foul prison-hole — over there.

        Step slowly!
        Speak lowly!
    These rocks may have life.
        Lay me down in this hollow;
    We are cut of the strife.
By heavens! the foemen may track me in blood,
For this hole in my breast is outpouring a flood.
No! no surgeon for me; he can give me no aid;
The surgeon I want is pickaxe and spade.
What, Morris, a tear? Why, shame on ye, man!
I thought you a hero; but since you began
To whimper a cry like a girl in her teens,
By George! I don't know what the devil it means!

Well! well! I am rough; 't is a very rough school,
This life of a trooper, — but yet I 'm no fool!
I know a brave man, and a friend from a foe;
And, boys, that you love me I certainly know;
        But was n't it grand
When they came down the hill over sloughing and sand!
But we stood — did we not? — like immovable rock,
Unheeding their balls and repelling their shock.
        Did you mind the loud cry
        When, as turning to fly,
Our men sprang upon them, determined to die?
        O, was n't it grand!

God help the poor wretches that fell in that fight ;
No time was there given for prayer or for flight ;
They fell by the score, in the crash, hand to hand,
And they mingled their blood with the sloughing and sand.
Huzza !
Great Heavens ! this bullet-hole gapes like a grave ;
A curse on the aim of the traitorous knave !
Is there never a one of ye knows how to pray,
Or speak for a man as his life ebbs away ?
Pray !
Pray !

Our Father ! our Father ! why don't ye proceed ?
Can't you see I am dying ? Great God, how I bleed !
Ebbing away !
Ebbing away !
The light of the day
Is turning to gray.
Pray !
Pray !

Our Father in Heaven — boys, tell me the rest,
While I stanch the hot blood from this hole in my breast.
There 's something about a forgiveness of sin.
Put that in ! put that in ! — and then
I 'll follow your words and say an amen.

Here, Morris, old fellow, get hold of my hand ;
And, Wilson, my comrade — O, was n't it grand
When they came down the hill like a thunder-charged
cloud !
Where 's Wilson, my comrade ? — Here, stoop down your
head ;
Can't you say a short prayer for the dying and dead ?

"Christ God, who died for sinners all,
Hear thou this suppliant wanderer's cry ;
Let not e'en this poor sparrow fall
Unheeded by thy gracious eye.

> Throw wide thy gates to let him in,
>   And take him, pleading, to thine arms;
> Forgive, O Lord! his life-long sin,
>   And quiet all his fierce alarms."

God bless you, my comrade, for singing that hymn;
It is light to my path when my eye has grown dim.
I am dying — bend down till I touch you once more —
Don't forget me, old fellow, — God prosper this war!
Confusion to enemies! — keep hold of my hand —
And float our dear flag o'er a prosperous land!

———◇———

HOW KAISER WILHELM'S SISTER WAS WON.

THE betrothal and marriage of the Princess Charlotte of
Prussia with Nicholas, who was then only a grand duke,
but became afterward Emperor of Russia, forms one of the
sweetest and most romantic love-episodes in the world of
European courts, which is usually so devoid of love and
romance, and would, on that account alone, deserve being
remembered, quite regardless of the historical interest which
will henceforth adhere to all the members of the family of
the conqueror of France.

Princess Charlotte was born in the year 1798, and was the
eldest daughter of King Frederick William the Third of
Prussia, and his beautiful and accomplished wife, Queen
Louisa. Her early childhood elapsed amidst scenes of terror
and humiliation for the royal family of Prussia, and nobody
would at that time have ventured to predict for her the brilliant career which Providence kept in store for this child,
born and brought up under such fatal auspices. We might,
indeed, make an exception in favor of her mother, who, with
that prophetic intuition which seems to have been the distin-
guishing feature of that high-minded woman, wrote one day
to her father, the Duke of Mecklenburg, the following lines
about her daughter: —

" Charlotte is given to silence and reserve, but under her apparent coldness she conceals a warm and loving heart. Her indifference and pride are but the dull outside of a diamond of the purest water, which some day will shine forth in its brilliant lustre. Her bearing and manners are noble and dignified. She has but few friends, but these few are warmly attached to her. I know her value, and predict for her a brilliant future, if she lives long enough."

The young princess was, indeed, a very frail and delicate creature, — one of those tender flowers which seem to wait for the kind hand of the gardener to transplant them into a warmer clime. She was charming and handsome ; but her beauty was rather that of a pale lily than that of a blooming rose.

Charlotte was just sixteen when, in the year 1814, the Grand Duke Nicholas, on his way to the camp of the allied armies in France, passed through Berlin, and was warmly welcomed as an honored guest at the royal palace.

The description which those who saw and knew the grand duke at that time have given of the incomparable graces of his person and mind makes it easy for us to imagine that the heart of a young girl just budding into womanhood was captivated and charmed by him almost at first sight. Well he might have said, like Cæsar, " I came, I saw, I conquered." The princess fell in love with him, and fortunately for her the young grand duke returned her love fully as passionately.

The Grand Duke Nicholas had the reputation of being one of the handsomest, if not the very handsomest man of his times ; and his majestic and stately form, which measured no less than six feet and two inches, was considered unequalled in beauty, not only in Russia, but in all Europe. He was vigorous, strong, full of life and health, with broad shoulders and chest, while his small hands and feet were of the most aristocratic elegance ; his whole figure realized the perfect model of manly and commanding beauty which the divine art of a sculptor of antiquity has immortalized under the features of the Apollo Belvedere. His features were of the

Grecian cast, — forehead and nose formed a straight line, — and his large blue, sincere eyes showed a singular combination of composure, sternness, self-reliance, and pride, among which it would have been difficult for the observer to name the predominant expression. Those who would have looked closely and attentively into those remarkable eyes would have easily believed that their threatening glances would suffice to suppress a rebellion, to terrify and disarm a murderer, or to frighten away a supplicant; but there would have been but few to believe that the sternness of these eyes could be so entirely softened as to beam forth nothing but love and kindness. Among these few was, however, the young Prussian princess, who had drunk deep in their intoxicating fervor. It is true that she was the only person in the world in whose presence the Olympian gravity of his features gave way to a radiant cheerfulness, which made his manly beauty perfectly irresistible.

In such moments his magnificent brow, always the seat of meditation and thought, exhibited the serene beauty and Attic grace of a young Athenian; the serious Pericles seemed, by the invisible wand of a magician, to have been transformed into the youthful Alcibiades.

Such is the flattering picture which his contemporaries have drawn of the personal appearance of the Grand Duke Nicholas at the time of his arrival at Berlin.

At that time, however, the matchless personal charms of the grand duke were not enhanced by political prospects of the most exalted character. He was not even eventually considered an heir to the imperial crown of Russia. It is true, Alexander the First, his brother, had no children, but in the case of his death, which could not be expected soon, the Grand Duke Constantine was to inherit the throne of Peter the Great, and leave to Nicholas at best but the position of a prince of the first blood. Nevertheless, Frederick William, charmed alike by the beauty and intellect of his guest, and by the hope of uniting the sovereign houses of Prussia and Russia by the close ties of a family union, greeted the prospect of a marriage between the grand duke and his daughter with enthusiasm, especially when he discovered that the young folks themselves were very fond of each other.

The king then delicately insinuated to his daughter that if she had taken a liking to the grand duke, and had reason to believe that the prince entertained similar feelings toward her, their marriage would meet with no objection on his part.

But the young princess, although secretly delighting in a hope which so fully responded to the secret wishes of her heart, was either too proud or too bashful to confess to her father her love for the grand duke, who had not yet made any declaration to her.

In this manner the day approached on which the grand duke was to leave Berlin. On the eve of his departure a grand gala supper was given in his honor at the royal palace, and, by way of accident or policy, the young Princess Charlotte was seated by the side of her distinguished admirer.

The grand duke was uncommonly taciturn during the evening. His high forehead was clouded, and his gloomy eyes seemed to follow in the space vague phantoms flitting before his imagination. Repeatedly he neglected to reply to questions addressed to him, and when he was asked to respond to a toast which one of the royal princes had proposed in his honor, he seemed to awake from a profound dream which had entirely withdrawn him from his surroundings.

Suddenly, as if by a mighty effort of his will, he turned to his fair neighbor, and whispered so as only to be understood by her, —

"So I shall leave Berlin to-morrow!"

He paused abruptly, and looked at the princess as if he was waiting for an answer which expressed sorrow and grief on her part. But the princess was fully as proud as the grand duke, and, overcoming the violent throbbing of her heart, she said politely to him, —

"We are all very sorry to see your Imperial Highness leave

us so soon. Would it not have been possible for you to defer your departure ? "

"You will all be very sorry ? " muttered the grand duke, not entirely satisfied with the vagueness of sorrow which these words of the princess implied. "But you in particular, madame ? " he added, after some hesitation. "For it will depend on you alone whether I shall stay here or depart."

"Ah ! " replied Charlotte, with her sweetest smile, "and what have I to do to keep your Imperial Highness here ? "

"You must permit me to address my admiration and homage to you."

"Is that all ? "

"And you must encourage me to please you."

"That is much more difficult," said the princess, with a deep blush, but at the same time her eyes beamed forth so much affection and delight that the prince could see at a glance that his fondest hopes had been realized beforehand.

"During my short stay at Berlin," the grand duke continued, in the same tone of voice, "I have taken pains to study your character and your affections, and this study has satisfied me that you would render me very happy, while on the other hand I have some qualities which would secure your own happiness."

The princess was overcome by emotion, and in her confusion did not know what to answer. At last she said, "But here, in the presence of the whole court, at the public table, you put such a question to me ! "

"O," replied the prince, "you need not make any verbal reply. It will be sufficient for you to give me some pledge of your affection. I see there on your hand a small ring whose possession would make me very happy. Give it to me."

"What do you think of ? Here in the presence of a hundred spectators ? "

"Ah, it can be easily done without being seen by anybody. Now we are chatting so quietly with each other that there is not one among the guests who suspects in the least what we are speaking about. Press the ring into a morsel of bread and leave it on the table; I will take the talisman, and nobody will notice it."

" This ring is really a talisman."

" I expected so. May I hope to hear its history ? "

" Why not ? My first governess was a Swiss lady by the name of Wildermatt. Once she went to Switzerland in order to enter upon an inheritance which had been bequeathed to her by a distant relative. When she came back to Berlin, a few weeks afterward, she showed me quite a collection of pretty and costly jewelry, which formed part of the inheritance. 'This is a curious old ring,' said I to her, as I put this little old-fashioned ring on my finger. 'Does it not look queer and cunning ? Perhaps it is an old relic or talisman, and may have been worn centuries ago by a pious lady who had received it from her knight, starting for the Holy Land.' I tried to take the ring from my finger again, but I could not get it off; for I was a little fleshier then than now," said Charlotte, smilingly. " My governess insisted on my keeping the ring as a souvenir. I accepted her present, and the ring has been on my finger ever since. Some time afterward, when I was contemplating its strange workmanship, I succeeded in pulling it from my finger, and was much surprised at seeing engraved on the inside some words which, though nearly rubbed out by the wear of time, were still legible. Now, your Imperial Highness, what do you think were the words engraved upon it ? I think when you hear them you will take some interest in the ring."

" Ah ! and pray what were they ? "

" The words engraved upon the inside were, '*Empress of Russia.*' This ring had undoubtedly been presented by an Empress of Russia to the relative of Mrs. Wildermatt, for I was told that both this lady and her mother had formerly belonged to the household of the czarina, your august grandmother."

" This is really remarkable," said the grand duke, thoughtfully. " I am quite superstitious, and I am really inclined to regard this ring, if I should be happy enough to receive it from you as a pledge of your love, as an omen of very auspicious significance."

In answer to this second and even more direct appeal to her heart, the princess took a small piece of bread, played carelessly with it, and managed to press the ring into the soft crumbs. Then she dropped it playfully on the table quite close to the plate of her neighbor. And after this adroit exhibition of her skill as an actress she continued to eat as unconcernedly as if she had performed the most insignificant action of her life.

With the same apparent coolness and indifference the grand duke picked up the bread enclosing the ring, took the latter out of its ingenious envelope, and concealed it in his breast, for it was too small to fit any of his fingers. It was this ring — both the pledge of Charlotte's love and the auspicious omen of his own elevation to the imperial dignity — which Nicholas wore on a golden chain around his neck to the very last day of his life, and which, if we are not mistaken, has even descended with him into the vault of his ancestors.

Three years after, in 1817, Princess Charlotte, then only nineteen years of age, and in the full splendor of beauty and happiness, made her entry into St. Petersburg by the side of her husband, whose eye had never looked prouder, and whose Olympian brow had never been more serene than at this happiest moment of his life. As he looked down upon the vast multitude who had flocked together from all parts of the vast empire to greet the young princess with shouts and rejoicings, and then again upon his fair young bride, perhaps the inscription of the ring recurred to his mind ; for, bending his head quite close to the ear of Charlotte, he whispered, " Now empress of the hearts, and some day, perhaps, empress of the realm."

At this moment the procession reached the main entrance of the Winter Palace, where Alexander the First, the Emperor, surrounded by a brilliant suit of generals and courtiers, came to meet his beautiful sister-in-law, and conducted her into the sumptuous drawing-rooms of the magnificent palace of the czars. Who would believe that eight short years afterward the brilliant young emperor had breathed his last, and that Nicholas and Charlotte would succeed him on the throne of Russia? Truly the inscription of the engagement-ring had proven prophetic!

* * *

A LEGEND OF BREGENZ. — Adelaide Procter.

GIRT round with rugged mountains
    The fair Lake Constance lies;
In her blue heart reflected,
    Shine back the starry skies;
And watching each white cloudlet
    Float silently and slow,
You think a piece of heaven
    Lies on our earth below!

Midnight is there: and silence,
    Enthroned in heaven, looks down
Upon her own calm mirror,
    Upon a sleeping town;
For Bregenz, that quaint city
    Upon the Tyrol shore,
Has stood above Lake Constance
    A thousand years and more.

Her battlements and towers
    Upon their rocky steep
Have cast their trembling shadow
    For ages on the deep;
Mountain and lake and valley
    A sacred legend know,
Of how the town was saved one night,
    Three hundred years ago.

Far from her home and kindred
  A Tyrol maid had fled,
To serve in the Swiss valleys,
  And toil for daily bread ;
And every year that fleeted
  So silently and fast
Seemed to bear farther from her
  The memory of the past.

She served kind gentle masters,
  Nor asked for rest or change ;
Her friends seemed no more new ones,
  Their speech seemed no more strange ;
And when she led her cattle
  To pasture every day,
She ceased to look and wonder
  On which side Bregenz lay.

She spoke no more of Bregenz
  With longing and with tears ;
Her Tyrol home seemed faded
  In a deep mist of years.
She heeded not the rumors
  Of Austrian war and strife ;
Each day she rose contented,
  To the calm toils of life.

Yet, when her master's children
  Would clustering round her stand,
She sang them the old ballads
  Of her own native land ;
And when at morn and evening
  She knelt before God's throne,
The accents of her childhood
  Rose to her lips alone.

And so she dwelt : the valley
  More peaceful year by year ;

When suddenly strange portents
  Of some great deed seemed near.
The golden corn was bending
  Upon its fragile stalk,
While farmers, heedless of their fields,
  Paced up and down in talk.

The men seemed stern and altered,
  With looks cast on the ground;
With anxious faces, one by one,
  The women gathered round;
All talk of flax or spinning,
  Or work, was put away;
The very children seemed afraid
  To go alone to play.

One day, out in the meadow,
  With strangers from the town,
Some secret plan discussing,
  The men talked up and down;
Yet now and then seemed watching
  A strange uncertain gleam,
That looked like lances 'mid the trees
  That stood below the stream.

At eve they all assembled,
  All care and doubt were fled;
With jovial laugh they feasted,
  The board was nobly spread.
The elder of the village
  Rose up, his glass in hand,
And cried, " We drink the downfall
  Of an accursed land!

" The night is growing darker, —
  Ere one more day is flown,
Bregenz, our foeman's stronghold,
  Bregenz shall be our own! "

The women shrank in terror,
  (Yet pride, too, had her part,)
But one poor Tyrol maiden
  Felt death within her heart.

Before her stood fair Bregenz,
  Once more her towers arose ;
What were the friends beside her ?
  Only her country's foes !
The faces of her kinsfolk,
  The days of childhood flown,
The echoes of her mountains,
  Reclaimed her as their own.

Nothing she heard around her
  (Though shouts rang forth again),
Gone were the green Swiss valleys,
  The pasture and the plain ;
Before her eyes one vision,
  And in her heart one cry,
That said, " Go forth, save Bregenz,
  And then, if need be, die ! "

With trembling haste and breathless,
  With noiseless step she sped ;
Horses and weary cattle
  Were standing in the shed ;
She loosed the strong white charger,
  That fed from out her hand ;
She mounted, and she turned his head
  Towards her native land.

Out — out into the darkness, —
  Faster, and still more fast ;
The smooth grass flies behind her,
  The chestnut wood is past ;
She looks up ; clouds are heavy :
  Why is her steed so slow ? —

Scarcely the wind beside them
　　Can pass them as they go.

"Faster!" she cries, "O, faster!"
　　Eleven the church-bells chime;
"O God," she cries, "help Bregenz,
　　And bring me there in time!"
But louder than bells' ringing,
　　Or lowing of the kine,
Grows nearer in the midnight
　　The rushing of the Rhine.

Shall not the roaring waters
　　Their headlong gallop check?
The steed draws back in terror,
　　She leans above his neck
To watch the flowing darkness,—
　　The bank is high and steep,—
One pause—he staggers forward
　　And plunges in the deep.

She strives to pierce the blackness,
　　And looser throws the rein;
Her steed must breast the waters
　　That dash above his mane.
How gallantly, how nobly,
　　He struggles through the foam!
And see—in the far distance
　　Shine out the lights of home!

Up the steep bank he bears her,
　　And now they rush again
Towards the heights of Bregenz,
　　That tower above the plain.
They reach the gate of Bregenz
　　Just as the midnight rings,
And out come serf and soldier,
　　To meet the news she brings.

Bregenz is saved ! ere daylight
  Her battlements are manned ;
Defiance greets the army
  That marches on the land.
And if to deeds heroic
  Should endless fame be paid,
Bregenz does well to honor
  The noble Tyrol maid.

Three hundred years are vanished,
  And yet upon the hill
An old stone gateway rises,
  To do her honor still.
And there, when Bregenz women
  Sit spinning in the shade,
They see in quaint old carving
  The Charger and the Maid.

And when, to guard old Bregenz,
  By gateway, street, and tower,
The warder paces all night long,
  And calls each passing hour :
" Nine," " ten," " eleven," he cries aloud,
  And then (O crown of Fame !)
When midnight pauses in the skies,
  He calls the maiden's name !

THE VOICES AT THE THRONE. — *T. Westwood.*

A LITTLE child,
  A little meek-faced, quiet village child,
Sat singing by her cottage door at eve
A low, sweet sabbath song. No human ear
Caught the faint melody, — no human eye
Beheld the upturned aspect, or the smile
That wreathed her innocent lips while they breathed

The oft-repeated burden of the hymn,
" Praise God ! Praise God ! "
                                        A seraph by the throne
In full glory stood.   With eager hand
He smote the golden harp-string, till a flood
Of harmony on the celestial air
Welled forth, unceasing.   There with a great voice,
He sang the " Holy, holy evermore,
Lord God Almighty ! " and the eternal courts
Thrilled with the rapture, and the hierarchies,
Angel, and rapt archangel, throbbed and burned
With vehement adoration.
                                        Higher yet
Rose the majestic anthem, without pause,
Higher, with rich magnificence of sound,
To its full strength ; and still the infinite heavens
Rang with the " Holy, holy evermore ! "
Till, trembling with excessive awe and love,
Each sceptred spirit sank before the Throne
With a mute hallelujah.
                                        But even then,
While the ecstatic song was at its height,
Stole in an alien voice, — a voice that seemed
To float, float upward from some world afar, —
A meek and childlike voice, faint, but how sweet !
That blended with the spirits' rushing strain,
Even as a fountain's music, with the roll
Of the reverberate thunder.
                                        Loving smiles
Lit up the beauty of each angel's face
At that new utterance, smiles of joy that grew
More joyous yet, as ever and anon
Was heard the simple burden of the hymn,
" Praise God ! praise God ! "
                                        And when the seraph's song
Had reached its close, and o'er the golden lyre
Silence hung brooding, — when the eternal courts

10

Rang with the echoes of his chant sublime,
Still through the abysmal space that wandering voice
Came floating upward from its world afar,
Still murmured sweet on the celestial air,
"Praise God! praise God!"

———◆———

ABOU EL MAHR AND HIS HORSE.

ALGER'S *Oriental Poetry.*

IT is Abou el Mahr, the gallant Sheik of Al Azeed;
How fondly he is stroking Lahla, his unrivalled steed!

Among the hills of Schem the tents of Al Azeed are pitched,
And close by every warrior's door the favorite horse is hitched.

For valor none can stand the men of Al Azeed beside;
And Houri only with their maids comparison can bide.

This tribe the unchallenged banner, too, throughout Arabia
bears,
For the wondrous strength and beauty of their stallions and
their mares.

But first among their warriors stands the Sheik, Abou el Mahr,
And conscious Lahla shines, among their steeds, the peerless
star.

When clasps Abou proud Lahla's neck to kiss his veinéd cheek,
The courser looks his love as plainly as if he could speak.

Abou caresses him before the people gathered there,
Who gaze with wonder at his loving and his haughty air.

And Leila, Selim, Zar — the wife and children of the Sheik —
Will pat and kiss him, and his hoof within their bosoms take.

And twenty chiefs press near, their servants ranged in ordered
    bands,
The privilege to claim that he shall eat from out their hands.

For Lahla is of Al Azeed the crowning joy and pride ;
The envy and despair of all the Arab tribes beside.

Another horse so celebrated never spurned the earth ;
Through white Koureen, the mare of Solomon, he draws his
    birth ;

And traces back, in straight, untainted rill, his royal blood
To thrice illustrious Hûfafâ, great Abraham's sable stud.

Hang o'er his spotless forehead, which is white as whitest milk,
Soft tufts of handsome hair as glossy as the finest silk.

Those tufts compose a veil which every breeze in openwork
    hems,
And underneath it glimpse his rapid eyes, two burning gems.

His neck and chest the graces of a swan's in nothing lack ;
A gorgeous mantle, woven of silk and gold, beclothes his back.

His pedigree, two hundred high descents, his bosom wears
In bag of musk, wherewith two precious amulets he wears.

His limbs and sockets so elastic, all his motions are
So swift and smooth, the rider scarcely feels a start or jar.

Abou el Mahr would on his back, in rapid gallop still,
A brimming cup of sherbet quaff, and not a droplet spill.

Indeed, a bard so mounted might receive the fancy bold,
His courser was a bird whose wings an unseen movement hold.

No price or bribe could cause the Sheik, nor any desperate need,
To part with his redoubtable and idolized steed.

.   .   .   .   .

It is Abou el Mahr, with twelve choice men of Al Azeed ;
And they to seize the hostile Bagdad caravan proceed.

Soon through the Synor pass into the open plain they wind,
And shake their spears, and shout, their blue caftáns stream
      wide behind.

Abou, his Lahla's sinews strung with fire, is far before,
As on the undefended, scattering caravan they pour.

To guard their goods two merchants of Damascus bravely stand,
But in an instant both are stretched in death upon the sand.

The Sheik and his good men of Al Azeed pile all the spoil
Upon the camels, and their homeward way begin to toil.

At noon they halt to rest awhile beside a desert spring ;
Ah ! who can tell what utter ruin one thoughtless hour may
      bring ?

Their foe, the fierce Pacha of Acre, leads his horsemen there.
Cries, " Strike ! and I command you, save Abou, not one to
      spare ! "

So all are slain.   The Sheik, in his right arm a fearful wound,
His darling Lahla led before, is on a camel bound.

They journey on until they reach the mountains of Saphàd,
Just as the sun drops out of sight, and night falls dark and sad.

The old Pacha commands each soldier there to pitch his tent,
And takes good care the escape of horse or camel to prevent.

The keeper of the Sheik has tied him fast both hand and foot,
And fallen asleep, and dreams of fighting, routing, and pursuit.

But the poor captive, restless with his torturing wound, still
      wakes,
And Lahla's low, disconsolate neigh his anguish sharper makes.

Bound as he is, he rolls and crawls one last caress to give
The steed from whom he had not thought to part while he
    should live.

"O Lahla!" sighs Abou, "no more shall I rejoice with thee
To skim the waste, the wild Simoom not prouder or more free;

"No more with thee the Jordan swim, whose spurnéd water
    drips
From off thy side, as white and pure as foam from off thy lips.

"A bitter fate consigns me to my unrelenting foe;
But thou, bright gem of Al Azeed, in liberty shalt go.

"What wouldst thou do, poor friend, shut in the close and
    wretched khan
Of some Turk huckster not deserving to be called a man?

"No, whether fortune dooms me for a slave or here to die,
Thou shalt, O jewel of a thousand hearts, in freedom fly.

"Go to the tents thou knowest so well, amid the hills of Schem,
And say, Abou el Mahr will nevermore return to them.

"Thy head put through the door where my dear wife and chil-
    dren are,
And lick the hands of Leila, Selim, and sweet little Zar.

"O Lahla, Lahla! must I now from thee forever part?
Farewell, farewell, belovéd comrade of my life and heart!"

So saying, with his teeth laboriously he gnawed apart
The tethering cord that went around the stake, and bade him
    start!

But the sagacious soul bounds not away.   The bonds he smells
That bind his master's limbs.   Each fact to him its secret tells.

With tenderness he licks the blood upon the shattered arm,
Gives forth a low and painful whine, but raises no alarm.

His teeth the girdle seize ; he lifts Abou, so spare and tall ;
Now, foolish guards, now, old Pacha, defiance to you all !

Great Lahla proves himself a steed of living steel and fire ;
To reach him vain are all the struggles of their mad desire.

For the hills of Schem he aims his way through the open, lus-
        trous night,
Straight as an arrow goes, swift as the lightning in its flight.

The stars one after one go down behind the desert's rim,
But the pale and eager moon rushes in even pace with him.

The palm-clumps on oases lift their heads of yellow green
Above the downs of endless sand, and vanish soon as seen.

The lagging sun comes up ; twelve weary, mighty leagues are
        passed ;
The lovely haunts and tents of Al Azeed appear at last.

The anxious tribe, whose thirteen best are out, is all astir ;
The mother deems it time her sons should have returned to her.

Ha ! what upon the far horizon moves ?   A single steed ?
Is this what we looked for with such intensity of greed ?

Nearer ! can it be Lahla ?   In his mouth a bundle ?   No,
The matchless Lahla never from adventure came so slow.

The godlike steed, with staggering steps, faint pantings, almost
        spent,
The girdle bites, reels up, and lays Abou before his tent.

One instant stands he, looking round, as if reward to reap
From those who, thrilled with grateful love and wonder, gaze
        and weep.

Then, while the congregated tribe break forth in piercing cries,
The noble creature, gasping, falls, all blood and foam, and dies.

Thabêt Ben Ali, poet of the tribe, leaps through the crowd,
With soul on fire, and sings the feat in panegyric proud.

To thrilling tones of love and pride he smites his burning lyre ;
With raining eyes and heaving bosoms all as one respire.

" No *man*," he says, " not even Hatim Täi, could have done
A nobler deed, a more impassioned gratitude have won.

" Long as the Horse shall be the friend and servant of our race,
The glorious fame of Lahla shall resound through time and
      space."

Full many a day has passed since Ali sang his touching song,
And from the vale the tents of Al Azeed have vanished long ;

But in the night of Arab lore still shineth, like a star,
The story of the peerless Lahla and Abou el Mahr.

UNDER THE SNOW.

UNDER the snow our baby lies,
    The fringed lids dropped o'er her eyes ;
The tiny hands upon her breast,
Like twin-born lilies taking rest ;
While o'er her grave the rough winds blow ;
Under the snow, — under the snow.

Under the snow our baby lies,
While we sit at home and list for her cries ;
And her mother asks (she is very lone),
" Why has my little baby gone ? "

Ah ! happy, she feeleth not our woe ;
Under the snow, — under the snow.

Under the snow our baby lies,
As pure as the clouds far up the skies, —
Those delicate banners of vapor, furled
Beyond the breath of this noisome world.
'T is the blood of Christ hath made her so ;
Under the snow, — under the snow.

Above the snow our baby dwells,
Where never the solemn death-bell knells ;
Where Sin and Death are never known,
Nor dark-browed Pain with her voice of moan ;
Where the angels move on wings that glow,
Above the snow, — above the snow.

Above the snow our baby dwells,
And we dry our tears when we think she swells
The song of the angels and just men there,
With a voice so sweet and a face so fair.
And we 're glad we 've sent them a voice from below
Above the snow, — above the snow.

HATS. — OLIVER WENDELL HOLMES.

THE old gentleman who sits opposite, finding that spring had fairly come, mounted a white hat one day, and walked into the street. It seems to have been a premature or otherwise exceptionable exhibition. When the old gentleman came home, he looked very red in the face, and complained that he had been "made sport of." By sympathizing questions, I learned from him that a boy had called him "old daddy," and asked him when he had his hat whitewashed.

This incident led me to make some observations at table

the next morning, which I here repeat for the benefit of the readers of this record. The hat is the vulnerable point in the artificial integument. I learned this in early boyhood. I was once equipped in a hat of Leghorn straw, having a brim of much wider dimensions than were usual at that time, and sent to school in that portion of my native town which lies nearest to this metropolis. On my way I was met by a " Port-chuck," as we used to call the young gentlemen of that locality, and the following dialogue ensued : —

The Port Chuck. — Hullo, you-sir, joo know th' wuz gon-to be a race to-morrah ?

Myself. — No. Who 's gon-to run, 'n' wher's 't gon-to be ?

The Port Chuck. — Squire Mico 'n' Doctor Williams, round the brim o' your hat.

These two much-respected gentlemen being the oldest inhabitants at that time, and the alleged race-course being out of the question, the Port-chuck also winking and thrusting his tongue into his cheek, I perceived that I had been trifled with, and the effect has been to make me sensitive and observant respecting this article of dress ever since. Here is an axiom or two relating to it.

A hat which has been *popped,* or exploded by being sat down upon, is never itself again afterwards.

It is a favorite illusion of sanguine natures to believe the contrary.

Shabby gentility has nothing so characteristic as its hat. There is always an unnatural calmness about its nap, and an unwholesome gloss, suggestive of a wet brush. The last effort of decayed fortune is expended in smoothing its dilapidated castor. The hat is the *ultimum moriens* of " respectability."

The old gentleman took all these remarks and maxims very pleasantly, saying, however, that he had forgotten most of his French except the word for potatoes, — *pummies de tare.* *Ultimum moriens,* I told him, is old Italian, and signifies *last thing to die.* With this explanation he was well contented, and looked quite calm when I saw him afterwards in the entry with a black hat on his head and the white one in his hand.

10* o

AN ORDER FOR A PICTURE. — Alice Cary.

O GOOD painter, tell me true,
   Has your hand the cunning to draw
Shapes of things that you never saw ?
Ay ? Well, here is an order for you.

Woods and cornfields, a little brown, —
   The picture must not be over-bright, —
   Yet all in the golden and gracious light
Of a cloud, when the summer sun is down.

   Alway and alway, night and morn,
    Woods upon woods, with fields of corn
     Lying between them, not quite sere,
And not in the full, thick, leafy bloom,
When the wind can hardly find breathing-room
     Under their tassels, — cattle near,
Biting shorter the short green grass,
And a hedge of sumach and sassafras,
With bluebirds twittering all around, —
(Ah, good painter, you can't paint sound !) —
   These, and the house where I was born,
Low and little, and black and old,
With children, many as it can hold,
All at the windows, open wide, —
Heads and shoulders clear outside,
And fair young faces all ablush :
    Perhaps you may have seen, some day,
    Roses crowding the selfsame way,
Out of a wilding, wayside bush.

   Listen closer. When you have done
    With woods and cornfields and grazing herds,
   A lady, the loveliest ever the sun
Looked down upon, you must paint for me ;
O, if I only could make you see

The clear blue eyes, the tender smile,
The sovereign sweetness, the gentle grace,
The woman's soul, and the angel's face
    That are beaming on me all the while ! —
    I need not speak these foolish words :
    Yet one word tells you all I would say, —
She is my mother : you will agree
    That all the rest may be thrown away.

Two little urchins at her knee
You must paint, sir : one like me, —
    The other with a clearer brow,
    And the light of his adventurous eyes
    Flashing with boldest enterprise :
At ten years old he went to sea, —
    God knoweth if he be living now, —
    He sailed in the good ship Commodore, —
Nobody ever crossed her track
To bring us news, and she never came back.
    Ah, 't is twenty long years and more
Since that old ship went out of the bay
    With my great-hearted brother on her deck ;
    I watched him till he shrank to a speck,
And his face was toward me all the way.

Bright his hair was, a golden brown,
    The time we stood at our mother's knee :
That beauteous head, if it did go down,
    Carried sunshine into the sea !

Out in the fields one summer night
    We were together, half afraid
    Of the corn-leaves' rustling, and of the shade
    Of the high hills, stretching so still and far, —
Loitering till after the low little light
    Of the candle shone through the open door,
And over the haystack's pointed top,

All of a tremble, and ready to drop;
 The first half-hour, the great yellow star,
 That we, with staring, ignorant eyes,
Had often and often watched to see
 Propped and held in its place in the skies
By the fork of a tall red mulberry-tree,
 Which close in the edge of our flax-field grew, —
Dead at the top, — just one branch full
Of leaves, notched round, and lined with wool,
 From which it tenderly shook the dew
Over our heads, when we came to play
In its handbreadth of shadow, day after day : —
 Afraid to go home, sir ; for one of us bore
A nest full of speckled and thin-shelled eggs, —
The other, a bird, held fast by the legs,
Not so big as a straw of wheat :
The berries we gave her she would n't eat,
But cried and cried, till we held her bill,
So slim and shining, to keep her still.

At last we stood at our mother's knee.
 Do you think, sir, if you try,
 You can paint the look of a lie ?
 If you can, pray have the grace
 To put it solely in the face
Of the urchin that is likest me :
 I think 't was solely mine, indeed :
 But that 's no matter, — paint it so ;
 The eyes of our mother — (take good heed) —
Looking not on the nestful of eggs,
Nor the fluttering bird, held so fast by the legs,
But straight through our faces down to our lies,
And O, with such injured, reproachful surprise !
 I felt my heart bleed where that glance went, as though
 A sharp blade struck through it.

       You, sir, know,
That you on the canvas are to repeat

Things that are fairest, things most sweet, ·—
Woods and cornfields and mulberry-tree, —
The mother, — the lads, with their bird, at her knee :
   But, O, that look of reproachful woe !
High as the heavens your name I 'll shout,
If you paint me the picture, and leave that out.

BARBARA. — ALEXANDER SMITH.

ON the Sabbath day,
   Through the churchyard old and gray,
Over the crisp and yellow leaves, I help my rustling way ;
And amid the words of mercy, falling on the soul like balms ;
'Mong the gorgeous storms of music in the mellow organ-calms ;
'Mong the upward-streaming prayers, and the rich and solemn
         psalms,
      I stood heedless, Barbara !

My heart was otherwhere,
While the organ filled the air,
And the priest with outspread hands blessed the people with
      a prayer.
But when rising to go homeward, with a mild and saintlike shine
Gleamed a face of airy beauty with its heavenly eyes on mine, —
Gleamed and vanished in a moment.   O the face was like to
      thine,
      Ere you perished, Barbara !

O that pallid face !
Those sweet, earnest eyes of grace !
When last I saw them, dearest, it was in another place ;
You came running forth to meet me with my love-gift on your
      wrist,
And a cursed river killed thee, aided by a murderous mist.
O, a purple mark of agony was on the mouth I kissed,
      When last I saw thee, Barbara !

Those dreary years, eleven,
Have you pined within your heaven,
And is this the only glimpse of earth that in that time was
           given?
And have you passed unheeded all the fortunes of your race —
Your father's grave, your sister's child, your mother's quiet
           face —
To gaze on one who worshipped not within a kneeling place ?
        Are you happy, Barbara ?

'Mong angels do you think
Of the precious golden link
I bound around your happy arm while sitting on yon brink ?
Or when that night of wit and wine, of laughter and guitars,
Was emptied of its music, and we watched through lattice-bars
The silent midnight heaven moving o'er us with its stars,
        Till the morn broke, Barbara ?

In the years I 've changed,
Wild and far my heart has ranged,
And many sins and errors deep have been on me avenged ;
But to you I have been faithful, whatsoever good I 've lacked ;
I loved you, and above my life still hangs that love intact,
Like a mild, consoling rainbow o'er a savage cataract.
        Love has saved me, Barbara !

O Love ! I am unblest,
With monstrous doubts opprest
Of much that 's dark and nether, much that 's holiest and best.
Could I but win you for an hour from off that starry shore,
The hunger of my soul were stilled ; for Death has told you more
Than the melancholy world doth know, — things deeper than
           all lore.
        Will you teach me, Barbara ?

In vain, in vain, in vain !
You will never come again : —

There droops upon the dreary hills a mournful fringe of rain,
The gloaming closes slowly round, unblest winds are in the tree,
Round selfish shores forever moans the hurt and wounded sea :
There is no rest upon the earth, peace is with Death and thee, —
  I am weary, Barbara !

THE BOAT OF GRASS. — Miss Kemble Butler.

FOR years the slave endured his yoke,
 Down-trodden, wronged, misused, opprest ;
Yet life-long serfdom could not choke
 The seeds of freedom in his breast.

At length, upon the north-wind came
 A whisper stealing through the land ;
It spread from hut to hut like flame, —
 " Take heart ! the hour is near at hand."

The whisper spread, and lo ! on high
 The dawn of an unhoped-for day !
"Be glad ! the Northern troops are nigh, —
 The fleet is in Port-Royal Bay ! "

Responsive to the words of cheer,
 An inner voice said, " Rise and flee !
Be strong, and cast away all fear :
 Thou art a man, and thou art free ! "

And full of new-born hope and might,
 He started up, and seaward fled ;
By day he turned aside, by night
 He followed where the North Star led.

Through miles of barren pine and waste,
 And endless breadth of swamp and sedge,

By streams, whose tortuous path is traced
 In tangled growth along their edge,

Two nights he fled, — no sound was heard,
 He met no creature on his way ;
Two days crouched in the bush ; the third
 He hears the bloodhounds' distant bay.

They drag him back to stripes and shame,
 And bitter, unrequited toil ;
With red-hot gyves his feet they maim,
 All future thought of flight to foil.

We, shuddering, turn from such a cup,
 Nor dare to look on his despair ;
For them, O, let us offer up
 The Saviour's sacrificial prayer !

But the celestial voice, that spake
 Erst in his soul, might not be hushed ;
The sense of birthright, once awake,
 Could never, nevermore be crushed.

And, brave of heart and strong of will,
 He kept his purpose, laid his plan ;
Though crippled, chained and captive still,
 A slave no longer, but a man.

Eleven months his soul he steeled
 To toil and wait in silent pain,
But in the twelfth his wounds were healed, —
 He burst his bonds, and fled again.

A weary winding stream he sought,
 And crossed its waters to and fro, —
An Indian wile, to set at naught
 The bloody instinct of his foe.

The waters widen to a fen,
   And, while he hid him, breathless, there,
With brutal cries of dogs and men,
   The hunt went round and round his lair.

The baffled hounds had lost the track :
   With many a curse and many a cry,
The angry owners called them back ;
   And so the wild pursuit went by.

The deadly peril seemed to pass ;
   And then he dared to raise his head
Above the waving marish grass,
   That mantled o'er the river-bed.

Those long broad leaves that round him grew
   He had been wont to bind and plait ;
And well, with simple skill, he knew
   To shape the basket and the mat.

Now, in their tresses sad and dull
   He saw the hope of his escape,
And patiently began to cull,
   And weave them in canoe-like shape.

To give the reedy fabrics light
   An armor 'gainst the soaking brine,
With painful care he sought by night
   The amber weepings of the pine.

And since on the Egyptian wave,
   The Hebrew launched her little ark,
Faith never to God's keeping gave
   So great a hope, so frail a bark.

O silent river of the South,
   Whose lonely stream ne'er felt the oar

In all its course, from rise to mouth,
   What precious freight was that you bore !

The grizzled oak and tall dark pine
   Stretch out their boughs, from either bank,
Across the stream, and many a vine
   Festoons them with luxuriance rank.

The yellow jasmine fills the shade
   With golden light, and downward shed,
From slender wreaths that lightly swayed,
   Her fragrant stars upon his head.

But still the boat, from dawn to dark,
   'Neath overhanging shrubs was drawn ;
And, loosed at eve, the little bark
   Safe floated on from dark to dawn.

At length, in that mysterious hour
   That comes before the break of day,
The current gained a swifter power,
   The boat began to rock and sway.

He felt the wave beneath him swell,
   His nostrils drank a fresh salt breath,
The boat of rushes rose and fell :
   " Lord ! is it life or is it death ? "

He saw the eastern heaven spanned
   With a slow-spreading belt of gray ;
Tents glimmered, ghost-like, on the sand ;
   And phantom ships before him lay.

The sky grew bright, the day awoke,
   The sun flashed up above the sea,
From countless drum and bugle broke
   The joyous Northern reveillé.

O white-winged warriors of the deep!
  No heart e'er hailed you so before;
No castaway on desert steep,
  Nor banished man, his exile o'er,

Nor drowning wretch lashed to a spar,
  So blessed your rescuing sails as he
Who on them first beheld from far
  The morning light of Liberty!

THE IDIOT BOY. — Southey.

IT had pleased God to form poor Ned
  A thing of idiot mind,
Yet to the poor, unreasoning boy
  God had not been unkind.

Old Sarah loved her helpless child,
  Whom helplessness made dear,
And life was everything to him
  Who knew no hope or fear.

She knew his wants, she understood,
  Each half-artic'late call,
For he was everything to her,
  And she to him was all.

And so for many a year they lived,
  Nor knew a wish beside;
But age at length on Sarah came,
  And she fell sick and died.

He tried in vain to waken her,
  He called her o'er and o'er;

They told him she was dead, — the word
  To him no import bore.

They closed her eyes and shrouded her,
  Whilst he stood wondering by,
And when they bore her to the grave
  He followed silently.

They laid her in the narrow house,
  And sung the funeral stave,
And when the mournful train dispersed
  He loitered by the grave.

The rabble boys that used to jeer
  Whene'er they saw poor Ned,
Now stood and watched him at the grave,
  And not a word was said.

They came and went and came again,
  And night at last drew on ;
Yet still he lingered at the place
  Till every one had gone.

And when he found himself alone
  He quick removed the clay,
And raised the coffin in his arms
  And bore it quick away.

Straight went he to his mother's cot
  And laid it on the floor,
And with the eagerness of joy
  He barred the cottage door.

At once he placed his mother's corpse
  Upright within her chair,
And then he heaped the hearth and blew
  The kindling fire with care.

She was now in her wonted chair,
  It was her wonted place,
And bright the fire blazed and flashed,
  Reflected from her face.

Then, bending down, he 'd feel her hands,
  Anon her face behold ;
" Why, mother, do you look so pale,
  And why are you so cold ? "

And when the neighbors on next morn
  Had forced the cottage door,
Old Sarah's corpse was in the chair,
  And Ned's was on the floor.

It had pleased God from this poor boy
  His only friend to call ;
Yet God was not unkind to him,
  For death restored him all.

THE MAD ENGINEER.

THIS thrilling story is furnished by a Prussian railroad
  conductor.

My train left Dantzic in the morning generally about eight
o'clock ; but once a week we had to wait for the arrival of the
steamer from Stockholm. It was the morning of the steamer's arrival that I came down from the hotel and found that
my engineer had been so seriously injured that he could not
perform his work. A railway-carriage had run over him, and
broken one of his legs. I went immediately to the engine-
house to procure another engineer, for I knew there were three
or four in reserve there, but I was disappointed. I inquired
for Westphal, but was informed that he had gone to Sreegen
to see his mother. Gondolpho had been sent to Konigsberg,

on the road. But where was Mayne? He had leave of absence for two days, and had gone no one knew whither.

Here was a fix. I heard the puffing of the steamer, and the passengers would be on hand in fifteen minutes. I ran to the guards and asked them if they knew where there was an engineer, but they did not. I then went to the firemen and asked them if any one of them felt competent to run the engine to Bromberg. No one dared to attempt it. The distance was nearly one hundred miles. What was to be done?

The steamer stopped at the wharf, and those who were going on by rail came flocking to the station. They had eaten breakfast on board the boat, and were all ready for a fresh start. The baggage was checked and registered, the tickets bought, the different carriages assigned to the various classes of passengers, and the passengers themselves seated. The train was in readiness in the long station-house, and the engine was steaming and puffing away impatiently in the distant firing-house.

It was past nine o'clock.

"Come, why don't we start?" growled an old fat Swede, who had been watching me narrowly for the last fifteen minutes.

And upon this there was a general chorus of anxious inquiry, which soon settled to downright murmuring. At this juncture some one touched me on the elbow. I turned and saw a stranger by my side. I expected that he was going to remonstrate with me for my backwardness. In fact, I began to have strong temptations to pull off my uniform, for every anxious eye was fixed upon the glaring badges which marked me as the chief officer of the train.

However, this stranger was a middle-aged man, tall and stout, with a face of great energy and intelligence. His eye was black and brilliant, — so brilliant that I could not for the life of me gaze steadily into it; and his lips, which were very thin, seemed more like polished marble than human flesh. His dress was black throughout, and not only set with exact nicety, but was scrupulously clean and neat.

"You want an engineer, I understand," he said, in a low, cautious tone, at the same time gazing quietly about him, as though he wanted no one to hear what he said.

"I do," I replied. "My train is all ready, and we have no engineer within twenty miles of this place."

"Well, sir, I am going to Bromberg ; I must go, and I will run the engine for you ! "

"Ha ! " I uttered, "are you an engineer ? "

"I am, sir, — one of the oldest in the country, — and am now on my way to make arrangements for a great improvement I have invented for the application of steam to a locomotive. My name is Martin Kroller. If you wish, I will run as far as Bromberg ; and I will show you running that is running."

Was I not fortunate ? I determined to accept the man's offer at once, and so I told him. He received my answer with a nod and a smile. I went with him to the house, where we found the iron-horse in charge of the fireman, and all ready for a start. Kroller got upon the platform, and I followed him. I had never seen a man betray such peculiar aptness amid machinery as he did. He let on the steam in an instant, but yet with care and judgment, and he backed up to the baggage-carriage with the most exact nicety. I had seen enough to assure me that he was thoroughly acquainted with the business, and I felt composed once more. I gave my engine up to the new man, and then hastened away to the office. Word was passed for all the passengers to take their seats, and soon afterward I waved my hand to the engineer. There was a puff, — a groaning of the heavy axletrees, — a trembling of the building, — and the train was in motion. I leaped upon the platform of the guard-carriage, and in a few minutes more the station-house was far behind us.

In less than an hour we reached Dirsham, where we took up the passengers that had come on the Königsberg railway. Here I went forward and asked Kroller how he liked the engine. He replied that he liked it very much.

"But," he added, with a strange sparkling of the eye, "wait

until I get my improvement, and then you will see travelling. By the soul of the Virgin Mother, sir, I could run an engine of my construction to the moon in four-and-twenty hours!"

I smiled at what I thought his enthusiasm, and then went back to my station. As soon as the Königsberg passengers were all on board, and their baggage-carriage attached, we started on again. Soon after, I went into the guard-carriage, and sat down. An early train from Königsberg had been through two hours before reaching Bromberg, and that was at Little Oscue, where we took on board the Western mail.

"How we go!" uttered one of the guard, some fifteen minutes after we had left Dirsham.

"The new engineer is trying the speed," I replied, not yet having any fear.

But erelong I began to apprehend he was running a little too fast. The carriages began to sway to and fro, and I could hear exclamations of fright from the passengers.

"Good heavens!" cried one of the guard, coming in at that moment, "what is that fellow doing? Look, sir, and see how we are going."

I looked at the window, and found that we were dashing along at a speed never before travelled on that road. Posts, fences, rocks, and trees flew by in one undistinguished mass, and the carriages now swayed fearfully. I started to my feet, and met a passenger on the platform. He was one of the chief owners of our road, and was just on his way to Berlin. He was pale and excited.

"Sir," he gasped, "is Martin Kroller on the engine?"

"Yes," I told him.

"Holy Virgin! did n't you know him?"

"Know?" I repeated, somewhat puzzled; "what do you mean? He told me his name was Kroller, and that he was an engineer. We had no one to run the engine, and — "

"You took *him*!" interrupted the man. "Good heavens, sir, he is as crazy as a man can be! He turned his brain over a new plan for applying steam power. I saw him at the station, but did not fully recognize him, as I was in a hurry.

Just now one of your passengers told me that your engineers were all gone this morning, and that you found one that was a stranger to you. Then I knew that the man whom I had seen was Martin Kroller. He had escaped from the hospital at Stettin. You must get him off somehow."

The whole fearful truth was now open to me. The speed of the train was increasing every moment, and I knew that a few more miles per hour would launch us all into destruction. I called to the guard, and then made my way forward as quick as possible. I reached the after platform of the after tender, and there stood Kroller upon the engine-board, his hat and coat off, his long black hair floating wildly in the wind, his shirt unbuttoned at the front, his sleeves rolled up, with a pistol in his teeth, and thus glaring upon the fireman, who lay motionless upon the fuel. The furnace was stuffed till the very latch of the door was red hot, and the whole engine was quivering and swaying as though it would shiver to pieces.

" Kroller ! Kroller ! " I cried at the top of my voice.

The crazy engineer started and caught the pistol in his hand. O, how those great black eyes glared, and how ghastly and frightful the face looked !

" Ha ! ha ! ha ! " he yelled demoniacally, glaring upon me like a roused lion.

" They swore that I could not make it ! But see ! see ! See my new power ! See my new engine ! I made it, and they are jealous of me ! I made it, and when it was done, they stole it from me. But I have found it ! For years I have been wandering in search of my great engine, and they swore it was not made. But I have found it ! I knew it this morning when I saw it at Dantzic, and I was determined to have it. And I 've got it ! Ho ! ho ! ho ! we 're on the way to the moon, I say ! By the Virgin Mother, we 'll be in the moon in four-and-twenty hours. Down, down, villain ! If you move, I 'll shoot you."

This was spoken to the poor fireman, who at that moment attempted to rise, and the frightened man sank back again.

" Here 's Little Oscue just before us ! " cried out one of the

11   P

guard. But even as he spoke the buildings were at hand. A sickening sensation settled upon my heart, for I supposed that we were now gone. The houses flew by like lightning. I knew if the officers here had turned the switch as usual, we should be hurled into eternity in one fearful crash. I saw a flash, — it was another engine, — I closed my eyes; but still we thundered on! The officers had seen our speed, and, knowing that we would not head up in that distance, they had changed the switch, so that we went forward.

But there was sure death ahead, if we did not stop. Only fifteen miles from us was the town of Schwartz, on the Vistula; and at the rate we were going we should be there in a few minutes, for each minute carried us over a mile. The shrieks of the passengers now rose above the crash of the rails, and more terrific than all else arose the demoniac yells of the mad engineer.

"Merciful heavens!" gasped the guardsman, "there's not a moment to lose; Schwartz is close. But hold," he added; "let's shoot him."

At that moment a tall, stout German student came over the platform where we stood, and we saw that the madman had his heavy pistol aimed at us. He grasped a huge stick of wood, and, with a steadiness of nerve which I could not have commanded, he hurled it with such force and precision that he knocked the pistol from the maniac's hand. I saw the movement, and on the instant that the pistol fell I sprang forward, and the German followed me. I grasped the man by the arm; but I should have been nothing in his mad power, had I been alone. He would have hurled me from the platform, had not the student at that moment struck him upon the head with a stick of wood which he caught as he came over the tender.

Kroller settled down like a dead man, and on the next instant I shut off the steam and opened the valve. As the freed steam shrieked and howled in its escape, the speed began to decrease, and in a few minutes more the danger was passed. As I settled back, entirely overcome by the wild emotions that had raged within me, we began to turn the river; and before I was fairly recovered, the fireman had stopped the train in the station-house at Schwartz.

Martin Kroller, still insensible, was taken from the platform; and, as we carried him to the guard-room, one of the guard recognized him, and told us that he had been there about two weeks before.

"He came," said the guard, "and swore that an engine which stood near by was his. He said it was one he had made to go to the moon in, and that it had been stolen from him. We sent for more help to arrest him, and he fled."

"Well," I replied with a shudder, "I wish he had approached me in the same way; but he was more cautious at Dantzic."

At Schwartz we found an engineer to run the engine to Bromberg; and having taken out the Western mail for the next Northern mail to carry along, we saw that Kroller would be properly attended to, and then started on.

The rest of the trip we ran in safety, though I could see the passengers were not wholly at ease, and would not be until they were entirely clear of the railway. A heavy purse was made up by them for the German student, and he accepted it with much gratitude, and I was glad of it; for the current of gratitude to him may have prevented a far different current of feeling which might have poured upon my head for having engaged a madman to run a railroad train.

But this is not the end. Martin Kroller remained insensible from the effects of the blow nearly two weeks; and when he recovered from that, he was sound again, his insanity was all gone. I saw him about three weeks afterward, but he had no recollection of me. He remembered nothing of the past year, not even his mad freak on my engine.

But I remembered it, and I remember it still; and the people need never fear that I shall be imposed upon again by a *crazy engineer.*

ROCK ME TO SLEEP. — Mrs. Akers.

BACKWARD, turn backward, O Time, in your flight,
Make me a child again, just for to-night !
Mother, come back from the echoless shore,
Take me again to your heart as of yore, —
Kiss from my forehead the furrows of care,
Smooth the few silver threads out of my hair,
Over my slumbers your loving watch keep, —
Rock me to sleep, mother, — rock me to sleep !

Backward, flow backward, O tide of the years !
I am so weary of toil and of tears, —
Toil without recompense, tears all in vain —
Take them and give me my childhood again !
I have grown weary of dust and decay,
Weary of flinging my soul-wealth away, —
Weary of sowing for others to reap ; —
Rock me to sleep, mother, — rock me to sleep !

Tired of the hollow, the base, the untrue,
Mother, O mother, my heart calls for you !
Many a summer the grass has grown green,
Blossomed and faded — our faces between —
Yet with strong yearning and passionate pain,
Long I to-night for your presence again ;
Come from the silence so long and so deep, —
Rock me to sleep, mother, — rock me to sleep !

Over my heart in the days that are flown
No love like mother-love ever has shone, —
No other worship abides and endures,
Faithful, unselfish, and patient like yours, —
None like a mother can charm away pain
From the sick soul and world-weary brain ;
Slumber's soft calm o'er my heavy lids creep, –
Rock me to sleep, mother, — rock me to sleep !

Come, let your brown hair, just lighted with gold,
Fall on your shoulders again as of old, —
Let it drop over my forehead to-night,
Shading my faint eyes away from the light !
For, with its sunny-edged shadows once more,
Haply will throng the visions of yore,
Lovingly, softly, its bright billows sweep, —
Rock me to sleep, mother, — rock me to sleep !

Mother, dear mother ! the years have been long
Since last I listened your lullaby song.
Sing, then, and unto my soul it shall seem
Womanhood's years have been only a dream ;
Clasped to your heart in a loving embrace,
With your light lashes just sweeping my face,
Never hereafter to wake or to weep,
Rock me to sleep, mother, — rock me to sleep !

———◆———

THE BRIDGE OF SIGHS. — Hood.

"Drowned ! drowned !" — *Hamlet.*

ONE more unfortunate,
  Weary of breath,
Rashly importunate,
Gone to her death !

Take her up tenderly,
Lift her with care ;
Fashioned so slenderly,
Young, and so fair !

Look at her garments
Clinging like cerements,
Whilst the wave constantly
Drips from her clothing ;

Take her up instantly,
Loving, not loathing.

Touch her not scornfully ;
Think of her mournfully,
Gently and humanly, —
Not of the stains of her ;
All that remains of her
Now is pure womanly.

Make no deep scrutiny
Into her mutiny,
Rash and undutiful ;
Past all dishonor,
Death has left on her
Only the beautiful.

Still, for all slips of hers, —
One of Eve's family, —
Wipe those poor lips of hers
Oozing so clammily.

Loop up her tresses
Escaped from the comb, —
Her fair auburn tresses, —
Whilst wonderment guesses
Where was her home ?

Who was her father ?
Who was her mother ?
Had she a sister ?
Had she a brother ?
Or was there a dearer one
Still, and a nearer one
Yet, than all other ?

Alas for the rarity
Of Christian charity

Under the sun !
Oh, it was pitiful !
Near a whole city full,
Home she had none.

Sisterly, brotherly,
Fatherly, motherly
Feelings had changed :
Love, by harsh evidence,
Thrown from its eminence ;
Even God's providence
Seeming estranged.

Where the lamps quiver
So far in the river,
With many a light
From window and casement,
From garret to basement,
She stood with amazement,
Houseless by night.

The bleak winds of March
Made her tremble and shiver ;
But not the dark arch,
Or the black flowing river ;
Mad from life's history,
Glad to death's mystery,
Swift to be hurled —
Anywhere, anywhere
Out of the world !

In she plunged boldly, —
No matter how coldly
The rough river ran, —
Picture it, — think of it,
Dissolute man !

Lave in it, drink of it,
Then, if you can.

Take her up tenderly,
Lift her with care ;
Fashioned so slenderly,
Young, and so fair !

Ere her limbs frigidly
Stiffen too rigidly,
Decently, kindly,
Smooth and compose them ;
And her eyes, close them,
Staring so blindly !
Dreadfully staring,
Through muddy impurity,
As when with the daring
Last look of despairing
Fixed on futurity !

Perishing gloomily,
Spurred by contumely,
Cold inhumanity,
Burning insanity,
Into her rest !
Cross her hands humbly,
As if praying dumbly,
Over her breast !

Owning her weakness,
Her evil behavior,
And leaving, with meekness,
Her sins to her Saviour !

MONA'S WATERS.

O MONA'S waters are blue and bright
   When the sun shines out like a gay young lover ;
But Mona's waves are dark as night
   When the face of heaven is clouded over.
The wild wind drives the crested foam
   Far up the steep and rocky mountain,
And booming echoes drown the voice,
   The silvery voice, of Mona's fountain.

Wild, wild, against that mountain's side
   The wrathful waves were up and beating,
When stern Glenvarloch's chieftain came ;
   With anxious brow, and hurried greeting,
He bade the widowed mother send,
   (While loud the tempest's voice was raging,)
Her fair young son across the flood,
   Where winds and waves their strife were waging.

And still that fearful mother prayed,
   " O yet delay, delay till morning,
For weak the hand that guides our bark,
   Though brave his heart, all danger scorning."
Little did stern Glenvarloch heed :
   " The safety of my fortress tower
Depends on tidings he must bring
   From Fairlee bank, within the hour.

" See'st thou, across the sullen wave,
   A blood-red banner, wildly streaming ?
That flag a message brings to me
   Of which my foes are little dreaming.
The boy *must* put his boat across
   (Gold shall repay his hour of danger),
And bring me back, with care and speed,
   Three letters from the light-browed stranger."

11 *

The orphan boy leaped lightly in;
  Bold was his eye and brow of beauty,
And bright his smile as thus he spoke:
  " I do but pay a vassal's duty;
Fear not for me, O mother dear;
  See how the boat the tide is spurning;
The storm will cease, the sky will clear,
  And thou wilt watch me safe returning."

His bark shot on, — now up, now down,
  Over the waves, — the snowy-crested;
Now like a dart it sped along,
  Now like a white-winged sea-bird rested;
And ever when the wind sank low,
  Smote on the ear that woman's wailing,
As long she watched, with streaming eyes,
  That fragile bark's uncertain sailing.

He reached the shore, — the letters claimed;
  Triumphant, heard the stranger's wonder
That one so young should brave alone
  The heaving lake, the rolling thunder.
And once again his snowy sail
  Was seen by her, — that mourning mother;
And once she heard his shouting voice, —
  That voice the waves were soon to smother.

Wild burst the wind, wide flapped the sail,
  A crashing peal of thunder followed;
The gust swept o'er the water's face,
  And caverns in the deep lake hollowed.
The gust swept past, the waves grew calm,
  The thunder died along the mountain;
But where was he who used to play,
  On sunny days, by Mona's fountain?

His cold corpse floated to the shore
  Where knelt his lone and shrieking mother;

And bitterly she wept for him,
  The widow's son, who had no brother!
She raised his arm, — the hand was closed;
  With pain his stiffened fingers parted,
And on the sand three letters dropped!—
  His last dim thought, — the faithful-hearted.

Glenvarloch gazed, and on his brow
  Remorse with pain and grief seemed blending;
A purse of gold he flung beside
  That mother, o'er her dead child bending.
O, wildly laughed that woman then,
  "Glenvarloch! would ye dare to measure
The holy life that God has given
  Against a heap of golden treasure?

"Ye spurned my prayer, for we were poor;
  But know, proud man, that God hath power
To smite the king on Scotland's throne,
  The chieftain in his fortress tower.
Frown on! frown on! I fear ye not;
  We've done the last of chieftain's bidding,
And cold he lies, for whose young sake
  I used to bear your wrathful chiding.

"Will gold bring back his cheerful voice
  That used to win my heart from sorrow?
Will silver warm the frozen blood,
  Or make my heart less lone to-morrow?
Go back and seek your mountain home,
  And when ye kiss your fair-haired daughter
Remember him who died to-night
  Beneath the waves of Mona's water."

Old years rolled on, and new ones came, —
  Foes dare not brave Glenvarloch's tower;
But naught could bar the sickness out
  That stole within fair Annie's bower.

The o'erblown floweret in the sun
  Sinks languid down, and withers daily,
And so she sank, her voice grew faint,
  Her laugh no longer sounded gayly.

Her step fell on the old oak floor
  As noiseless as the snow-shower's drifting ;
And from her sweet and serious eyes
  They seldom saw the dark lid lifting.
" Bring aid ! bring aid ! " the father cries ;
  " Bring aid ! " each vassal's voice is crying ;
" The fair-haired beauty of the isles,
  Her pulse is faint, — her life is flying ! "

He called in vain ; her dim eyes turned
  And met his own with parting sorrow,
For well she knew, that fading girl,
  That he must weep and wail the morrow.
Her faint breath ceased ; the father bent
  And gazed upon his fair-haired daughter.
What thought he on ? The widow's son,
  And the stormy night by Mona's water.

HIGHER VIEWS OF THE UNION. — WENDELL PHILLIPS.

I CONFESS the pictures of the mere industrial value of the Union make me profoundly sad. I look, as beneath the skilful pencil trait after trait leaps to glowing life, and ask at last, Is this all ? Where are the nobler elements of national purpose and life ? Is this the whole fruit of ages of toil, sacrifice, and thought, — those cunning fingers, the overflowing lap, labor vocal on every hillside, and commerce whitening every sea ? All the dower of one haughty, overbearing race, the zeal of the Puritan, the faith of the Quaker, a century of colonial health, and then this large civilization, — does it result only in a workshop, — fops melted in baths and perfumed, and men grimed with toil? Raze out, then, the Eagle from our banner, and paint instead Niagara used as a cotton-mill!

O no! not such the picture my glad heart sees when I look forward. Once plant deep in the national heart the love of right, let there grow out of it the firm purpose of duty, and then from the higher plane of Christian manhood we can put aside, on the right hand and the left, these narrow, childish, and mercenary considerations.

> " Leave to the soft Campanian
>   His baths and his perfumes;
> Leave to the sordid race of Tyre
>   Their dyeing vats and looms;
> Leave to the sons of Carthage
>   The rudder and the oar,
> Leave to the Greek his marble nymph
>   And scrolls of wordy lore"; —

but for us, the children of a purer civilization, the pioneers of a Christian future, it is for us to found a Capitol whose corner-stone is Justice, and whose top-stone is Liberty; within the sacred precinct of whose Holy of Holies dwelleth One who is no respecter of persons, but hath made of one blood all nations of the earth to serve him.

Crowding to the shelter of its stately arches, I see old and young, learned and ignorant, rich and poor, native and foreign, Pagan, Christian, and Jew, black and white, in one glad, harmonious, triumphant procession!

> " Blest and thrice blest the Roman
>   Who sees Rome's brightest day;
> Who sees that long victorious pomp
>   Wind down the sacred way,
> And through the bellowing Forum,
>   And round the suppliant's Grove,
> Up to the everlasting gates
>   Of Capitolian Jove!"

THE BELLS. — Edgar A. Poe.

HEAR the sledges with the bells, —
　　　Silver bells !
What a world of merriment their melody foretells !
　　How they tinkle, tinkle, tinkle,
　　　In the icy air of night !
　　While the stars that oversprinkle
　　All the heavens seem to twinkle
　　　With a crystalline delight ;
　　Keeping time, time, time,
　　In a sort of Runic rhyme,
To the tintinabulation that so musically wells
　　From the bells, bells, bells, bells,
　　　Bells, bells, bells, —
From the jingling and the tinkling of the bells.

　　Hear the mellow wedding bells, —
　　　Golden bells !
What a world of happiness their harmony foretells !
　　Through the balmy air of night
　　How they ring out their delight !
　　From the molten-golden notes,
　　　And all in tune,
　　What a liquid ditty floats
To the turtle-dove that listens, while she gloats
　　　On the moon !
O, from out the sounding cells,
What a gush of euphony voluminously wells !
　　　How it swells !
　　　How it dwells
　　On the Future ! how it tells
　　Of the rapture that impels
　　To the swinging and the ringing
　　Of the bells, bells, bells,
　　Of the bells, bells, bells, bells,

Bells, bells, bells, —
To the rhyming and the chiming of the bells !

Hear the loud alarum bells, —
Brazen bells !
What a tale of terror, now, their turbulency tells !
In the startled ear of night
How they scream out their affright !
Too much horrified to speak,
They can only shriek, shriek,
Out of tune,
In a clamorous appealing to the mercy of the fire,
In a mad expostulation with the deaf and frantic fire,
Leaping higher, higher, higher,
With a desperate desire,
And a resolute endeavor
Now — now to sit or never,
By the side of the pale-faced moon.
O the bells, bells, bells,
What a tale their terror tells,
Of Despair !
How they clang and clash and roar !
What a horror they outpour
On the bosom of the palpitating air !
Yet the ear it fully knows,
By the twanging,
And the clanging,
How the danger ebbs and flows ;
Yet the ear distinctly tells,
In the jangling,
And the wrangling,
How the danger sinks and swells,
By the sinking or the swelling in the anger of the bells, —
Of the bells, —
Of the bells, bells, bells, bells,
Bells, bells, bells, —
In the clamor and the clangor of the bells !

Hear the tolling of the bells, —
Iron bells !
What a world of solemn thought their monody compels !
In the silence of the night,
How we shiver with affright
At the melancholy menace of their tone !
For every sound that floats
From the rust within their throats
Is a groan.
And the people — ah, the people —
They that dwell up in the steeple,
All alone,
And who tolling, tolling, tolling,
In that muffled monotone,
Feel a glory in so rolling
On the human heart a stone, —
They are neither man nor woman,
They are neither brute nor human,
They are Ghouls :
And their king it is who tolls ;
And he rolls, rolls, rolls,
Rolls,
A pæan from the bells, —
And his merry bosom swells
With the pæan of the bells !
And he dances and he yells ;
Keeping time, time, time,
In a sort of Runic rhyme,
To the pæan of the bells, —
Of the bells :
Keeping time, time, time,
In a sort of Runic rhyme,
To the throbbing of the bells, —
Of the bells, bells, bells, —
To the sobbing of the bells ;
Keeping time, time, time,
As he knells, knells, knells,

In a happy Runic rhyme,
　　To the rolling of the bells, —
Of the bells, bells, bells,
　　To the tolling of the bells,
Of the bells, bells, bells, bells,
　　Bells, bells, bells, —
To the moaning and the groaning of the bells.

THE DRUM-CALL IN 1861. — E. J. CUTLER.

THE drum's wild roll awakes the land; the fife is calling
　　shrill;
Ten thousand starry banners blaze on town and bay and hill;
The thunders of the rising war drown Labor's peaceful hum,
And heavy to the ground the first dark drops of battle come.

Wake, sons of heroes, wake!　The age of heroes dawns again;
Truth takes in hand her ancient sword, and calls her loyal men.
Lo! brightly o'er the breaking day shines Freedom's holy
　　star;
Peace cannot cure the sickly time.　All hail the healer,
　　War!

That voice the Empire City heard; 't was heard in Boston Bay;
Then to the lumber-camps of Maine sped on its eager way.
Over the breezy prairie lands, by bluff and lake it went,
To where the Mississippi shapes the plastic continent;
Then on, by cabin and by fort, by stony wastes and sands,
It rang exultant down the sea where the Golden City stands.
And wheresoe'er the summons came, there rose an angry din,
As when upon a rocky coast a stormy tide sets in.

Sweet is the praise of harvest-home, of sylvan haunts and
　　brooks,

Q

Of red swords into ploughshares beat, of spears to pruning-
hooks,
Of the long splendor of the Arts the fervid years disclose ;
But mid the victories of Peace, the heart a-straying goes.

.   .   .   .   .

But sweeter than the song of Peace, the ringing battle-shout, —
When Error's thistle-calyx bursts, Truth's purple blossoms
out ;
And lovelier than the waving grain, the battle-flag unfurled
Amid the din of trump and drum to lead the onward world !
Then mothers, sisters, daughters ! spare the tears you fain
would shed.
Who seem to die in such a cause, you cannot call them dead !
O, length of days is not a boon the brave man prayeth for !
There are a thousand evils worse than death or any war :
Oppression, with his iron strength fed on the souls of men ;
And License, with the hungry brood that kennel in his den.
But Law, the form of Liberty ! God's light is on thy brow ;
And Liberty, the soul of Law ! God's very self art thou.
Divine ideas ! we write your names across our banner's fold ;
For you the sluggard's brain is fire, for you the coward bold.
Fair daughter of the bleeding Past ! Bright hope the Prophets
saw !
God give us Law in Liberty, and Liberty in Law !

Hurrah ! the drums are beating ; the fife is calling shrill ;
Ten thousand starry banners flame on town and bay and
hill ;
The thunders of the rising war hush Labor's drowsy hum ;
Thank God that we have lived to see the saffron morning
come ! —
The morning of the battle-call, to every soldier dear.
O joy ! the cry is " Forward ! " O joy ! the foe is near !
For all the crafty men of peace have failed to purge the land.
Hurrah ! the ranks of battle close ; God takes his cause in
hand !

THE GALLEY–SLAVE. — Henry Abbey.

THERE lived in France, in days not long now dead,
   A farmer's sons, twin brothers, like in face ;
And one was taken in the other's stead
   For a small theft, and sentenced in disgrace
To serve for years a hated galley-slave,
   Yet said no word his prized good name to save.

Trusting remoter days would be more blessed,
   He set his will to wear the verdict out,
And knew most men are prisoners at best
   Who some strong habit ever drag about,
Like chain and ball ; then meekly prayed that he
Rather the prisoner he was should be.

But best resolves are of such feeble thread,
   They may be broken in Temptation's hands.
After long toil the guiltless prisoner said :
   " Why should I thus, and feel life's precious sands
The narrow of my glass, the present, run,
For a poor crime that I have never done ? "

Such questions are like cups, and hold reply ;
   For when the chance swung wide the prisoner fled,
And gained the country road, and hastened by
   Brown furrowed fields and skipping brooklets fed
By shepherd clouds, and felt 'neath sapful trees
The soft hand of the mesmerizing breeze.

Then, all that long day having eaten naught,
   He at a cottage stopped, and of the wife
A brimming bowl of fragrant milk besought.
   She gave it him ; but as he quaffed the life,
Down her kind face he saw a single tear
   Pursue its wet and sorrowful career.

Within the cot he now beheld a man
　　And maiden also weeping.　" Speak," said he,
And tell me of your grief; for if I can,
　　I will disroot the sad tear-fruited tree."
The cotter answered :　" In default of rent
We shall to-morrow from this roof be sent."

Then said the galley-slave :　" Whoso returns
　　A prisoner escaped may feel the spur
To a right action, and deserves and earns
　　Proffered reward.　I am a prisoner !
Bind these my arms, and drive me back my way,
That your reward the price of home may pay."

Against his wish the cotter gave consent,
　　And at the prison-gate received his fee,
Though some made it a thing for wonderment
　　That one so sickly and infirm as he,
When stronger would have dared not to attack,
Could capture this bold youth and bring him back.

Straightway the cotter to the mayor hied
　　And told him all the story, and that lord
Was much affected, dropping gold beside
　　The pursed sufficient silver of reward ;
Then wrote his letter in authority,
　　Asking to set the noble prisoner free.

There is no nobler, better life on earth
　　Than that of conscious, meek self-sacrifice.
Such life our Saviour, in his lowly birth
　　And holy work, made his sublime disguise,
Teaching this truth, still rarely understood :
'T is sweet to suffer for another's good.

THE DIVER. — Schiller.

" O WHERE is the knight or the squire so bold
    As to dive to the howling charybdis below? —
I cast into the whirlpool a goblet of gold,
    And o'er it already the dark waters flow;
Whoever to me may the goblet bring
Shall have for his guerdon that gift of his king."

He spoke, and the cup from the terrible steep
    That, rugged and hoary, hung over the verge
Of the endless and measureless world of the deep,
    Swirled into the maelstrom that maddened the surge.
"And where is the diver so stout to go —
I ask ye again — to the deep below?"

And the knights and the squires that gathered around
    Stood silent, and fixed on the ocean their eyes;
They looked on the dismal and savage profound,
    And the peril chilled back every thought of the prize.
And thrice spoke the monarch, — "The cup to win,
Is there never a wight who will venture in?"

And all as before heard in silence the king,
    Till a youth with an aspect unfearing but gentle,
'Mid the tremulous squires, stept out from the ring,
    Unbuckling his girdle, and doffing his mantle;
And the murmuring crowd, as they parted asunder,
On the stately boy cast their looks of wonder.

As he strode to the marge of the summit, and gave
    One glance on the gulf of that merciless main;
Lo! the wave that forever devours the wave
    Casts roaringly up the charybdis again;
And, as with the swell of the far thunder-boom,
Rushes foamingly forth from the heart of the gloom.

And it bubbles and seethes, and it hisses and roars,
  As when fire is with water commixed and contending;
And the spray of its wrath to the welkin up-soars,
  And flood upon flood hurries on, never ending.
And it never *will* rest, nor from travail be free,
Like a sea that is laboring the birth of a sea.

And at last there lay open the desolate realm!
  Through the breakers that whitened the waste of the swell,
Dark, dark yawned a cleft in the midst of the whelm,
  The path to the heart of that fathomless hell.
Round and round whirled the waves — deep and deeper still
    driven,
Like a gorge through the mountainous main thunder-riven.

The youth gave his trust to his Maker!   Before
  That path through the riven abyss closed again —
Hark! a shriek from the crowd rang aloft from the shore,
  And, behold! he is whirled in the grasp of the main!
And o'er him the breakers mysteriously rolled,
And the giant-mouth closed on the swimmer so bold.

O'er the surface grim silence lay dark and profound,
  But the deep from below murmured hollow and fell;
And the crowd, as it shuddered, lamented aloud, —
  "Gallant youth, noble heart, fare thee well, fare thee
    well!"
And still ever deepening that wail as of woe,
More hollow the gulf sent its howl from below.

If thou shouldst in those waters thy diadem fling,
  And cry, "Who may find it shall win it, and wear,"
Gods wot, though the prize were the crown of a king,
  A crown at such hazard were valued too dear.
For never did lips of the living reveal
What the deeps that howl yonder in terror conceal.

O many a ship, to that breast grappled fast,
    Has gone down to the fearful and fathomless grave ;
Again, crashed together, the keel and the mast
    To be seen, tossed aloft in the glee of the wave. —
Like the growth of a storm ever louder and clearer,
Grows the roar of the gulf rising nearer and nearer.

And it bubbles and seethes, and it hisses and roars,
    As when fire is with water commixed and contending ;
And the spray of its wrath to the welkin up-soars,
    And flood upon flood hurries on, never ending ;
And, as with the swell of the far thunder-boom,
Rushes roaringly forth from the heart of the gloom.

And lo ! from the heart of that far-floating gloom
    What gleams on the darkness so swanlike and white ?
Lo ! an arm and a neck, glancing up from the tomb ! —
    They battle, — the Man's with the Element's might.
It is he ! it is he ! — in his left hand behold,
As a sign, as a joy, shines the goblet of gold !

And he breathéd deep, and he breathéd long,
    And he greeted the heavenly delight of the day.
They gaze on each other ; they shout as they throng, —
    " He lives, — lo, the ocean has rendered its prey !
And out of the grave where the Hell began,
His valor has rescued the living man ! "

And he comes with the crowd in their clamor and glee,
    And the goblet his daring has won from the water
He lifts to the king as he sinks on his knee ;
    And the king from her maidens has beckoned his daughter,
And he bade her the wine to his cup-bearer bring,
And thus spake the Diver, — " Long life to the king !

" Happy they whom the rose-hues of daylight rejoice,
    The air and the sky that to mortals are given !

May the horror below nevermore find a voice,
　　Nor man stretch too far the wide mercy of Heaven!
Nevermore, nevermore may he lift from the mirror
The veil which is woven with NIGHT and with TERROR!

"Quick brightening like lightning, it tore me along,
　　Down, down, till the gush of a torrent at play
In the rocks of its wilderness caught me, and strong
　　As the wings of an eagle, it whirled me away.
Vain, vain were my struggles; the circle had won me;
Round and round in its dance the wild element spun me.

"And I called on my God, and my God heard my prayer,
　　In the strength of my need, in the gasp of my breath,
And showed me a crag that rose up from the lair,
　　And I clung to it, trembling, and baffled the death.
And, safe in the perils around me, behold,
On the spikes of the coral, the goblet of gold!

"Below, at the foot of that precipice drear,
　　Spread the gloomy and purple and pathless obscure, —
A silence of horror that slept on the ear,
　　That the eye more appalled might the horror endure!
Salamander, snake, dragon, — vast reptiles that dwell
In the deep, — coiled about the grim jaws of their hell.

"Dark crawled, glided dark the unspeakable swarms,
　　Like masses unshapen, made life hideously.
Here clung and here bristled the fashionless forms;
　　Here the hammer-fish darkened the dark of the sea;
And with teeth grinning white, and a menacing motion,
Went the terrible shark, the hyena of ocean.

"There I hung, and the awe gathered icily o'er me,
　　So far from the earth where man's help there was none;
The one human thing, with the goblins before me, —
　　Alone, in a loneness so ghastly, — ALONE!

Fathom-deep from man's eye in the speechless profound,
With the death of the main and the monsters around.

"Methought, as I gazed through the darkness, that now
   A hundred-limbed creature caught sight of its prey,
And darted —   O God ! from the far-flaming bough
   Of the coral, I swept on the horrible way ;
And it seized me, — the wave with its wrath and its roar, —
   It seized me to save, — King, the danger is o'er ! "

On the youth gazed the monarch, and marvelled ; quoth he,
   " Bold diver, the goblet I promised is thine ;
And this ring will I give, a fresh guerdon to thee, —
   Never jewels more precious shone up from the mine, —
If thou 'lt bring me fresh tidings, and venture again
To say what lies hid in the *innermost* main ! "

Then outspake the daughter in tender emotion,
   " Ah ! father, my father, what more can there rest ?
Enough of this sport with the pitiless ocean ;
   He has served thee as none would, thyself has confest.
If nothing can slake thy wild thirst of desire,
Be your knights not, at least, put to shame by the squire ! "

The king seized the goblet ; he swung it on high,
   And, whirling, it fell in the roar of the tide :
" But bring back that goblet again to my eye,
   And I 'll hold thee the dearest that rides by my side ;
And thine arms shall embrace as thy bride, I decree,
The maiden whose pity now pleadeth for thee."

In his heart, as he listened, there leapt the wild joy,
   And the hope and the love through his eyes spoke in fire.
On that bloom, on that blush, gazed, delighted, the boy ;
   The maiden she faints at the feet of her sire.
Here the guerdon divine, there the danger beneath ;
He resolves ! — To the strife with the life and the death !

12

They hear the loud surges sweep back in their swell ;
   Their coming the thunder-sound heralds along !
Fond eyes yet are tracking the spot where he fell —
   They come, the wild waters in tumult and throng,
Rearing up to the cliff, roaring back as before ;
But no wave ever brought the lost youth to the shore.

DEATH OF LEONIDAS. — CROLY.

IT was the wild midnight, — a storm was in the sky,
  The lightning gave its light, and the thunder echoed by ;
The torrent swept the glen, the ocean lashed the shore, —
Then rose the Spartan men, to make their bed in gore !

Swift from the deluged ground three hundred took the shield ;
Then, silent, gathered round the leader of the field.
He spoke no warrior-word, he bade no trumpet blow ;
But the signal thunder roared, and they rushed upon the foe.

The fiery element showed, with one mighty gleam,
Rampart and flag and tent, like the spectres of a dream ;
All up the mountain side, all down the woody vale,
All by the rolling tide, waved the Persian banners pale.

And King Leonidas, among the slumbering band,
Sprang foremost from the pass, like the lightning's living brand ;
Then double darkness fell, and the forest ceased to moan,
But there came a clash of steel, and a distant dying groan.

Anon, a trumpet blew, and a fiery sheet burst high,
That o'er the midnight threw a blood-red canopy :
A host glared on the hill, a host glared by the bay ;
But the Greeks rushed onward still, like leopards in their play.

The air was all a yell, and the earth was all a flame,
Where the Spartan's bloody steel on the silken turbans came ;
And still the Greeks rushed on, beneath the fiery fold,
Till, like a rising sun, shone Xerxes' tent of gold.

They found a royal feast, his midnight banquet, there !
And the treasures of the East lay beneath the Doric spear ;
Then sat to the repast the bravest of the brave, —
That feast must be their last, that spot must be their grave!

They pledged old Sparta's name in cups of Syrian wine,
And the warrior's deathless fame was sung in strains divine ;
They took the rose-wreathed lyres from eunuch and from
    slave,
And taught the languid wires the sounds that Freedom gave.

But now the morning star crownéd Œta's twilight brow,
And the Persian horn of war from the hill began to blow ;
Up rose the glorious rank, to Greece one cup poured high,
Then, hand in hand, they drank, — " To Immortality ! "

Fear on King Xerxes fell, when, like spirits from the tomb,
With shout and trumpet-knell, he saw the warriors come ;
But down swept all his power, with chariot and with charge, —
Down poured the arrowy shower, till sank the Dorian targe.

They marched within the tent, with all their strength unstrung;
To Greece one look they sent, then on high their torches flung ;
To heaven the blaze uprolled, like a mighty altar-fire,
And the Persians' gems and gold were the Grecians' funeral
    pyre.

Their king sat on his throne, his captains by his side,
While the flame rushed roaring on, and their pæan loud replied!
Thus fought the Greek of old !   Thus will he fight again !
Shall not the selfsame mould bring forth the selfsame men ?

MY EXPERIENCE IN ELOCUTION. — John Neal.

IN the academy I attended, elocution was taught in a way I never shall forget, — never! We had a yearly exhibition, and the favorites of the preceptor were allowed to speak a piece; and a pretty time they had of it. Somehow, I was never a favorite with any of my teachers after the first two or three days; and, as I went barefooted, I dare say it was thought unseemly, or perhaps cruel, to expose me upon the platform. And then, as I had no particular aptitude for public speaking, and no relish for what was called oratory, it was never my luck to be called up.

Among my schoolmates, however, was one, — a very amiable, shy boy, — to whom was assigned, at the last exhibition I attended, that passage in Pope's Homer beginning with "*Aurora*, now fair daughter of the dawn." This the poor boy gave with so much emphasis and discretion that, to me, it sounded like "O roarer!" and I was wicked enough, out of sheer envy I dare say, to call him "O roarer!" — a nickname which clung to him for a long while, though no human being ever deserved it less; for in speech and action both, he was quiet, reserved, and sensitive.

My next experience in elocution was still more disheartening, so that I never had a chance of showing what I was capable of in that way, till I set up for myself. Master Moody, my next instructor, was thought to have uncommon qualifications for teaching oratory. He was a large, handsome, heavy man, over six feet high; and having understood that the first, second, and third prerequisite in oratory was *action*, the boys he put in training were encouraged to most vehement and obstreperous manifestations. Let me give an example, and one that weighed heavily on my conscience for many years after the poor man passed away.

Among his pupils were two boys, brothers, who were thought highly gifted in elocution. The master, who was evidently of that opinion, had a habit of parading them on all occasions before visitors and strangers; though one had lost his upper front teeth and lisped badly, and the other had the voice of a penny-trumpet. Week after week, these boys went through the quarrel of Brutus and Cassius, for the benefit of myself and others, to see if their example would not provoke us to a generous competition for all the honors.

How it operated on the other boys in after life I cannot say; but the effect on me was decidedly unwholesome — discouraging, indeed — until I was old enough to judge for myself, and to carry into operation a system of my own; believing that men should always *talk* — I do not say they should talk *always* — on paper and off, on the platform and at the bar, in the senate-chamber and at the dinner-table, — if they would not forego all the advantages of experience in private life, when they launch into public life.

On coming to the passage, " Be ready, gods, with all your thunderbolts, — dash him in pieces! " the elder of the two gave it after the following fashion : " Be ready, godths, with all your thunderbolths, — dath him in pietheth ! " — bringing his right fist down into his left palm with all his strength, and his lifted foot upon the platform, which was built like a sounding-board, so that the master himself, who had suggested the action, and obliged the poor boy to rehearse it over and over again, appeared to be utterly carried away by the magnificent demonstration ; while to me — so deficient was I in rhetorical taste — it sounded like the crash of broken crockery, intermingled with chicken-peeps.

I never got over it; and to this day, cannot endure stamping, nor even tapping with the foot, nor clapping the hands together, nor thumping the table for illustration ; having an idea that such noises are not oratory, and that untranslatable sounds are not language.

My next essay was of a somewhat different kind. I took the field in person, being in my nineteenth year, well proportioned, and already beginning to have a sincere relish for poetry, if not for declamation. I had always been a great reader ; and in the course of my foraging depredations I had met with "The Sailor-Boy's Dream," and "The Lake of the Dismal Swamp," both of which I had committed to memory before I knew it.

And one day, happening to be alone with my sister, and newly rigged out in a student's gown, such as the lads at Brunswick sported when they came to show off among their old companions, I proposed to astonish her by rehearsing these two poems in appropriate costume. Being very proud of her brother, and very obliging, she consented at once, — upon the condition, however, that our dear mother, who had never seen anything of the sort, should be invited to make one of the audience.

On the whole, I rather think that I succeeded in astonishing both. I well remember their looks of amazement — for they had never seen anything better or — worse — in all their lives, and were no judges of acting — as I swept to and fro in that magnificent robe, with outstretched arms and uplifted eyes, when I came to passages like the following, where an apostrophe was called for : —

> "And near him the she-wolf stirred the brake,
>   And the copper-snake breathed in his ear,
> Till, starting, he cried, from his dream awake,
> ' O, when shall I see the dusky lake,
>   And the white canoe of my dear ? ' "

Or like this : —

> "O sailor-boy ! sailor-boy ! peace to thy shade !
> Around thy white bones the red coral shall grow,
> Of thy fair yellow hair threads of amber be made,
> And every part suit to thy mansion below" ; —

throwing up my arms, and throwing them out in every possible direction as the spirit moved me, or the sentiment prompted ; for I always encouraged my limbs and features to think for themselves, and to act for themselves, and never predetermined — never forethought — a gesture nor an intonation in all my life ; and should as soon think of counterfeiting another's look or step or voice, or of modulating my own by a pitch-pipe, — as the ancient orators did, with whom oratory was acting-elocution, a branch of the dramatic art, — as of adopting or imitating the gestures or tones of the most celebrated rhetorician I ever saw.

The result was quite encouraging. My mother and sister were both satisfied. At any rate, they said nothing to the contrary. Being only in my nineteenth year, what might I not be able to accomplish after a little more experience ?

How little did I think, while rehearsing before my mother and sister, that anything serious would ever come of it, or that I was laying the foundations of character for life, or that I was beginning what I should not be able to finish within the next forty or fifty years following. Yet so it was. I had broken the ice without knowing it. These things were but the foreshadowing of what happened long afterward.

THE KINGDOM. — Lizzie Doten.

'TWAS the ominous month of October, —
 How the memories rise in my soul,
How they swell like a sea in my soul ! —
When a spirit, sad, silent, and sober,
 Whose glance was a word of control,
Drew me down to the black Lake Avernus,
 In the desolate kingdom of Death, —
To the mist-covered Lake of Avernus,
 In the ghoul-haunted kingdom of Death.

And there, while I shivered and waited,
 I talked with the souls of the dead ;
The lawless, the lone, and the hated,
 Who broke from their bondage and fled.
Each word was a burning eruption,
 That leaped from a crater of flame, —

A red lava-tide of corruption,
    That out of life's sediment came
From the scoriac natures God gave them,
    Compounded of glory and shame.

"Aboard ! " cried our pilot and leader ;
    Then wildly we rushed to embark,
And forth, in our ghostly *Edida,*
    We swept in the silence and dark.
O God ! on that black Lake Avernus,
    Where vampires drink even the breath,
On that terrible Lake of Avernus,
    Leading down to the whirlpool of death !

It was there the Eumenides found us,
    In sight of no shelter or shore,
They lashed up the white waves around us, —
    We sank in the waters' wild roar.
But not to the regions infernal,
    Through billows of sulphurous flame,
But unto the city eternal,
    The home of the blest, we came.

To the gate of the beautiful city,
    All fainting and weary, we pressed :
"O Heart of the Holy, take pity,
    And welcome us home to our rest !
Pursued by the Fates and the Furies,
    In danger and darkness we fled ;
From the pitiless Fates and the Furies,
    Through the desolate realms of the dead."

Like the song of a bird that yet lingers,
    Like the wind-harp by Æolus blown,
As if touched by the lightest of fingers,
    Wide open the portals were thrown.

And there, in a mystical splendor,
  Stood a golden-haired, azure-eyed child;
With a look that was touching and tender
  She stretched forth her white hand and smiled.
" Ay, welcome ! thrice welcome, poor mortals !
  O, why do you linger and wait ?
Come fearlessly in at these portals,
  No warder keeps watch at the gate."

" *Gloria Deo !   Te Deum laudamus !* "
  Exclaimed a proud prelate, " I 'm safe into heaven !
By the blood of the Lamb, and the martyrs who claim us,
  My soul has been purchased, my sins are forgiven ;
I tread where the saints and the martyrs have trod,
Lead on, thou fair child, to the temple of God ! "

The child stood in silence and wondered,
  And bowed down her beautiful head,
  And even as fragrance is shed
By the lily the waves have swept under,
  She meekly and tenderly said :
" In vain do you seek to behold Him ;
  He dwells in no temple apart ;
The height of the heavens cannot hold him,
  And yet he is here in my heart, —
    He is here, and he will not depart."

Then forth from the mystical splendor,
  The scintillant, crystalline light,
Gleamed faces more touching and tender
  Than ever had greeted our sight.
And they sang, " Welcome home to this kingdom,
  Ye earth-born and serpent-beguiled !
The Lord is the light of this kingdom,
  And his temple the heart of a child ! "

THE SONG OF THE COSSACK TO HIS HORSE. —
BERANGER.

TRANSLATED BY " FATHER PROUT " (REV. FRANCIS MAHONY).

COME, arouse thee up, my gallant horse, and bear thy
rider on !
The comrade thou, and the friend, I trow, of the dweller on
the Don.
Pillage and Death have spread their wings ! 't is the hour to
hie thee forth,
And with thy hoofs an echo wake to the trumpets of the
North !
Nor gems nor gold do men behold upon thy saddle-tree ;
But earth affords the wealth of lords for thy master and for
thee.
Then fiercely neigh, my charger gray ! — thy chest is proud
and ample !
Thy hoofs shall prance o'er the fields of France, and the pride
of her heroes trample !

Europe is weak, — she hath grown old, — her bulwarks are
laid low ;
She is loath to hear the blast of war, — she shrinketh from a
foe !
Come, in our turn, let us sojourn in her goodly haunts of
joy, —
In the pillared porch to wave the torch, and her palaces
destroy !
Proud as when first thou slakedst thy thirst in the flow of
conquered Seine,
Aye, shalt thou lave, within that wave, thy blood-red flanks
again.
Then fiercely neigh, my gallant gray ! — thy chest is strong
and ample !
Thy hoofs shall prance o'er the fields of France, and the pride
of her heroes trample !

Kings are beleaguered on their thrones by their own vassal
 crew ;
And in their den quake noblemen, and priests are bearded too ;
And loud they yelp for the Cossacks' help to keep their bonds-
 men down,
And they think it meet, while they kiss *our* feet, to wear a
 tyrant's crown !
The sceptre now to my lance shall bow, and the crosier and
 the cross
Shall bend alike, when I lift my pike, and aloft THAT SCEPTRE
 toss !
Then proudly neigh, my gallant gray ! — thy chest is broad
 and ample !
Thy hoofs shall prance o'er the fields of France, and the pride
 of her heroes trample !

In a night of storm I have seen a form ! — and the figure was
 a GIANT,
And his eye was bent on the Cossack's tent, and his look was
 all defiant ;
Kingly his crest, — and towards the West with his battle-axe
 he pointed ;
And the "form" I saw *was* ATTILA ! of this earth the scourge
 anointed.
From the Cossacks' camp let the horseman's tramp the coming
 crash announce ;
Let the vulture whet his beak sharp set, on the carrion field
 to pounce ;
And proudly neigh, my charger gray ! — O, thy chest is
 broad and ample !
Thy hoofs shall prance o'er the fields of France, and the pride
 of her heroes trample !

What boots old Europe's boasted fame, on which she builds
 reliance,
When the North shall launch its *avalanche* on her works of
 art and science ?

Hath she not wept her cities swept by our hordes of tramp-
    ling stallions,
And tower and arch crushed in the march of our barbarous
    battalions?
Can *we* not wield our fathers' shield? the same war-hatchet
    handle?
Do our blades want length, or the reapers strength, for the
    harvest of the Vandal?
Then proudly neigh, my gallant gray, for thy chest is strong
    and ample;
And thy hoofs shall prance o'er the fields of France, and the
    pride of her heroes trample!

DOROTHY IN THE GARRET. — J. T. Trowbridge.

IN the low-raftered garret, stooping
    Carefully over the creaking boards,
Old Maid Dorothy goes a-groping
    Among its dusty and cobwebbed hoards;
Seeking some bundle of patches, hid
    Far under the eaves, or bunch of sage,
Or satchel hung on its nail, amid
    The heirlooms of a bygone age.

There is the ancient family chest,
    There the ancestral cards and hatchel;
Dorothy, sighing, sinks down to rest,
    Forgetful of patches, sage, and satchel.
Ghosts of faces peer from the gloom
    Of the chimney, where, with swifts and reel,
And the long-disused, dismantled loom,
    Stands the old-fashioned spinning-wheel.

She sees it back in the clean-swept kitchen,
    A part of her girlhood's little world;

Her mother is there by the window, stitching ;
  Spindle buzzes, and reel is whirled
With many a click : on her little stool
  She sits, a child, by the open door,
Watching, and dabbling her feet in the pool
  Of sunshine spilled on the gilded floor.

Her sisters are spinning all day long;
  To her wakening sense the first sweet warning
Of daylight come is the cheerful song
  To the hum of the wheel in the early morning.
Benjie, the gentle, red-cheeked boy,
  On his way to school, peeps in at the gate ;
In neat white pinafore, pleased and coy,
  She reaches a hand to her bashful mate ;

And under the elms, a prattling pair,
  Together they go, through glimmer and gloom : —
It all comes back to her, dreaming there
  In the low-raftered garret-room ;
The hum of the wheel, and the summer weather,
  The heart's first trouble, and love's beginning,
Are all in her memory linked together ;
  And now it is she herself that is spinning.

With the bloom of youth on cheek and lip,
  Turning the spokes with the flashing pin,
Twisting the thread from the spindle-tip,
  Stretching it out and winding it in,
To and fro, with a blithesome tread,
  Singing she goes, and her heart is full,
And many a long-drawn golden thread
  Of fancy is spun with the shining wool.

Her father sits in his favorite place,
  Puffing his pipe by the chimney-side ;
Through curling clouds his kindly face
  Glows upon her with love and pride.

Lulled by the wheel, in the old arm-chair
   Her mother is musing, cat in lap,
With beautiful drooping head, and hair
   Whitening under her snow-white cap.

One by one, to the grave, to the bridal,
   They have followed her sisters from the door ;
Now they are old, and she is their idol : —
   It all comes back on her heart once more.
In the autumn dusk the hearth gleams brightly,
   The wheel is set by the shadowy wall, —
A hand at the latch, — 't is lifted lightly,
   And in walks Benjie, manly and tall.

His chair is placed ; the old man tips
   The pitcher, and brings his choicest fruit ;
Benjie basks in the blaze, and sips,
   And tells his story, and joints his flute :
O, sweet the tunes, the talk, the laughter !
   They fill the hour with a glowing tide ;
But sweeter the still, deep moments after,
   When she is alone by Benjie's side.

But once with angry words they part :
   O, then the weary, weary days !
Ever with restless, wretched heart,
   Plying her task, she turns to gaze
Far up the road ; and early and late
   She harks for a footstep at the door,
And starts at the gust that swings the gate,
   And prays for Benjie, who comes no more.

Her fault ? O Benjie, and could you steel
   Your thoughts toward one who loved you so ? —
Solace she seeks in the whirling wheel,
   In duty and love that lighten woe ;
Striving with labor, not in vain,
   To drive away the dull day's dreariness, —

Blessing the toil that blunts the pain
   Of a deeper grief in the body's weariness.

Proud and petted and spoiled was she :
   A word, and all her life is changed !
His wavering love too easily
   In the great, gay city grows estranged :
One year : she sits in the old church pew ;
   A rustle, a murmur, — O Dorothy ! hide
Your face and shut from your soul the view !
   'T is Benjie leading a white-veiled bride !

Now father and mother have long been dead,
   And the bride sleeps under a churchyard stone,
And a bent old man with grizzled head
   Walks up the long dim aisle alone.
Years blur to a mist ; and Dorothy
   Sits doubting betwixt the ghost she seems
And the phantom of youth, more real than she,
   That meets her there in that haunt of dreams.

Bright young Dorothy, idolized daughter,
   Sought by many a youthful adorer,
Life, like a new risen-dawn on the water,
   Shining an endless vista before her !
Old Maid Dorothy, wrinkled and gray,
   Groping under the farm-house eaves, —
And life is a brief November day
   That sets on a world of withered leaves !

Yet faithfulness in the humblest part
   Is better at last than proud success,
And patience and love in a chastened heart
   Are pearls more precious than happiness ;
And in that morning when she shall wake
   To the spring-time freshness of youth again,
All trouble will seem but a flying flake,
   And life-long sorrow a breath on the pane.

RAVENSWOOD AND LUCY ASHTON. — Scott.

Lucy Ashton has solemnly plighted her faith to Ravenswood, a poor but high-spirited nobleman ; and as a mutual pledge they have broken a piece of gold together. Lucy's mother, finding a rich suitor for her daughter, urges her to write a letter of dismissal to Ravenswood, and consent to a union with Bucklaw. Lucy, driven to despair, at length yields to the will of her imperious mother, after many threats and entreaties. The marriage day has come. The marriage contract is to be signed. Bucklaw, the bridegroom, Craigengelt, his parasite, Bide-the-bent, the clergyman, Lucy's parents and brother are present.

THE business of the day now went forward ; Sir William Ashton signed the contract with legal solemnity and precision ; his son, with military *nonchalance ;* and Bucklaw, having subscribed as rapidly as Craigengelt could manage to turn the leaves, concluded by wiping his pen on that worthy's new laced cravat.

It was now Miss Ashton's turn to sign the writings, and she was guided by her watchful mother to the table for that purpose. At her first attempt, she began to write with a dry pen, and when the circumstance was pointed out, seemed unable, after several attempts, to dip it in the massive silver ink-standish, which stood full before her. Lady Ashton's vigilance hastened to supply the deficiency. I have myself seen the fatal deed, and in the distinct characters in which the name of Lucy Ashton is traced on each page, there is only a very slight tremulous irregularity, indicative of her state of mind at the time of the subscription. But the last signature is incomplete, defaced, and blotted ; for, while her hand was employed in tracing it, a hasty tramp of a horse was heard at the gate, succeeded by a step in the outer gallery, and a voice, which, in a commanding tone, bore down the opposition of the menials. The pen dropped from Lucy's fingers, as she exclaimed with a faint shriek, " He is come, — he is come ! "

Hardly had Miss Ashton dropped the pen, when the door of the apartment flew open, and the Master of Ravenswood entered the apartment.

Lockhard and another domestic, who had in vain attempted to oppose his passage through the gallery, or antechamber, were seen standing on the threshold transfixed with surprise, which was instantly communicated to the whole party in the state-room. That of Colonel Douglas Ashton was mingled with resentment ; that of Bucklaw, with haughty and affected indifference ; the rest, even Lady Ashton herself, showed signs of fear, and Lucy seemed stiffened to stone by this unexpected apparition. Apparition it might well be termed, for Ravenswood had more the appearance of one returned from the dead than of a living visitor.

He planted himself full in the middle of the apartment, opposite to the table at which Lucy was seated, on whom, as if she had been alone in the chamber, he bent his eyes with a mingled expression of deep grief and deliberate indignation. His dark-colored riding-cloak, displaced from one shoulder, hung around one side of his person in the ample folds of the Spanish mantle. The rest of his rich dress was travel-soiled, and deranged by hard riding. He had a sword by his side, and pistols in his belt. His slouched hat, which he had not removed at entrance, gave an additional gloom to his dark features, which, wasted by sorrow, and marked by the ghastly look communicated by long illness, added to a countenance naturally somewhat stern and wild a fierce and even savage expression. The matted and dishevelled locks of hair which escaped from under his hat, together with his fixed and unmoved posture, made his head more resemble that of a marble bust than that of a living man. He said not a single word, and there was a deep silence in the company for more than two minutes.

It was broken by Lady Ashton, who in that space partly recovered her natural audacity. She demanded to know the cause of this unauthorized intrusion.

" That is a question, madam," said her son, " which I have the best right to ask, and I must request of the Master of Ravenswood to follow me, where he can answer it at leisure."

Bucklaw interposed, saying, " No man on earth should usurp his previous right in demanding an explanation from the Master. — Craigengelt," he added, in an undertone, " why do you stand staring as if you saw a ghost ? fetch me my sword from the gallery."

" I will relinquish to none," said Colonel Ashton, " my right of calling to account the man who has offered this unparalleled affront to my family." . . . .

" Silence ! " exclaimed Ravenswood, "let him who really seeks danger take the fitting time when it is to be found ; my mission here will be shortly accomplished. Is *that* your handwriting, madam ? " he added in a softer tone, extending towards Miss Ashton her last letter.

A faltering " Yes," seemed rather to escape from her lips, than to be uttered as a voluntary answer.

" And is *this* also your handwriting ? " extending towards her the mutual engagement.

Lucy remained silent. Terror, and a yet stronger and more confused feeling, so utterly disturbed her understanding, that she probably scarcely comprehended the question that was put to her.

" If you design," said Sir William Ashton, " to found any legal claim on that paper, sir, do not expect to receive any answer to an extrajudicial question."

" Sir William Ashton, " said Ravenswood, " I pray you, and all who hear me, that you will not mistake my purpose. If this young lady, of her own free will, desires the restoration of this contract, as her letter would seem to imply, there is not a withered leaf which this autumn wind strews on the heath, that is more valueless in my eyes. But I must and will hear the truth from her own mouth, — without this satisfaction I will not leave this spot. Murder me by numbers you possibly may ; but I am an armed man, I am a desperate man, and I will not die without ample vengeance. This is my resolution, take it as you may. I WILL hear her determination from her own mouth ; from her own mouth, alone, and without witnesses, will I hear it. Now, choose."

he said, drawing his sword with the right hand, and with the left, by the same motion, taking a pistol from his belt and cocking it, but turning the point of one weapon and the muzzle of the other to the ground, — " choose if you will have this hall floated with blood, or if you will grant me the decisive interview with my affianced bride which the laws of God and the country alike entitle me to demand."

All recoiled at the sound of his voice, and the determined action by which it was accompanied ; for the ecstasy of real desperation seldom fails to overpower the less energetic passions by which it may be opposed. The clergyman was the first to speak. " In the name of God," he said, " receive an overture of peace from the meanest of his servants. What this honorable person demands, albeit it is urged with over-violence, hath yet in it something of reason. Let him hear from Miss Lucy's own lips that she hath dutifully acceded to the will of her parents, and repenteth her of her covenant with him ; and when he is assured of this, he will depart in peace unto his own dwelling, and cumber us no more. Alas ! the workings of the ancient Adam are strong even in the regenerate, — surely we should have long-suffering with those who, being yet in the gall of bitterness and bond of iniquity, are swept forward by the uncontrollable current of worldly passion. Let, then, the Master of Ravenswood have the interview on which he insisteth ; it can but be as a passing pang to this honorable maiden, since her faith is now irrevocably pledged to the choice of her parents. Let it, I say, be thus ; it belongeth to my functions to entreat your honor's compliance with this healing overture."

" Never," answered Lady Ashton, whose rage had now overcome her first surprise and terror, — " never shall this man speak in private with my daughter, the affianced bride of another ! Pass from this room who will, I remain here. I fear neither his violence nor his weapons, though some," she said, glancing a look towards Colonel Ashton, " who bear my name, appear more moved by them."

" For God's sake, madam," answered the worthy divine,

"add not fuel to firebrands. The Master of Ravenswood cannot, I am sure, object to your presence, the young lady's state of health being considered, and your maternal duty. I myself will also tarry ; peradventure my gray hairs may turn away wrath."

"You are welcome to do so, sir," said Ravenswood, "and Lady Ashton is also welcome to remain, if she shall think proper ; but let all others depart." . . . .

Ravenswood sheathed his sword, uncocked and returned his pistol to his belt, walked deliberately to the door of the apartment, which he bolted, returned, raised his hat from his forehead, and, gazing upon Lucy with eyes in which an expression of sorrow overcame their late fierceness, spread his dishevelled locks back from his face, and said, "Do you know me, Miss Ashton? I am still Edgar Ravenswood." She was silent, and he went on with increasing vehemence, " I am still that Edgar Ravenswood, who, for your affection, renounced the dear ties by which injured honor bound him to seek vengeance. I am that Ravenswood, who, for your sake, forgave, nay, clasped hands in friendship with the oppressor and pillager of his house, — the traducer and murderer of his father."

"My daughter," answered Lady Ashton, interrupting him, " has no occasion to dispute the identity of your person ; the venom of your present language is sufficient to remind her that she speaks with the mortal enemy of her father."

"I pray you to be patient, madam," answered Ravenswood ; " my answer must come from her own lips. Once more, Miss Lucy Ashton, I am that Ravenswood to whom you granted the solemn engagement, which you now desire to retract and cancel."

Lucy's bloodless lips could only falter out the words, "It was my mother."

"She speaks truly," said Lady Ashton ; "it *was* I, who, authorized alike by the laws of God and man, advised her, and concurred with her, to set aside an unhappy and precipitate engagement, and to annul it by the authority of Scripture itself." . . . .

"And is this all?" said Ravenswood, looking at Lucy; "are you willing to barter sworn faith, the exercise of free-will, and the feelings of mutual affection, to this wretched hypocritical sophistry?"

"Hear him!" said Lady Ashton, looking at the clergy-man, — "hear the blasphemer!"

"May God forgive him," said Bide-the-bent, "and enlighten his ignorance!"

"Hear what I have sacrificed for you," said Ravenswood, still addressing Lucy, " ere you sanction what has been done in your name. The honor of an ancient family, the urgent advice of my best friends, have been in vain used to sway my resolution; neither the arguments of reason nor the portents of superstition have shaken my fidelity. The very dead have arisen to warn me, and their warning has been despised. Are you prepared to pierce my heart for its fidelity with the very weapon which my rash confidence intrusted to your grasp?"

"Master of Ravenswood," said Lady Ashton, "you have asked what questions you thought fit. You see the total incapacity of my daughter to answer you. But I will reply for her, and in a manner which you cannot dispute. You desire to know whether Lucy Ashton, of her own free will, desires to annul the engagement into which she has been trepanned. You have her letter under her own hand, de-manding the surrender of it; and, in yet more full evidence of her purpose, here is the contract which she has this morning subscribed, in presence of this reverend gentleman, with Mr. Hayston of Bucklaw."

Ravenswood gazed upon the deed, as if petrified. "And it was without fraud or compulsion," said he, looking towards the clergyman, "that Miss Ashton subscribed this parch-ment?"

"I vouch it upon my sacred character."

"This is indeed, madam, an undeniable piece of evidence," said Ravenswood, sternly; "and it will be equally unneces-sary and dishonorable to waste another word in useless remonstrance or reproach. There, madam," he said, laying down before Lucy the signed paper and the broken piece of gold, — "there are the evidences of your first engagement; may you be more faithful to that which you have just formed! I will trouble you to return the corresponding tokens of my ill-placed confidence, — I ought rather to say, of my egregious folly."

Lucy returned the scornful glance of her lover with a gaze from which perception seemed to have been banished; yet she seemed partly to have understood his meaning, for she raised her hands as if to undo a blue ribbon which she wore around her neck. She was unable to accomplish her purpose, but Lady Ashton cut the ribbon asunder, and detached the broken piece of gold which Miss Ashton had till then worn concealed in her bosom; the written counterpart of the lovers' engagement she for some time had had in her own possession. With a haughty courtesy, she delivered both to Ravenswood, who was much softened when he took the piece of gold.

"And she could wear it thus," he said, speaking to himself, — "could wear it in her very bosom, — could wear it next to her heart — even when — But complaint avails not," he said, dashing from his eye the tear which had gathered in it, and resuming the stern composure of his manner. He strode to the chimney, and threw into the fire the paper and piece of gold, stamping upon the coals with the heel of his boot, as if to insure their destruction. "I will be no longer," he then said, "an intruder here. Your evil wishes, and your worse offices, Lady Ashton, I will only return, by hoping these will be your last machinations against your daughter's honor and happiness. And to you, madam," he said, addressing Lucy, "I have nothing further to say, except to pray to God that you may not become a world's wonder for this act of wilful and deliberate perjury." Having uttered these words, he turned on his heel, and left the apartment.

THE SILENT TOWER OF BOTTREAUX.

Bottreaux is the old name for Boscastle. The church at Bottreaux, in Cornwall, has no bells, while the neighboring tower of Tintagel contains a fine peal of six. It is said that a peal of bells for Bottreaux was once cast at a foundry on the Continent, and that the vessel which was bringing them went down within sight of the church-tower.

TINTAGEL bells ring o'er the tide,
 The boy leans on his vessel's side,
He hears that sound, while dreams of home
Soothe the wild orphan of the foam.
     "Come to thy God in time,"
     Thus said their pealing chime;
     "Youth, manhood, old age past,
     Come to thy God at last."

But why are Bottreaux's echoes still?
Her tower stands proudly on the hill,
Yet the strange chough that home hath found,
The lamb lies sleeping on the ground.
     "Come to thy God in time,"
     Should be her answering chime;
     "Come to thy God at last,"
     Should echo on the blast.

The ship rode down with courses free,
The daughter of a distant sea,
Her sheet was loose, her anchor stored,
The merry Bottreaux bells on board.
     "Come to thy God in time,"
     Rung out Tintagel chime;
     "Youth, manhood, old age past,
     Come to thy God at last."

The pilot heard his native bells
Hang on the breeze in fitful spells.

"Thank God," with reverent brow, he cried,
"We make the shore with evening's tide."
    "Come to thy God in time,"
    It was his marriage chime;
    "Youth, manhood, old age past,
    Come to thy God at last."

"Thank God, thou whining knave, on land,
But thank at sea the steersman's hand";
The captain's voice rose o'er the gale,
"Thank the good ship and ready sail."
    "Come to thy God in time,"
    Sad grew the boding chime;
    "Come to thy God at last,"
    Boomed heavy on the blast.

Uprose that sea as if it heard
The mighty Master's signal word.
What thrills the captain's whitening lip?
The death groans of his sinking ship.
    "Come to thy God in time,"
    Swung deep the funeral chime;
    "Grace, mercy, kindness past,
    Come to thy God at last."

Long did the rescued pilot tell,
When gray hairs o'er his forehead fell,
While those around would hear and weep,
That fearful judgment of the deep.
    "Come to thy God in time,"
    He read his native chime;
    "Youth, manhood, old age past,
    Come to thy God at last."

Still, when the storm of Bottreaux's waves
Is waking in his weedy caves,

Those bells, that sullen surges hide,
Peal their deep tones beneath the tide.
    "Come to thy God in time,"
    Thus saith the ocean chime;
"Storm, whirlwind, billows past,
    Come to thy God at last."

THE HIRELING SWISS REGIMENT. — Victor Hugo.

WHEN the regiment of the Halberdiers is proudly march-
        ing by,
The eagle of the mountains screams from out his stormy sky;
Who speaketh to the precipice, and to the chasm sheer;
Who hovers o'er the throne of kings, and bids the caitiffs
    fear.
King of the peak and glacier; king of the cold, white scalps, —
He lifts his head, at that close tread, the eagle of the Alps.

O shame, those men that march below! O ignominy dire!
Are the sons of my free mountains sold for imperial hire?
Ah, the vilest in the dungeon! — Ah, the slave upon the
    seas, —
Is great, is pure, is glorious, is grand compared with these,
Who, born amid my holy rocks, in solemn places high,
Where the tall pines bend like rushes when the storm goes
    sweeping by,
Yet give the strength of foot they learned by perilous path
    and flood,
And from their blue-eyed mothers won, the old, mysterious
    blood;
The daring that the good south-wind into their nostrils
    blew,
And the proud swelling of the heart with each pure breath
    they drew;

13   s

The graces of the mountain glens, with flowers in summer
    gay ;
And all the glory of the hills, to earn a lackey's pay.

Their country free and joyous, — she of the rugged sides, —
She of the rough peaks arrogant, whereon the tempest rides ;
Mother of the unconquered thought and of the savage form,
Who brings out of her sturdy heart the hero and the storm ;
Who giveth freedom unto man, and life unto the beast ;
Who hears her silver torrents ring like joy-bells at a feast ;
Who hath her caves for palaces, and where her châlets
    stand, —
The proud old archer of Altorf, with his good bow in his
    hand ; —
Is she to suckle jailers ? shall shame and glory rest,
Amid her lakes and mountains, like twins upon her breast ?
Shall the two-headed eagle, marked with her double blow,
Drink of her milk through all those hearts whose blood he
    bids to flow ?

Say was it pomp ye needed, and all the proud array
Of courtliness and high parade upon a gala day ?
Look up ; have not my valleys, their torrents white with
    foam,
Their lines of silver bullion on the blue hills of home ?
Doth not sweet May embroider my rocks with pearls and
    flowers ?
Her fingers trace a richer lace than yours in all my bowers,
Are not my old peaks gilded when the sun rises proud,
And each one shakes a white mist plume out of the thunder-
    cloud ?
O neighbors of the golden sky, — sons of the mountain
    sod, —
Why wear a base king's colors for the livery of God ?

O shame ! despair ! to see my Alps their giant shadows fling
Into the very waiting-room of tyrant and of king !

O thou deep heaven, unsullied yet, into thy gulfs sublime,
Up azure tracts of flaming light, let my free pinion climb ;
Till from my sight, in that clear light, earth and her crimes
    be gone, —
The men who act the evil deeds, the caitiffs who look on ;
Far, far into that space immense, beyond the vast white veil,
Where distant stars come out and shine, and the great sun
    grows pale.

THE AVENGING CHILDE. — Lockhart.

HURRAH! hurrah! avoid the way of the Avenging
    Childe ;
His horse is swift as sands that drift, — an Arab of the wild ;
His gown is twisted round his arm, — a ghastly cheek he
    wears ;
And in his hand, for deadly harm, a hunting-knife he bears.

Avoid that knife in battle strife, that weapon short and thin ;
The dragon's gore hath bathed it o'er, seven times 't was
    steeped therein ;
Seven times the smith hath proved its pith, — it cuts a
    coulter through ;
In France the blade was fashioned, from Spain the shaft it
    drew.

He sharpens it, as he doth ride, upon his saddle-bow ;
He sharpens it on either side, he makes the steel to glow.
He rides to find Don Quadros, that false and faitour * knight ;
His glance of ire is hot as fire, although his cheek be white.

He found him standing by the king, within the judgment-
    hall ;
He rushed within the barons' ring, — he stood before them all.

* Vagabond.

Seven times he gazed and pondered if he the deed should do ;
Eight times distraught he looked and thought, then out his
    dagger flew.

He stabbed therewith at Quadros, — the king did step be-
    tween ;
It pierced his royal garment of purple wove with green.
He fell beneath the canopy, upon the tiles he lay.
"Thou traitor keen, what dost thou mean, — thy king why
    wouldst thou slay ?"

"Now, pardon, pardon," cried the Childe ; "I stabbed not,
    king, at thee,
But him, that caitiff, blood-defiled, who stood beside thy
    knee :
Eight brothers were we, — in the land might none more
    loving be, —
They all are slain by Quadros' hand, — they all are dead but
    me.

"Good king, I fain would wash the stain, — for vengeance is
    my cry ;
This murderer with sword and spear to battle I defy."
But all took part with Quadros, except one lovely May, —
Except the king's fair daughter, none word for him would
    say.

She took their hands, she led them forth into the court
    below ;
She bade the ring be guarded, she bade the trumpet blow ;
From lofty place, for that stern race, the signal she did
    throw, —
"With truth and right the Lord will fight ; together let
    them go."

The one is up, the other down, the hunter's knife is bare ;
It cuts the lace beneath the face, it cuts through beard and
    hair ;

Right soon that knife hath quenched his life, — the head is
    sundered sheer;
Then gladsome smiled the Avenging Childe, and fixed it on
    his spear.

But when the king beholds him bring that token of his
    truth,
Nor scorn nor wrath his bosom hath, — "Kneel down, thou
    noble youth;
Kneel down, kneel down, and kiss my crown, I am no more
    thy foe;
My daughter now may pay the vow she plighted long ago."

FAIR SUFFERERS.

BY fair sufferers we mean about ninety-nine out of every
hundred of those poor dear young ladies, condemned,
through the accident of their birth, to languish in silk and
satin, beneath the load of a fashionable existence.

Ah! little think the gay licentious paupers, who have no
plays, operas, and evening parties to be forced to go to, and
no carriages to be obliged to ride about in, of the miseries
which are endured by the daughters of affluence!

It is a well-known fact, that scarcely one of those tender
creatures can be in a theatre or a concert-room ten minutes
without being seized with a violent headache, which, more
frequently than not, obliges her to leave before the perform-
ance is over, and drag a brother, husband, lover, or attentive
young man away with her. If spared the headache, how
often is she threatened with a fainting fit, — nay, now and·
then seized with it, — to the alarm and disturbance of her
company! Not happening to feel faint exactly, still there is
a sensation, "a something," as she describes it, "she does n't
know what," which she is almost sure to be troubled with.
Unvisited by these afflictions, nevertheless, either the cold, or

the heat, or the glare of the gas, or some other source of pain, oppresses or excruciates her susceptible nerves. And when we take one such young lady, and put together all the public amusements which she must either go to — or die — in the course of a season ; and when we add up all the head-aches and swoons and the "somethings-she-does-n't-know-what," the shiverings, burnings, and other agonizing sensations which she has undergone by the end of it, the result is an aggregate of torture truly frightful to contemplate.

Suppose she is obliged to walk, — this is sometimes actually the case ; — happy is she if she can go twenty yards without some pain or other, in the side, the back, the shoulder, the great toe. Thus the pleasure of shopping, promenading, or a picnic is imbittered.

If she reads a chapter in a novel, the chances are that her temples throb for it. She tries to embroider a corsair ; doing more than an arm of him at a time strains her eyes. Employ herself in what way she will, she feels fatigued afterwards, and may think herself well off if she is not worse.

Without a care to vex her, save, perhaps, some slight misgivings respecting "the captain," she is unable to rest, though on a couch of down. Exercise would procure her slumber ; but O, she cannot take it !

Whether a little less confinement of the waist, earlier hours, plainer luncheons, more frequent airings in the green fields, and mental and bodily exertion, generally, than what, in these respects, is the fashionable usage, would in any way alleviate the miseries of our "fair sufferers," may be questioned. It may also be inquired how far such miseries are imaginary, and to what extent a trifling exercise of resolution would tend to mitigate them. Otherwise supposing them to be ills that woman is necessarily heiress to, — unavoidable, irremediable, — what torments, what anguish, must fishwomen, washerwomen, charwomen, and haymakers, — to say nothing of servants of all work, — and even ladies' maids, endure every day of their lives !

APPLEDORE IN A STORM. — J. R. Lowell.

HOW looks Appledore in a storm?
       I have seen it when its crags seemed frantic,
   Butting against the mad Atlantic,
When surge on surge would heap enorme,
   Cliffs of emerald topped with snow,
   That lifted and lifted, and then let go
A great white avalanche of thunder,
   A grinding, blinding, deafening ire
Monadnock might have trembled under;
   And the island, whose rock-roots pierce below
   To where they are warmed with the central fire,
You could feel its granite fibres racked,
   As it seemed to plunge with a shudder and thrill
   Right at the breast of the swooping hill,
And to rise again snorting a cataract
Of rage-froth from every cranny and ledge,
   While the sea drew its breath in hoarse and deep,
And the next vast breaker curled its edge,
   Gathering itself for a mightier leap.

North, east, and south there are reefs and breakers
   You would never dream of in smooth weather,
That toss and gore the sea for acres,
   Bellowing and gnashing and snarling together;
Look northward, where Duck Island lies,
And over its crown you will see arise,
Against a background of slaty skies,
   A row of pillars still and white,
   That glimmer, and then are out of sight,
As if the moon should suddenly kiss,
   While you crossed the gusty desert by night,
The long colonnades of Persepolis;
Look southward for White Island light,
   The lantern stands ninety feet o'er the tide;

There is first a half-mile of tumult and fight,
Of dash and roar and tumble and fright,
   And surging bewilderment wild and wide,
Where the breakers struggle left and right,
   Then a mile or more of rushing sea,
And then the lighthouse slim and lone;
And wherever the weight of the ocean is thrown
Full and fair on White Island head,
   A great mist-jotun you will see.
   Lifting himself up silently
High and huge o'er the lighthouse top,
With hands of wavering spray outspread,
   Groping after the little tower,
   That seems to shrink and shorten and cower,
Till the monster's arms of a sudden drop,
   And silently and fruitlessly
   He sinks again into the sea.

You, meanwhile, where drenched you stand,
   Awaken once more to the rush and roar,
And on the rock-point tighten your hand,
As you turn and see a valley deep,
   That was not there a moment before,
Suck rattling down between you and a heap
Of toppling billow, whose instant fall
   Must sink the whole island once for all;
Or watch the silenter, stealthier seas
   Feeling their way to you more and more;
If they once should clutch you high as the knees,
They would whirl you down like a sprig of kelp,
Beyond all reach of hope or help; —
   And such in a storm is Appledore.

I HOLD STILL. — Julius Sturm.

PAIN'S furnace-heat within me quivers,
    God's breath upon the flame doth blow,
And all my heart in anguish shivers,
    And trembles at the fiery glow;
And yet I whisper, As God will!
And in his hottest fire hold still.

He comes and lays my heart, all heated,
    On the hard anvil, minded so
Into his own fair shape to beat it
    With his great hammer, blow on blow;
And yet I whisper, As God will!
And at his heaviest blows hold still.

He takes my softened heart and beats it,
    The sparks fly off at every blow;
He turns it o'er and o'er and heats it,
    And lets it cool and makes it glow;
And yet I whisper, As God will!
And in his mighty hand hold still.

Why should I murmur? for the sorrow
    Thus only longer lived would be;
Its end may come, and will, to-morrow,
    When God has done his work in me;
So I say, trusting, As God will!
And, trusting to the end, hold still.

He kindles for my profit purely
    Affliction's glowing fiery brand,
And all his heaviest blows are surely
    Inflicted by a master hand;
So I say, praying, As God will!
And hope in him, and suffer still.

13*

A THANKSGIVING DINNER. — Mrs. Ann S. Stephens.

> O, I love an old-fashioned thanksgiving,
>   When the crops are all safe in the barn ;
> When the chickens are plump with good living,
>   And the wool is all spun into yarn.
>
> It is pleasant to draw round the table,
>   When uncles and cousins are there,
> And grandpa, who scarcely is able,
>   Sits down in his old oaken chair.
>
> It is pleasant to wait for the blessing,
>   With a heart free from malice and strife,
> While a turkey that 's portly with dressing
>   Lies meekly awaiting the knife.

CHRISTMAS, New Year, the Fourth of July, in short, all the holidays of the year, were crowded into one by Mrs. Gray. During the whole twelve months she commemorated Thanksgiving only. You should have seen the old lady as Thanksgiving week drew near.

You should have seen her surrounded by raisins, black currants, pumpkin sauce, peeled apples, sugar-boxes, and plates of golden butter, her plump hand pearly with flour-dust, the whole kitchen redolent with ginger, allspice, and cloves ! You should have seen her grating orange-peel and nutmegs, the border of her snow-white cap rising and falling to the motion of her hands, and the soft gray hair underneath tucked hurriedly back of the ear on one side, where it had threatened to be in the way.

You should have seen her in that large, splint-bottomed rocking-chair, with a wooden bowl in her capacious lap, and a sharp chopping-knife in her right hand ; with what a soft, easy motion the chopping-knife fell ! with what a quiet and smiling air the dear old lady would take up a quantity of the pow-dered beef on the flat of her knife, and observe, as it show-ered softly down to the tray again, that "meat chopped too fine for mince-pies was sure poison."

Yes, you should have seen Mrs. Gray at this very time, in order to appreciate fully the perfections of an old-fashioned New England housewife. They are departing from the land. Railroads and steamboats are sweeping them away. In a little time this very description will have the dignity of an antique subject. Women who cook their own dinners and take care of the work-hands are getting to be legendary even now.

The day came at last, bland as the smile of a warm heart; a breath of summer seemed whispering with the over-ripe leaves. The sunshine was of that warm, golden yellow which belongs to the autumn. A few hardy flowers glowed in the front yard, richly tinted dahlias, marigolds, chrysanthemums, and China-asters, with the most velvety amaranths, still kept their bloom, for those huge old maples sheltered them like a tent, and flowers always blossomed later in that house than elsewhere. No wonder! Inside and out, all was pleasant and genial. The fall flowers seemed to thrive upon Mrs. Gray's smiles. Her rosy countenance, as she overlooked them, seemed to warm up their leaves like a sunbeam. Everything grew and brightened about her. Everything combined to make this particular Thanksgiving one to be remembered.

Mrs. Gray had done wonders that morning. The dinner was in a most hopeful state of preparation. The great red-crested, imperious-looking turkey, that had strutted away his brief life in the barn-yard, was now snugly bestowed in the oven, — Mrs. Gray had not yet degenerated down to a cooking-stove, — his heavy coat of feathers was scattered to the wind. His head — that arrogant crimson head, that had so often awed the whole poultry-yard — lay all unheeded in the dust, close by the horse-block. There he sat, the poor denuded monarch, turned up in a dripping-pan, simmering himself down in the kitchen oven. Never, in all his pomp, had that bosom been so warm and distended, — yet the huge turkey had been a sad gourmand in his time. A rich thymy odor broke through every pore of his body; drops of luscious gravy dripped down his sides, filling the oven with an unctuous steam that penetrated a crevice in the door, and made the poor Irish girl cross herself devoutly. She felt her spirit so yearning after the good things of earth, and, never having seen Thanksgiving set down in the calendar, was shy of surrendering her heart to a holiday that had no saint to patronize it.

No wonder the odor that stole so insidiously to her nostrils was appetizing, for the turkey had plenty of companionship in the oven. A noble chicken-pie flanked his dripping-pan on the right; a delicate sucking-pig was drawn up to the left wing; in the rear towered a mountain of roast beef, while the mouth of the oven was choked up with a generous Indian pudding. It was an ovenful worthy of New England, worthy of the day.

The hours came creeping on when guests might be expected.

Mrs. Gray was ready for company, and tried her best to remain with proper dignity in the great rocking-chair that she had drawn to a window commanding a long stretch of the road; but every few moments she would start up, bustle across the room, and charge Kitty, the Irish girl, to be careful and watch the oven, to keep a sharp eye on the saucepans in the fireplace, and, above all, to have the mince-pies within range of the fire, that they might receive a gradual and gentle warmth by the time they were wanted. Then she would return to the room, arrange the branches of asparagus that hung laden with red berries over the looking-glass, or dust the spotless table with her handkerchief, just to keep herself busy, as she said.

At last she heard the distant sound of a wagon, turning down the cross-road toward the house. She knew the tramp of her own market horse even at that distance, and seated herself by the window, ready to receive her expected guests with becoming dignity.

The little one-horse wagon came down the road with a sort of dash quite honorable to the occasion. Mrs. Gray's hired man was beginning to enter into the spirit of a holiday; and the old horse himself made everything rattle again, he was so eager to reach home the moment it hove in sight.

The wagon drew up to the door-yard gate with a flourish worthy of the Third Avenue. The hired man sprang out, and, with some show of awkward gallantry, lifted a young girl in a pretty pink calico dress and a cottage bonnet down from the front seat. Mrs. Gray could maintain her position no longer ; for the young girl glanced that way with a look so eloquent, a smile so bright, that it warmed the dear old lady's heart like a flash of fire in the winter time. She started up, hastily shook loose the folds of her dress, and went out, rustling all the way like a tree in autumn.

"You are welcome, dear, — welcome as green peas in June, or radishes in March," she cried, seizing the little hand held toward her, and kissing the heavenly young face.

The girl turned with a bright look, and, making a graceful little wave of the hand toward an aged man who was tenderly helping a female from the wagon, seemed about to speak.

"I understand, dear, I know all about it ! the good old people, — grandpa and grandma, of course. How could I help knowing them ?" Mrs. Gray went up to the old people as she spoke, with a bland welcome in every feature of her face.

"Know them, of course I do !" she said, enfolding the old gentleman's hand with her plump fingers. "I — I — gracious goodness, now, it really does seem as if I had seen that face somewhere !" she added, hesitating, and with her eyes fixed doubtingly on the stranger, as if she were calling up some vague remembrance, — "strange, now is n't it ? but he looks natural as life."

The old man turned a warming glance toward his wife, and then answered, with a grave smile, "that, at any rate, Mrs. Gray could never be a stranger to them, — she who had done so much — "

She interrupted him with one of her mellow laughs. Thanks for a kind act always made the good woman feel awkward, and she blushed like a girl.

All truly benevolent persons shrink from spoken thanks. The gratitude expressed by looks and actions may give pleasure, but there is something too material in words, — they destroy all the refinement of a generous action. Good Mrs. Gray felt this the more sensitively, because her own words had seemed to challenge the thanks of her guest. The color came into her smooth cheek, and she began to arrange the folds of her dress with both hands, exhibiting a degree of awkwardness quite unusual to her. When she lifted her eyes again, they fell upon a young man coming down the cross-road on foot, with an eager and buoyant step.

"There he comes; I thought he would not be long on the way," she cried, while a flash of gladness radiated her face. "It's my nephew; you see him there, Mrs. Warren, — no, the maple branch is in the way! Here he is again, — now look! a noble fellow, is n't he?"

Mrs. Warren looked, and was indeed struck by the free air and superior appearance of the youth. He had evidently walked some distance, for a light over-sack hung across his arm, and his face was flushed with exercise. Seeing his aunt, the boy waved his hand; his lips parted in a joyous smile, and he hastened his pace almost to a run.

Mrs. Gray's little brown eyes glistened; she could not turn them from the youth even while addressing her guest.

"Is n't he handsome? and good, — you have no idea, ma'am, *how* good he is! There, that is just like him, the wild creature!" she continued, as the youth laid one hand upon the door-yard fence, and vaulted over, "right into my flower-beds, trampling over the grass there, — did you ever?"

"Could n't help it, Aunt Sarah," shouted the youth, with a careless laugh, "I'm in a hurry to get home, and the gate is too far off. Three kisses for every flower I tramp down, — will that do? Ha! what little lady is this?"

The last exclamation was drawn forth by Julia Warren, who had seated herself at the foot of the largest maple, and with her lap full of flowers, was arranging them into bouquets. On hearing Robert's voice she looked up with a glance of pleasant surprise, and a smile broke over her lips. There was something so rosy and joyous in his face, and in the tones of his voice, that it rippled through her heart as if a bird overhead had just broken into song. The youth looked upon her for a moment with his bright, gleeful eyes, then, throwing off his hat and sweeping back the damp chestnut curls from his forehead, he sat down by her side, and cast a glance of laughing defiance at his relative.

"Come out here and get the kisses, Aunt Sarah. I have made up my mind to stay among the flowers!"

Mrs. Gray laughed at the young rogue's impudence, as she called it, and came out to meet him.

At that moment the Irish girl came through the front door with an expression of solemn import in her face. She whispered in a flustered manner to her mistress, and the words "spoilt entirely" reached Robert's ear.

Away went the aunt, all in a state of excitement, to the kitchen.

Whatever mischief had happened in the kitchen, the dinner turned out magnificently. The turkey came upon the table a perfect miracle of cookery. The pig absolutely looked more beautiful than life, crouching in his bed of parsley, with his head up, and holding a lemon daintily between his jaws. The chicken-pie, pinched around the edge into a perfect embroidery by the two plump thumbs of Mrs. Gray, and then finished off by an elaborate border done in key work, would have charmed the most fastidious artist.

You have no idea how beautiful colors may be blended on a dinner-table, unless you have seen just the kind of feast to which Mrs. Gray invited her guests. The rich brown of the meats, the snow-white bread, the fresh, golden butter, the cranberry sauce, with its bright, ruby tinge, were daintily mingled with plates of pies, arranged after a most tempting fashion. Golden custard, the deep red tart, the brown mince, and tawny orange color of the pumpkin, were placed in alternate wedges, and, radiating from the centre of each plate like a star, stood at equal distances round the table. Water sparkling from the well, currant wine brilliantly red, contrasted with the sheeted snow of the tablecloth ; and the gleam of crystal ; then that old arm-chair at the head of the table, with its soft crimson cushions. I tell you again, reader, it was a Thanksgiving dinner worthy to be remembered. That poor family from the miserable basement in New York did remember it for many a weary day after. Mrs. Gray remembered it, for she had given delicious pleasure to those old people. She had, for that one day at least, lifted them from their toil and depression.

———◆———

THE WOLVES.—J. T. TROWBRIDGE.

YE that listen to stories told,
   When hearths are cheery and nights are cold,
Of the lone woodside, and the hungry pack
That howls on the fainting traveller's track,
The flame-red eyeballs that waylay,
By the wintry moon, the belated sleigh ;
The lost child sought in the dismal wood,
The little shoes, and the stains of blood
On the trampled snow, — ye that hear
With thrills of pity, or chills of fear,
Wishing some kind angel had been sent
To shield the hapless innocent, —
Know ye the fiend that is crueller far
Than the gaunt, gray herds of the forest are ?
Swiftly vanish the wild fleet tracks
Before the rifle and the woodman's axe.
But hark to the coming of unseen feet,
Pattering by night through the city street.
Each wolf that dies in the woodland brown
Lives a spectre, and haunts the town !
By square and market they slink and prowl,
In lane and alley they leap and howl ;
All night long they snuff and snarl before

The patched window and the broken door.
They paw the clapboards, and claw the latch ;
At every crevice they whine and scratch.
Children, crouched in corners cold,
Shiver, with tattered garments old ;
They start from sleep with bitter pangs
At the touch of the phantom's viewless fangs.
Weary the mother, and worn with strife,
Still she watches, and fights for life ;
But her hand is feeble, and her weapon small, —
One little needle, against them all.
In evil hour the daughter fled
From her poor shelter and wretched bed,
Through the city's pitiless solitude
To the door of sin, — the wolves pursued !
Fierce the father, and grim with want,
His heart was gnawed by the spectres gaunt.
Frenzied, stealing forth by night,
With whetted knife for the desperate fight,
He thought to strike the spectres dead, —
But killed his brother man instead.

O ye that listen to stories told
When hearths are cheery and nights are cold,
Weep no more at the tales you hear,
The danger is *close*, and the wolves are *near !*
Shudder not at the murderer's name,
Marvel not at the maiden's shame ;
Pass not by, with averted eye,
The door where the stricken children cry.
But when the beat of the unseen feet
Sound by night through the city street,
Follow thou, where the spectres glide
And stand, like hope, at the mother's side ;
And be *thyself* the angel sent
To shield the hapless innocent.
He gives but little who gives his tears,

T

He gives best who aids and cheers.
He does well in the forest wild
Who slays the monster and saves the child;
He does better, and merits more,
Who drives the wolf from the poor man's door.

————◆————

THE BANNER OF THE COVENANTERS. — C. E. Norton.

[One of the banners formerly belonging to the Covenanters is preserved among other curiosities at Mareschal College, Aberdeen. It is of white silk, with the motto "Spe Expecto" in red letters.]

WAKE! wave aloft, thou Banner! let every snowy fold
  Float on our wild, unconquered hills, as in the days
    of old;
Hang out, and give again to death a glory and a charm,
Where heaven's pure dew may freshen thee, and heaven's pure
    sunshine warm.
Wake! wave aloft! — I hear the silk low rustling on the
    breeze
Which whistles through the lofty fir, and bends the birchen
    trees.
I hear the tread of warriors armed to conquer or to die;
Their bed or bier the heathery hill, their canopy the sky.

What, what is life or death to them? *They* only feel and know
Freedom is to be struggled for, with an unworthy foe, —
Their homes, — their hearths, — the all for which their fathers,
    too, have fought,
And liberty to breathe the prayers their cradled lips were
    taught.
On, on they rush, — like mountain streams resistlessly they
    sweep, —
On! those who live are heroes now, — and martyrs those who
    sleep!

While still the snow-white Banner waves above the field of
    strife,
With a proud triumph, as it were a thing of soul and life.

They stand, — they bleed, — they fall! they make one brief
    and breathless pause,
And gaze with fading eyes upon the standard of their
    cause ; —
Again they brave the strife of death, again each weary limb
Faintly obeys the warrior soul, though earth's best hopes grow
    dim ; —
The mountain rills are red with blood ; the pure and quiet sky
Rings with the shouts of those who win, the groans of those
    who die ;
Taken, — retaken, — raised again, but soiled with clay and
    gore,
Heavily, on the wild free breeze, that Banner floats once
    more.

Heaven's dew hath drunk the crimson drops which on the
    heather lay,
The rills that were so red with gore go sparkling on their
    way ;
The limbs that fought, the hearts that swelled, are crumbled
    into dust ;
The souls which strove are gone to meet the spirits of the
    just ; —
But that frail silken flag for which, and under which, they
    fought
(And which e'en *now* retains its power upon the soul of
    thought)
Survives, — a tattered, senseless thing, — to meet the curious
    eye,
And wake a momentary dream of hopes and days gone by.

A momentary dream ! O, not for *one* poor transient hour,
Not for a brief and hurried day that flag exerts its power !

Full flashing on our dormant souls the firm conviction comes,
That what our fathers did for *theirs,* we too could for *our*
homes.
We, *too,* could brave the giant arm that seeks to chain each
word,
And rule what form of prayer alone shall by our God be heard ;
We, too, in triumph or defeat, could drain our heart's best
veins, .
While the good old cause of Liberty for Church and State
remains !

———————

HERVE RIEL. — ROBERT BROWNING.

ON the sea and at the Hogue, sixteen hundred ninety-two,
Did the English fight the French, — woe to France !
And, the thirty-first of May, helter-skelter through the blue,
Like a crowd of frightened porpoises a shoal of sharks pursue,
Came crowding ship on ship to St. Malo on the Rance,
With the English fleet in view.

'T was the squadron that escaped, with the victor in full
chase,
First and foremost of the drove, in his great ship, Damfre-
ville ;
Close on him fled, great and small,
Twenty-two good ships in all ;
And they signalled to the place,
" Help the winners of a race !
Get us guidance, give us harbor, take us quick, — or,
quicker still,
Here 's the English can and will ! "

Then the pilots of the place put out brisk and leaped on
board.
" Why, what hope or chance have ships like these to pass ? "
laughed they ;

"Rocks to starboard, rocks to port, all the passage scarred
        and scored,
Shall the Formidable here, with her twelve and eighty guns,
    Think to make the river-mouth by the single narrow way,
Trust to enter where 't is ticklish for a craft of twenty tons,
        And with flow at full beside?
        Now 't is slackest ebb of tide.
    Reach the mooring? Rather say,
While rock stands or water runs,
    Not a ship will leave the bay!"

Then was called a council straight;
Brief and bitter the debate:
"Here 's the English at our heels; would you have them
        take in tow
All that 's left us of the fleet, linked together stern and bow,
For a prize to Plymouth Sound?
Better run the ships aground!"
    (Ended Damfreville his speech.)
"Not a minute more to wait!
    Let the captains all and each
    Shove ashore, then blow up, burn the vessels on the beach!
France must undergo her fate."

"Give the word!"   But no such word
Was ever spoke or heard;
    For up stood, for out stepped, for in struck amid all these, —
A captain? A lieutenant? A mate, — first, second, third?
        No such man of mark, and meet
        With his betters to compete!
        But a simple Breton sailor pressed by Tourville for the
        fleet, —
    A poor coasting-pilot he, Hervé Riel the Croisickese.

And "What mockery or malice have we here?" cries Hervé
        Riel;
    Are you mad, you Malouins? Are you cowards, fools, or
        rogues?

Talk to me of rocks and shoals, me who took the soundings,
  tell
On my fingers every bank, every shallow, every swell
  'Twixt the offing here and Grève, where the river disem-
    bogues?
Are you bought by English gold? Is it love the lying 's for?
    Morn and eve, night and day,
    Have I piloted your bay,
Entered-free and anchored fast at the foot of Solidor.
    Burn the fleet, and ruin France? That were worse than
      fifty Hogues!
      Sirs, they know I speak the truth! Sirs, believe me,
        there 's a way!
Only let me lead the line,
    Have the biggest ship to steer,
    Get this Formidable clear,
Make the others follow mine,
And I lead them most and least by a passage I know well,
    Right to Solidor, past Grève,
      And there lay them safe and sound;
      And if one ship misbehave, —
        Keel so much as grate the ground, —
Why, I 've nothing but my life; here 's my head!" cries
    Hervé Riel.

Not a minute more to wait.
"Steer us in, then, small and great!
    Take the helm, lead the line, save the squadron!" cried its
      chief.
Captains, give the sailor place!
    He is admiral, in brief.
Still the north-wind, by God's grace.
See the noble fellow's face
As the big ship, with a bound,
Clears the entry like a hound,
Keeps the passage as its inch of way were the wide sea's
    profound!

See, safe through shoal and rock,
  How they follow in a flock.
Not a ship that misbehaves, not a keel that grates the
      ground,
  Not a spar that comes to grief !
The peril, see, is past,
All are harbored to the last ;
And just as Hervé Riel hollas " Anchor ! " — sure as fate,
Up the English come, too late.

So the storm subsides to calm ;
  They see the green trees wave
    On the heights o'erlooking Grève :
Hearts that bled are stanched with balm.
" Just our rapture to enhance,
  Let the English rake the bay,
Gnash their teeth and glare askance
  As they cannonade away !
'Neath rampired Solidor pleasant riding on the Rance ! "
How hope succeeds despair on each captain's countenance !
Outburst all with one accord,
  " This is Paradise for Hell !
    Let France, let France's King
    Thank the man that did the thing ! "
What a shout, and all one word,
  " Hervé Riel,"
As he stepped in front once more,
  Not a symptom of surprise
  In the frank blue Breton eyes,
Just the same man as before.

Then said Damfreville, " My friend,
I must speak out at the end,
  Though I find the speaking hard :
Praise is deeper than the lips ;
You have saved the king his ships,
  You must name your own reward.

Faith, our sun was near eclipse !
Demand whate'er you will,
France remains your debtor still.
Ask to heart's content, and have ! or my name 's not Damfre-
      ville."

Then a beam of fun outbroke
On the bearded mouth that spoke,
As the honest heart laughed through
Those frank eyes of Breton blue :
" Since I needs must say my say,
    Since on board the duty 's done,
      And from Malo Roads to Croisic Point, what is it but a
      run ? —
Since 't is ask and have I may, —
    Since the others go ashore, —
Come !   A good whole holiday !
    Leave to go and see my wife, whom I call the Belle
      Aurore ! "
    That he asked, and that he got, — nothing more.

Name and deed alike are lost ;
Not a pillar nor a post
    In his Croisic keeps alive the feat as it befell ;
Not a head in white and black
On a single fishing-smack,
In memory of the man but for whom had gone to wrack
    All that France saved from the fight whence England bore
      the bell.
Go to Paris ; rank on rank
    Search the heroes flung pell-mell
On the Louvre, face and flank ;
    You shall look long enough ere you come to Hervé Riel.
So, for better and for worse,
Hervé Riel, accept my verse !
In my verse, Hervé Riel, do thou once more
Save the squadron, honor France, love thy wife the Belle
    Aurore !

THE BESIEGED CASTLE. — Scott.

[Ivanhoe, an English knight, has been taken prisoner by the Normans, and is lying wounded and helpless in a chamber of the castle, under the care of Rebecca, the Jewess, who is also a prisoner.]

IN finding herself once more by the side of Ivanhoe, Rebecca was astonished at the keen sensation of pleasure which she experienced, even at a time when all around them both was danger, if not despair. As she felt his pulse, and inquired after his health, there was a softness in her touch and in her accents, implying a kinder interest than she would herself have been pleased to have voluntarily expressed. Her voice faltered and her hand trembled, and it was only the cold question of Ivanhoe, "Is it you, gentle maiden?" which recalled her to herself, and reminded her the sensations which she felt were not and could not be mutual. A sigh escaped, but it was scarce audible; and the questions which she asked the knight concerning his state of health were put in the tone of calm friendship. Ivanhoe answered her hastily that he was, in point of health, as well and better than he could have expected, — "thanks," he said, "dear Rebecca, to thy helpful skill."

"He calls me *dear* Rebecca," said the maiden to herself, "but it is in the cold and careless tone which ill suits the word. His war-horse, his hunting hound, are dearer to him than the despised Jewess!"

"My mind, gentle maiden," continued Ivanhoe, "is more disturbed by anxiety than my body with pain. From the speeches of these men who were my warders just now, I learn that I am a prisoner, and, if I judge aright of the loud hoarse voice which even now despatched them hence on some military duty, I am in the castle of Front-de-Bœuf. If so, how will this end, or how can I protect Rowena and my father?"

"He names not the Jew or Jewess," said Rebecca, internally; "yet what is our portion in him, and how justly am I punished by Heaven for letting my thoughts dwell upon

14

him!" She hastened, after this brief self-accusation, to give Ivanhoe what information she could; but it amounted only to this, that the Templar Bois-Guilbert and the Baron Front-de-Bœuf were commanders within the castle; that it was beleaguered from without, but by whom she knew not.

The voices of the knights were heard, animating their followers, or directing means of defence, while their commands were often drowned in the clashing of armor, or the clamorous shouts of those whom they addressed. Tremendous as these sounds were, and yet more terrible from the awful event which they presaged, there was a sublimity mixed with them, which Rebecca's high-toned mind could feel even in that moment of terror. Her eye kindled, although the blood fled from her cheeks; and there was a strong mixture of fear and of a thrilling sense of the sublime, as she repeated, half whispering to herself, half speaking to her companion, the sacred text, — "The quiver rattleth, the glittering spear and the shield, the noise of the captains and the shouting!"

But Ivanhoe was like the war-horse of that sublime passage, glowing with impatience at his inactivity, and with his ardent desire to mingle in the affray of which these sounds were the introduction. "If I could but drag myself," he said, "to yonder window, that I might see how this brave game is like to go, — if I had but a bow to shoot a shaft, or battle-axe to strike were it but a single blow for our deliverance! It is vain, — it is vain, — I am alike nerveless and weaponless!"

"Fret not thyself, noble knight," answered Rebecca; "the sounds have ceased of a sudden, — it may be they join not battle."

"Thou knowest naught of it," said Ivanhoe, impatiently; "this dead pause only shows that the men are at their posts on the walls, and expecting an instant attack; what we have heard was but the distant muttering of the storm, — it will burst anon in all its fury. Could I but reach yonder window!"

"Thou wilt but injure thyself by the attempt, noble

knight," replied his attendant. Observing his extreme solicitude, she firmly added, " I myself will stand at the lattice, and describe to you as I can what passes without."

" You must not, — you shall not ! " exclaimed Ivanhoe ; " each lattice, each aperture, will be soon a mark for the archers ; some random shaft — "

" It shall be welcome ! " murmured Rebecca, as with firm pace she ascended two or three steps, which led to the window of which they spoke.

" Rebecca, dear Rebecca ! " exclaimed Ivanhoe, " this is no maiden's pastime, — do not expose thyself to wounds and death, and render me forever miserable for having given the occasion ; at least, cover thyself with yonder ancient buckler, and show as little of your person at the lattice as may be."

Following with wonderful promptitude the directions of Ivanhoe, and availing herself of the protection of the large ancient shield, which she placed against the lower part of the window, Rebecca, with tolerable security to herself, could witness part of what was passing without the castle, and report to Ivanhoe the preparations which the assailants were making for the storm. She could observe, from the number of men placed for the defence of this post, that the besieged entertained apprehensions for its safety ; and from the mustering of the assailants in a direction nearly opposite to the outwork, it seemed no less plain that it had been selected as a vulnerable point of attack.

These appearances she hastily communicated to Ivanhoe, and added, " The skirts of the wood seem lined with archers, although only a few are advanced from its dark shadow."

" Under what banner ? " asked Ivanhoe.

" Under no ensign of war which I can observe," answered Rebecca.

" A singular novelty," muttered the knight, " to advance to storm such a castle without pennon or banner displayed ! Seest thou who they be that act as leaders ? "

" A knight, clad in sable armor, is the most conspicuous,"

said the Jewess; "he alone is armed from head to heel, and seems to assume the direction of all around him."

"What device does he bear on his shield?" replied Ivanhoe.

"Something resembling a bar of iron, and a padlock painted blue on the black shield!"

"A fetterlock and shacklebolt azure," said Ivanhoe; "I know not who may bear the device, but well I ween it might now be mine own. Canst thou not see the motto?"

"Scarce the device itself at this distance," replied Rebecca; "but when the sun glances fair upon his shield, it shows as I tell you."

"Seem there no other leaders?" exclaimed the anxious inquirer.

"None of mark and distinction that I can behold from this station," said Rebecca; "but, doubtless, the other side of the castle is also assailed. They appear even now preparing to advance. God of Zion, protect us! What a dreadful sight! Those who advance first bear huge shields, and defences made of plank; the others follow, bending their bows as they come on. They raise their bows! God of Moses, forgive the creatures thou hast made!"

Her description was here suddenly interrupted by the signal for assault, which was given by the blast of a shrill bugle, and at once answered by a flourish of the Norman trumpets from the battlements, which, mingled with the deep and hollow clang of the kettle-drums, retorted in notes of defiance the challenge of the enemy. The shouts of both parties augmented the fearful din, the assailants crying, "Saint George for merry England!" and the Normans answering them with cries of "*En avant De Bracy! — Beau-seant! Beau-seant! — Front-de-Bœuf à la rescousse!*" according to the war-cries of their different commanders.

"And I must lie here like a bedridden monk," exclaimed Ivanhoe, "while the game that gives me freedom or death is played out by the hand of others! Look from the window once again, kind maiden, but beware that you are not marked by the archers beneath. Look out once more, and tell me if they yet advance to the storm."

With patient courage, strengthened by the interval which she had employed in mental devotion, Rebecca again took post at the lattice, sheltering herself, however, so as not to be visible from beneath.

"What dost thou see, Rebecca?" again demanded the wounded knight.

"Nothing but the cloud of arrows flying so thick as to dazzle mine eyes, and to hide the bowmen who shoot them."

"That cannot endure," said Ivanhoe; "if they press not right on to carry the castle by pure force of arms, the archery may avail but little against stone walls and bulwarks. Look for the Knight of the Fetterlock, fair Rebecca, and see how he bears himself; for as the leader is, so will his followers be."

"I see him not," said Rebecca.

"Foul craven!" exclaimed Ivanhoe; "does he blench from the helm when the wind blows highest?"

"He blenches not! he blenches not!" said Rebecca. "I see him now; he heads a body of men close under the outer barrier of the barbican. They pull down the piles and palisades; they hew down the barriers with axes. His high black plume floats abroad over the throng, like a raven over the field of the slain. They have made a breach in the barriers, — they rush in, — they are thrust back! Front-de-Bœuf heads the defenders; I see his gigantic form above the press. They throng again to the breach, and the pass is disputed hand to hand, and man to man. God of Jacob! it is the meeting of two fierce tides, — the conflict of two oceans moved by adverse winds!"

She turned her head from the lattice, as if unable longer to endure a sight so terrible.

"Look forth again, Rebecca," said Ivanhoe, mistaking the cause of her retiring; "the archery must in some degree have ceased, since they are now fighting hand to hand. Look again, there is now less danger."

Rebecca again looked forth, and almost immediately exclaimed, " Holy prophets of the law ! Front-de-Bœuf and the Black Knight fight hand to hand on the breach, amid the roar of their followers, who watch the progress of the strife. Heaven strike with the cause of the oppressed and of the captive ! " She then uttered a loud shriek, and exclaimed, " He is down ! — he is down ! "

" Who is down ? " cried Ivanhoe ; " for our dear Lady's sake, tell me which has fallen ? "

" The Black Knight," answered Rebecca, faintly ; then instantly again shouted with joyful eagerness, " But no, — but no ! — the name of the Lord of Hosts be blessed ! — he is on foot again, and fights as if there were twenty men's strength in his single arm. His sword is broken, — he snatches an axe from a yeoman, — he presses Front-de-Bœuf with blow on blow. The giant stoops and totters like an oak under the steel of the woodman, — he falls, — he falls ! "

" Front-de-Bœuf ? " exclaimed Ivanhoe.

" Front-de-Bœuf ! " answered the Jewess ; " his men rush to the rescue, headed by the haughty Templar, — their united force compels the champion to pause, — they drag Front-de-Bœuf within the walls."

" The assailants have won the barriers, have they not ? " said Ivanhoe.

" They have, — they have ! " exclaimed Rebecca, "and they press the besieged hard upon the outer wall ; some plant ladders, some swarm like bees, and endeavor to ascend upon the shoulders of each other, — down go stones, beams, and trunks of trees upon their heads, and as fast as they bear the wounded to the rear, fresh men supply their places in the assault. Great God ! hast thou given men thine own image, that it should be thus cruelly defaced by the hands of their brethren ? "

" Think not of that," said Ivanhoe ; " this is no time for such thoughts. Who yield ? — who push their way ? "

" The ladders are thrown down," replied Rebecca, shuddering ; " the soldiers lie grovelling under them like crushed reptiles. The besieged have the better."

"Saint George strike for us!" exclaimed the knight; "do the false yeomen give way?"

"No!" exclaimed Rebecca, "they bear themselves right yeomanly. The Black Knight approaches the postern with his huge axe, — the thundering blows which he deals, you may hear them above all the din and shouts of the battle. Stones and beams are hailed down on the bold champion, — he regards them no more than if they were thistle-down or feathers!"

"By Saint John of Acre," said Ivanhoe, raising himself joyfully on his couch, "methought there was but one man in England that might do such a deed!"

"The postern-gate shakes," continued Rebecca; "it crashes, — it is splintered by his blows, — they rush in, — the outwork is won, — O God! — they hurl the defenders from the battlements, — they throw them into the moat. O men, if ye be indeed men, spare them that can resist no longer!"

"The bridge, — the bridge which communicates with the castle, — have they won that pass?" exclaimed Ivanhoe.

"No," replied Rebecca, "the Templar has destroyed the plank on which they crossed, — few of the defenders escaped with him into the castle, — the shrieks and cries which you hear tell the fate of the others, — alas! I see it is still more difficult to look upon victory than upon battle."

"What do they now, maiden?" said Ivanhoe; "look forth yet again, — this is no time to faint at bloodshed."

"It is over for the time," answered Rebecca; "our friends strengthen themselves within the outwork which they have mastered; and it affords them so good a shelter from the foemen's shot, that the garrison only bestow a few bolts on it from interval to interval, as if rather to disquiet than effectually to injure them."

"Our friends," said Ivanhoe, "will surely not abandon an enterprise so gloriously begun and so happily attained. O no! I will put my faith in the good knight whose axe hath rent heart-of-oak and bars of iron. Seest thou naught else, Rebecca, by which the Black Knight may be distinguished?"

"Nothing," said the Jewess; "all about him is black as the wing of the night raven. Nothing can I spy that can mark him further, — but having once seen him put forth his strength in battle, methinks I could know him again among a thousand warriors. He rushes to the fray as if he were summoned to a banquet. There is more than mere strength; there seems as if the whole soul and spirit of the champion were given to every blow which he deals upon his enemies. It is fearful, yet magnificent, to behold how the arm and heart of one man can triumph over hundreds."

"Rebecca," said Ivanhoe, "thou hast painted a hero; surely they rest but to refresh their force, or to provide the means of crossing the moat. Under such a leader as thou hast spoken this knight to be, there are no craven fears, no cold-blooded delays, no yielding up a gallant emprise; since the difficulties which render it arduous render it also glorious. I swear by the honor of my house, I vow by the name of my bright lady-love, would endure ten years' captivity to fight one day by that good knight's side in such a quarrel as this!"

"Alas!" said Rebecca, leaving her station at the window, and approaching the couch of the wounded knight, "this impatient yearning after action, this struggling with and repining at your present weakness, will not fail to injure your returning health. How couldst thou hope to inflict wounds on others ere that be healed which thou thyself hast received?"

"Rebecca," he replied, "thou knowest not how impossible it is for one trained to actions of chivalry to remain passive as a priest or a woman, when they are acting deeds of honor around him. The love of battle is the food upon which we live, — the dust of the *mêlée* is the breath of our nostrils! We live not, we wish not to live longer than while we are victorious and renowned. Such, maiden, are the laws of chivalry to which we are sworn, and to which we offer all that we hold dear.

"Thou art no Christian, Rebecca; and to thee are unknown those high feelings which swell the bosom of a noble maiden when her lover hath done some deed of emprise which sanctions his flame. Chivalry! — why, maiden, she is the nurse of pure and high affection, the stay of the oppressed, the redresser of grievances, the curb of the power of the tyrant. Nobility were but an empty name without her, and liberty finds the best protection in her lance and her sword."

"How little he knows this bosom," she said, "to imagine that cowardice or meanness of soul must needs be its guests, because I have censured the fantastic chivalry of the Nazarenes! Would to Heaven that the shedding of mine own blood, drop by drop, could redeem the captivity of Judah! Nay, would to God it could avail to set free my father, and this his benefactor, from the chains of the oppressor! The proud Christian should then see whether the daughter of God's chosen people dared not to die as bravely as the vainest Nazarene maiden, that boasts her descent from some petty chieftain of the rude and frozen North!"

She then looked toward the couch of the wounded knight.

"He sleeps," she said; "nature exhausted by sufferance and the waste of spirits, his wearied frame embraces the first moment of temporary relaxation to sink into slumber. Alas! is it a crime that I should look upon him, when it may be for the last time? When yet but a short space, and those fair features will be no longer animated by the bold and buoyant spirit which forsakes them not even in sleep! But I will tear this folly from my heart, though every fibre bleed as I rend it away!"

She wrapped herself closely in her veil, and sat down at a distance from the couch of the wounded knight, with her back turned towards it, fortifying, or endeavoring to fortify her mind, not only against the impending evils from without, but also against those treacherous feelings which assailed her from within.

Ivanhoe was awakened from his brief slumber by the noise of the battle; and his attendant, who had, at his anxious desire, again placed herself at the window to watch and report to him the fate of the attack, was for some time prevented from observing either, by the increase of the smouldering and stifling vapor. At length the volumes of smoke which rolled into the apartment, the cries for water, which were heard even above the din of the battle, made them sensible of the progress of this new danger.

"The castle burns," said Rebecca; "it burns! What can we do to save ourselves?"

"Fly, Rebecca, and save thine own life," said Ivanhoe, "for no human aid can avail me."

"I will not fly," answered Rebecca; "we will be saved or perish together!"

At this moment the door of the apartment flew open, and the Templar presented himself, — a ghastly figure, for his gilded armor was broken and bloody, and the plume was partly shorn away, partly burnt from his casque. "I have found thee," said he to Rebecca. "There is but one path to safety; I have cut my way through fifty dangers to point it to thee, — up, and instantly follow me."

"Alone," answered Rebecca, "I will not follow thee. If thou hast but a touch of human charity in thee, if thy heart be not as hard as thy breastplate, save this wounded knight!"

"A knight," answered the Templar, with his characteristic calmness, — "a knight, Rebecca, must encounter his fate, whether it meet him in the shape of sword or flame."

So saying, he seized on the terrified maiden.

At that instant the Black Knight entered the apartment.

"If thou be'st true knight," said Ivanhoe, "think not of me, save the Lady Rowena, look to the noble Cedric!"

"In their turn," answered he of the fetterlock; "but thine is first."

And, seizing upon Ivanhoe, he bore him off with as much ease as the Templar had carried off Rebecca, rushed with him to the postern, and having there delivered his burden to the care of two yeomen, he again entered the castle to assist in the rescue of the other prisoners.

One turret was now in bright flames, which flashed out furiously from window and shot-hole.

The towering flames had soon surmounted every obstruction, and rose to the evening skies one huge and burning beacon, seen far and wide through the adjacent country. Tower after tower crashed down, with blazing roof and rafter; and the combatants were driven from the court-yard. The vanquished, of whom very few remained, scattered and escaped into the neighboring wood. The victors, assembling in large bands, gazed with wonder, not unmixed with fear, upon the flames, in which their own ranks and arms glanced dusky red. At length, with a terrific crash, the whole turret gave way. The voice of Locksley was then heard, "Shout, yeomen!— the den of tyrants is no more!"

A VISION OF BATTLE. — S. DOBELL.

HIST! I see the stir of glamour far upon the twilight
    wold.
Hist! I see the vision rising! List! and as I speak behold!
These dull mists are mists of morning, and behind yon eastern hill
The hot sun abides my bidding; he shall melt them when I
    will.
All the night that now is past, the foe hath labored for the day,
Creeping through the stealthy dark, like a tiger to his prey.

Throw this window wider! Strain thine eyes along the dusky
    vale!
Art thou cold with horror? Has thy bearded cheek grown
    pale?
'T is the total Russian host, flooding up the solemn plain,
Secret as a silent sea, mighty as a moving main!

O my country! is there none to rouse thee to the rolling
    sight?

O thou gallant sentinel who hast watched so oft, so well, must
    thou sleep this only night?

So hath the shepherd lain on a rock above a plain,

Nor beheld the flood that swelled from some embowelled
    mount of woe,

Waveless, foamless, sure, and slow,

Silent o'er the vale below,

Till nigher still and nigher comes the seethe of fields on fire,

And the thrash of falling trees, and the steam of rivers dry,

And before the burning flood the wild things of the wood
    Skulk and scream and fight and fall and flee and fly.

A gun! and then a gun! I' the far and early sun
    Dost thou see by yonder tree a fleeting redness rise,

As if, one after one, ten poppies red had blown,
    And shed in a blinking of the eyes?

They have started from their rest with a bayonet at each
    breast,

    Those watchers of the west who shall never watch again!

'T is naught to die, but O, God's pity on the woe
    Of dying hearts that know they die in vain!

Beyond yon backward height that meets their dying sight,
    A thousand tents are white, and a slumbering army lies.

" Brown Bess," the sergeant cries, as he loads her while he
    dies,

" Let this devil's deluge reach them, and the good old cause
    is lost."

He dies upon the word, but his signal gun is heard,
    Yon ambush green is stirred, yon laboring leaves are tost,

And a sudden sabre waves, and like dead from opened graves,
    A hundred men stand up to meet a host.

Dumb as death, with bated breath,

Calm upstand that fearless band,
    And the dear old native land, like a dream of sudden
    sleep,

Passes by each manly eye that is fixed so stern and dry
  On the tide of battle rolling up the steep.

They hold their silent ground, I can hear each fatal sound
  Upon that summer mound which the morning sunshine
    warms,
The word so brief and shrill that rules them like a will,
  The sough of moving limbs, and the clank and ring of
    arms.
" Fire ! " and round that green knoll the sudden war-clouds
    roll,
  And from the tyrant's ranks so fierce an answering blast
Of whirling death came back that the green trees turned to
    black,
  And dropped their leaves in winter as it passed.

A moment on each side the surging smoke is wide,
  Between the fields are green, and around the hills are
    loud,
But a shout breaks out, and lo ! they have rushed upon the
    foe,
  As the living lightning leaps from cloud to cloud.
Fire and flash, smoke and crash,
  The fogs of battle close o'er friends and foes, and they are
    gone !
Alas, thou bright-eyed boy ! alas, thou mother's joy !
  With thy long hair so fair, that didst so bravely lead them
    on !

I faint with pain and fear.   Ah, Heaven ! what do I hear ?
  A trumpet-note so near ?
What are these that race like hunters at a chase ?
  Who are these that run a thousand men as one ?
What are these that crash the trees far in the waving rear ?
Fight on, thou young hero ! there 's help upon the way !
The light horse are coming, the great guns are coming,
  The Highlanders are coming; — good God, give us the day !

Hurrah for the brave and the leal ! Hurrah for the strong
and the true !
Hurrah for the helmets of steel ! Hurrah for the bonnets o'
blue !

A run and a cheer, the Highlanders are here ! a gallop and a
cheer, the light horse are here !
A rattle and a cheer, the great guns are here !
With a cheer they wheel round and face the foe !
As the troopers wheel about, their long swords are out,
With a trumpet and a shout, in they go !
Like a yawning ocean green, the huge host gulfs them in,
But high o'er the rolling of the flood,
Their sabres you may see like lights upon the sea
When the red sun is going down in blood.

As on some Scottish shore, with mountains frowning o'er,
The sudden tempests roar from the glen,
And roll the tumbling sea in billows to the lee,
Came the charge of the gallant Highlandmen !
And as one beholds the sea, though the wind he cannot see,
But by the waves that flee knows its might,
So I tracked the Highland blast by the sudden tide that past
O'er the wild and rolling vast of the fight.
Yes, glory be to God ! they have stemmed the foremost flood !
I lay me on the sod and breathe again !
In the precious moments won, the bugle-call has gone
To the tents where it never rang in vain,
And lo, the landscape wide is red from side to side,
And all the might of England loads the plain !

Like a hot and bloody dawn, across the horizon drawn,
While the host of darkness holds the misty vale,
As glowing and as grand our bannered legions stand,
And England's flag unfolds upon the gale !
At that great sign unfurled, as morn moves o'er the world
When God lifts his standard of light,

With a tumult and a voice, and a rushing mighty noise,
  Our long line moves forward to the fight.

Clarion and clarion defying,
Sounding, resounding, replying,
Trumpets braying, pipers playing, chargers neighing,
Near and far
The to-and-fro storm of the never-done hurrahing,
Through the bright weather-banner and feather rising and
      falling, bugle and fife
Calling, recalling, — for death or for life, —
Our host moved on to the war,
While England, England, England, England, England!
Was blown from line to line near and far,
And like the morning sea, our bayonets you might see,
Come beaming, gleaming, streaming,
Streaming, gleaming, beaming,
Beaming, gleaming, streaming, to the war.

Clarion and clarion defying,
Sounding, resounding, replying,
Trumpets braying, pipers playing, chargers neighing,
Near and far
The to-and-fro storm of the never-done hurrahing,
Through the bright weather, banner and feather rising and
      falling, bugle and fife
Calling, recalling, — for death or for life, —
Our long line moved forward to the war.

————•————

HARMOSAN. — Dean Trench.

NOW the third and fatal conflict for the Persian throne
      was done,
And the Moslem's fiery valor had the crowning victory won.
Harmosan, the last and boldest the invader to defy,
Captive, overborne by numbers, they were bringing forth to die.

Then exclaimed that noble captive, "Lo, I perish in my thirst;
Give me but one drink of water, and let then arrive the
worst!"
In his hand he took the goblet; but awhile the draught for-
bore,
Seeming doubtfully the purpose of the foeman to explore.

Well might then have paused the bravest, for around him
angry foes,
With a hedge of naked weapons, did that lonely man enclose.
"But what fearest thou?" cried the caliph.   "Is it, friend, a
secret blow?
Fear it not! our gallant Moslems no such treacherous dealing
know.

"Thou mayst quench thy thirst securely, for thou shalt not
die before
Thou hast drunk that cup of water, — this reprieve is thine,
— no more!"
Quick the satrap dashed the goblet down to earth with ready
hand,
And the liquid sank forever, lost amid the burning sand.

"Thou hast said that mine my life is, till the water of that
cup
I have drained; then bid thy servants that spilled water
gather up!"
For a moment stood the caliph as by doubtful passions
stirred, —
Then exclaimed, "Forever sacred must remain a monarch's
word.

"Bring another cup, and straightway to the noble Persian
give;
Drink, I said before, and perish, — now I bid thee drink and
live!"

OUR COUNTRY SAVED. — J. R. LOWELL.

BOOM, cannon, boom to all the winds and waves!
Clash out, glad bells, from every rocking steeple!
Banners, advance with triumph, bend your-staves!
   And from every mountain-peak
   Let beacon-fire to answering beacon speak,
   Katahdin tell Monadnock, Whiteface he,
And so leap on in light from sea to sea,
   Till the glad news be sent
   Across a kindling continent,
Making earth feel more firm and air breathe braver:
Be proud! for she is saved, and all have helped to save her!

   She that lifts up the manhood of the poor,
   She of the open soul and open door,
   With room about her hearth for all mankind!
   The fire is dreadful in her eyes no more;
   From her bold front the helm she doth unbind,
   Sends all her handmaid armies back to spin,
   And bids her navies, that so lately hurled
   Their crashing battle, to hold their thunders in,
Swimming like birds of calm along the unharmful shore.

   No challenge sends she to the elder world,
   That looked askance and hated; a light scorn
   Plays o'er her mouth, as round her mighty knees
   She calls her children back, and waits the morn
Of nobler day, enthroned between her subject seas.

   Bow down, dear land, for thou hast found release!
   Thy God, in these distempered days,
   Hath taught thee the sure wisdom of His ways,
   And through thine enemies hath wrought thee peace!
   Bow down in prayer and praise!
No poorest in thy borders but may now
Lift to the juster skies a man's enfranchised brow.

O Beautiful ! my Country ! ours once more !
Smoothing thy gold of war-dishevelled hair
O'er such sweet brows as never other wore,
    And letting thy set lips
      Freed from wrath's pale eclipse,
The rosy edges of their smile lay bare,
What words divine of lover or of poet
Could tell our love and make thee know it,
Among the nations bright beyond compare ?
    What were our lives without thee ?
    What all our lives to save thee ?
    We reck not what we gave thee ;
    We will not dare to doubt thee,
But ask whatever else, and we will dare !

THE BLUE AND THE GRAY. — F. M. FINCH.

[The women of Columbus, Mississippi, animated by nobler sentiments
than are many of their sisters, have shown themselves impartial in their
offerings made to the memory of the dead. They strewed flowers alike
on the graves of the Confederate and of the National soldiers.]

BY the flow of the inland river,
    Whence the fleets of iron have fled,
Where the blades of the grave-grass quiver,
    Asleep are the ranks of the dead ; —
      Under the sod and the dew,
        Waiting the judgment day ; —
      Under the one, the Blue ;
        Under the other, the Gray.

These in the robings of glory,
    Those in the gloom of defeat,
All with the battle-blood gory,
    In the dusk of eternity meet ; —
      Under the sod and the dew,
        Waiting the judgment day ; —

Under the laurel, the Blue ;
Under the willow, the Gray.

From the silence of sorrowful hours
The desolate mourners go,
Lovingly laden with flowers
Alike for the friend and the foe ; —
Under the sod and the dew,
Waiting the judgment day ; —
Under the roses, the Blue ;
Under the lilies, the Gray.

So with an equal splendor
The morning sun-rays fall,
With a touch, impartially tender,
On the blossoms blooming for all ; —
Under the sod and the dew,
Waiting the judgment day ; —
'Broidered with gold, the Blue ;
Mellowed with gold, the Gray.

So, when the summer calleth,
On forest and field of grain
With an equal murmur falleth
The cooling drip of the rain ; —
Under the sod and the dew,
Waiting the judgment day ; —
Wet with the rain, the Blue ;
Wet with the rain, the Gray.

Sadly, but not with upbraiding,
The generous deed was done ;
In the storm of the years that are fading,
No braver battle was won ; —
Under the sod and the dew,
Waiting the judgment day ; —
Under the blossoms, the Blue ;
Under the garlands, the Gray.

No more shall the war-cry sever,
  Or the winding rivers be red;
They banish our anger forever
  When they laurel the graves of our dead!
    Under the sod and the dew,
      Waiting the judgment day; —
    Love and tears for the Blue,
      Tears and love for the Gray.

———◆———

THE SENTRY ON THE TOWER. — Sacristan's Household.

[This incident really occurred in the German war of 1866.]

MIDNIGHT sounded with a thin, jangling voice from the belfry of the old tower of the church at Goldenau as Otto Hemmerich, having toiled up the winding, narrow stone staircase, stepped out upon the roof, prepared to watch through his term of sentinel duty in the dark solitude. Under his feet was the leaden roof, weather-scarred and stained. The platform whereon he could pace was rectangular and very limited. It was bounded on the outer side by a low parapet, scarcely reaching to his knee as he stood.

From the centre of the square tower sprang a tapering spire, which rose to no great height, and was surmounted by a creaking weathercock of gilded copper. Thus, whoso ventured to climb the steep, winding stair, and issue forth on the roof of the belfry by a low, straight doorway, found himself on the narrow strip of leaden roofing which surrounded the spire. To the summit of the spire itself there was no interior way of arriving.

One, two, three, and so on up to twelve, sounded the bell below. The bell, which was the clock's voice, hung nearly ten feet lower than the summit of the tower. Its tone was, as I have said, thin and jangling; yet more thin and jangling were the bells which chimed the quarters, — ting tang, ting tang, ting tang, ting tang, —like the querulous voice of an old man. Thus they sounded to one listening down in the village. Heard nearer, — in the belfry itself, — they had more resonance ; and there remained, after the clappers had ceased to swing, a long, quivering vibration, which seemed to pulse in the very core of the ancient stone-work, and the mouldering beams, and the dry, cracked tiling.

Otto stood by the parapet looking to the southeast as the last hum of the twelfth stroke died away in his ear. The night was dark and moonless ; too dark for it to be possible to see the landscape stretching far below. It was warm, too, as it had been all day ; although at that height, and in the neighborhood of the mountain range, there was not wanting a certain freshness in the air.

Looking downward, all dark, all blank. Only straining his eyes as they grew used to the dimness, Otto could discern a faint, steely gleam from the river, looking as though some soldier had dropped his bright bayonet upon the peaceful meadows. Here and there a blacker spot gloomed mysteriously ; and that he knew was thick tufty woodland. Not a light shone from the village ; not a footstep sounded in its straggling street.

Otto commenced to pace up and down with solitary regularity. One o'clock ; half past one ; two. Well, it was lonely up there, after all. — Ting tang, ting tang, ting tang. A quarter to three. Swoop came a sudden gust of wind, and wailed for a minute or two through the loop-holes and crannies of the spire, and the weathercock creaked up aloft complainingly. Then the atmosphere grew dead calm. It was darker than ever. The sun would rise at about a quarter of four. Otto knew that. He knew also that, according to the saying, " it is always darkest the hour before day." In a little more than an hour would come daylight and his release together.

Hark ! What was that sound, rising upward from the village ? That was surely the roll of a drum ? A single horse clattered up the street. Then there was a bugle-call, distinctly audible in the motionless air. Lights twinkled in more than one casement. What was going on ? The idea of a sudden night-attack by the enemy came into the head of the solitary sentinel watching from the tower; but after a while he dismissed it. There was no sharp crack of a rifle-volley, no crashing of a body of cavalry, no heavy rumbling artillery over the roads. Neither were any voices to be heard, such as would have arisen from the terrified villagers under such circumstances as their home being suddenly turned into a battle-ground.

Otto knelt down, and, leaning his chin on the parapet, listened intently. Surely men were gathering on the open space around the tower. Yes; more and more distinctly he could hear the sound of footsteps. Then another sharp, sudden roll of drums, startling the echoes far and wide. Again a momentary silence. A loud, clear voice giving out the word of command, "March!" — the measured tramp of feet, growing fainter as it receded from the village; doors and casements closed with a rattling noise; then again profound, and, thenceforward, unbroken silence.

"Strange!" thought Otto, as he rose from his knees, after some time. "They must be sending a detachment on toward the frontier. And yet we were so few here, I wonder that they thought it well to divide so small a body." As he turned to resume his march, the first streaks of dawn broke through the darkness in the east, and some birds began to stir in their nests amidst the stone-work of the steeple.

Ting tang, ting tang, ting tang, ting tang. Four o'clock in the morning! Cocks were crowing lustily down below. The swallows were all alive, and darted hither and thither through the fast brightening sky. The chattering of garrulous daws grew more and more voluble, as they flew with busy, flapping wing in and out of their haunts on the spire.

Silver-gray; rose-color; glowing purple and crimson; bright, gorgeous, dazzling gold! There was the sun at last, burnishing the old copper weathercock into temporary brilliancy, and making the river — steely pale erewhile — flash and flow like molten silver. Why, in Heaven's name, did they not come to relieve the guard? There was Otto, however, and

there it behooved him to remain. His duty was clear ; and a
duty that was clear he had never flinched from.

It was full, broad day. The old clock reported the hour to
be half past six. The good people of Goldenau were stirring
about their daily employments. A great portion of the high-
way to the village could be seen from the belfry. But neither
in the near streets and lanes, nor on the distant road, could
Otto discern a glimpse of a soldier's uniform. Not a dark
blue coat was to be seen anywhere. What did it mean ?
What could have become of all his comrades ?

On the other hand, there was an unusual gathering of the
citizens on the public square around the tower. Otto's keen
eyes could plainly see the gestures and the expression of their
faces, and he observed that he himself was obviously the subject of some discussion among them ; for every now and then
an old, stout, stolid-looking man, whom he (Otto) recognized
as the burgomaster of the place, raised his arm and pointed
upward to where the Prussian sentry's form was sharply relieved against the sky on the summit of the belfry-tower.

A faint suspicion of the truth began to dawn in Otto's
mind. He examined his cartridge-box, and made sure that
his rifle was in good working order. Then he stood quite still
at " attention," waiting for what should come next.

What did come next was that the burgomaster advanced
singly from the little crowd of men, on whose skirts a number of women and children were by this time hovering, and,
putting his hollowed hands to his mouth, bellowed out a long
speech, addressed to Otto upon the tower. The long speech
had the effect of making the stout burgomaster very red in the
face, and of exciting very evident approbation among his fel-
low-citizens ; but, further than that, it produced no result
whatever.

Otto shook his head and touched his ears, to signify that he
could not hear, and then stood still again. Upon this the
burgomaster, after giving an angry shrug at the deplorable
waste of his eloquence, beckoned, and waved his arms with an
imperious gesture of command, importing that the sentry was

at once to descend from the altitude of the tower, and appear
in his, the great man's presence on *terra firma.* To this Otto
vouchsafed no kind of reply, but shouldered his rifle, and
coolly resumed his march up and down on the leaden roof.
Coolly in appearance, that is to say ; for, as may be imagined,
his position was not a pleasant one, and he had shrewd misgivings that it would rapidly become decidedly unpleasant.

Two things were clear to him. Firstly, that the detachment of Prussians to which he belonged had left Goldenau ;
and, secondly, that the inhabitants of the place did not expect them to return. Otherwise, the burgomaster's swelling
port would undoubtedly have been modified. How or why
his comrades had gone ; whether they had remembered the
sentinel on the belfry, and purposely left him there, intending
to return ; or whether, in the hurry of a night-alarm, they
had forgotten his existence, and were now in the thick of some
hot skirmish with the foe, he could not tell.

It was well that his course appeared clear in the matter,
and that he needed no long time to decide upon what he should
do, for this is what happened as soon as the burgomaster and
the assembled crowd on the square clearly perceived, by the
sentry's resumption of his march up and down, that he intended to pay no attention to their summons. First the great
man drew back a little from the foot of the tower, and there
gathered around him a group of the chief inhabitants of the
place, who forthwith entered into an animated discussion, as
far as could be gathered by their gestures. Then the burgomaster, being apparently urged into the van by those behind
him, advanced with stately, although rather slow footsteps to
the postern-door, which gave access to the winding staircase
of the tower.

Otto peeped over the parapet, and saw the burgomaster
enter, followed by four or five other men. He was quite uncertain what would be the nature of the colloquy he was now
to hold with the authorities of Goldenau, but he opined that
it would probably not be a pacific one. But he would defend
himself to the uttermost, and had no more idea of abandon-

ing his post on the belfry without due authority from his superiors, than a brave sea-commander has of deserting the deck of his vessel. So he fixed his bayonet firmly, looked to the priming of his piece, and set himself with his back to the steeple, and exactly facing the low doorway which gave access to the roof of the tower.

"There 's no hurry," he told himself, "for the burgomaster is in the van, and it will take him some time to climb all those steps, even if he does not stick by the way in the narrow staircase."

In a few minutes he could hear the panting and puffing of the stout burgomaster, and the sound of his footsteps scraping heavy and springless on the stone steps. Quick as lightning Otto sprang to the doorway; pulled open the heavy oaken door, which opened outward; and remained with fixed bayonet directed toward the winding staircase.

"Yield, Prussian!" cried the burgomaster, huskily. He was not yet in sight, being hidden by a turn of the stairs.

"Who goes there?" answered Otto. "Speak, or I fire!"

"For Heaven's sake, don't fire! don't fire!"

There was a hustling noise on the steps, and a thud, as of some heavy body coming violently in contact with the wall.

"Oh!" exclaimed the voice of one in acute pain. "You have crushed my foot, Mr. Burgomaster! Let me go on if you 're afraid. I 'll tackle him!"

Thereupon the head and shoulders of the miller of Goldenau appeared in the open doorway.

"Go back there, unless you want my bayonet in your body. Back, I say!"

Otto made so threatening and resolute an advance that the miller withdrew in his turn, though much less precipitately than his predecessor, and remained on a lower step, so that his flour-dusted head alone was visible from the door on the roof.

"Come, sentry," said the miller, "don't be a fool! We have something to say to you. You can't refuse to listen."

"I don't know that. You have no business to talk to a

15   v

sentry on guard. And for that matter, you have no business here at all."

"Perhaps you are not aware of one circumstance," said the miller, with something like a sneer; "namely, that your friends have abandoned you here altogether. They are on their march into Bohemia."

"Enough talk! I have nothing to say to you."

"Indeed! But I have something to say to you. You are our prisoner!"

"Pooh!"

The burgomaster's voice was heard from the lower steps, coming muffled by the thick wall. "Hallo, there! Is that Prussian rascal to keep us here all day? Why don't you bring him down?"

"He won't come!"

"Won't come? Nonsense! Drag him down!"

"Would you like to try it, Mr. Burgomaster?"

"The first man who advances within three steps of the doorway I will send my bayonet into," said Otto.

The miller redescended to his friends. The position was rather difficult. The staircase wound like a corkscrew, and was very narrow withal; so that it was impossible to advance up it otherwise than in single file. Now, although *en masse* the Goldenauers were exceedingly anxious to perform the glorious exploit of taking a prisoner of war, no man was to be found willing to risk his individual life in the attempt.

"It would be useless for a broad-built man like myself to venture into the clutches of the rascal," said the burgomaster, looking wistfully at the spare figure of a man in the rear; "but if any light, slim, agile person were to make one spring, one sudden spring, so as to take the Prussian off his guard, I have no doubt the fellow would be captured easily, quite easily."

There was a dead pause. All at once the tavern-keeper made a brilliant suggestion. Why should they not reduce the enemy by famine? The idea was received with enthusiasm. It was resolved that the contumacious sentry should be informed that he would remain aloft there without a bit or drop until such time as he chose to submit himself to the civic authorities, and deliver up his needle-gun into their hands.

Otto listened with grave attention to the decision of the council of war. Then, after a short pause of deliberation, he made answer thus : —

" I am right sorry to find the Goldenauers showing such a bad spirit, and being so blind to which is the good side for the cause of Fatherland. Also I think it my duty to warn you that this trick of yours may have unpleasant consequences to yourselves when my comrades come to relieve me, — as of course they will. But as to your threat of starving me out, that 's all nonsense. I have a good supply of cartridges; I am a good shot ; this tower commands the square, and all the little lanes leading to it ; — and unless I am fed, and well fed, I swear to you solemnly that I will pick off every human being who approaches within a hundred yards of the well yonder to draw water. There ; deliver that message as my answer to the burgòmaster, and try to persuade him that I mean what I say."

With ludicrously chapfallen aspect the miller carried these bold, resolute words to his companions. Deliberations followed, hastened by the shrill importunities of all the women of Goldenau, who had somehow got wind of the matter, and who would rather, so they said, feed twenty Prussians than expose the lives of their husbands and children, not to mention their own. The result was, that Otto was left to sustain a siege on the top of the belfry, — a siege with the unusual circumstance that the besiegers were supplying the garrison with victuals.

For two days this singular state of things lasted ; the sentinel being formally called upon, morning and evening, to yield himself up prisoner, and the citizens being as formally warned that on any failure in the supply of food, the deadly needle-gun should do terrible execution on them and theirs. On the third day the regiment returned, and the guard was relieved.

When Otto descended from his airy station and appeared
on the square, his comrades there assembled greeted him with
a hearty ringing "Hurrah!" · And his captain said a few kind
words, applauding his fidelity and endurance. That was all.
The explanation of his having been abandoned was simply
that in the hurry of an unexpected summons he had been
forgotten. An outpost had received warning of an intended
attack by a party of Austrian cavalry. Their commander
had sent for assistance to the nearest Prussian detachment.
The contemplated attack had not taken place, however, and
Otto's regiment was now in full march to join the main army.

------◆------

BETSY AND I ARE OUT. — WILL M. CARLETON.

DRAW up the papers, lawyer, and make 'em good and stout;
    Things at home are cross-ways, and Betsy and I are out.
We who have worked together so long as man and wife
Must pull in single harness the rest of our nat'ral life.

"What is the matter?" say you. I swan! it's hard to tell!
Most of the years behind us we've passed by very well.
I have no other woman, she has no other man;
Only we've lived together as long as we ever can.

So I have talked with Betsy, and Betsy has talked with me;
So we've agreed together that we can't never agree.
Not that we've catched each other in any terrible crime;
We've been a gatherin' this for years, a little at a time.

There was a stock of temper we both had, for a start,
Though we ne'er suspected 't would take us two apart.
I had my various failings, bred in flesh and bone;
And Betsy, like all good women, had a temper of her own.

First thing I remember whereon we disagreed
Was somethin' concernin' heaven, — a difference in our creed.

We arg'ed the thing at breakfast, we arg'ed the thing at tea;
And the more we arg'ed the question, the more we did n't agree.

And the next that I remember was when we lost a cow;
She had kicked the bucket for certain, — the question was
   only — how?
I held my own opinion, and Betsy another had;
And when we were done a talkin', we both of us was mad.

And the next that I remember, it started in a joke;
But full for a week it lasted, and neither of us spoke.
And the next was when I scolded because she broke a bowl;
And she said I was mean and stingy, and had n't any soul.

And so that bowl kept pourin' dissensions in our cup;
And so that blamed old cow was always a comin' up;
And so that heaven we arg'ed no nearer to us got,
But it gives us a taste of somethin' a thousand times as hot.

And so the thing kept workin', and all the selfsame way;
Always somethin' to arg'e, and somethin' sharp to say.
And down on us come the neighbors, a couple dozen strong,
And lent their kindest sarvice to help the thing along.

And there has been days together — and many a weary week —
We was both of us cross and spunky, and both too proud to
   speak.
And I have been thinkin' and thinkin', the whole of the win-
   ter and fall,
If I can't live kind with a woman, why then I won't at all.

And so I have talked with Betsy, and Betsy has talked with
   me;
And we have agreed together that we can't never agree;
And what is hers shall be hers, and what is mine shall be
   mine,
And I 'll put it in the agreement, and take it to her to sign.

Write on the paper, lawyer, — the very first paragraph, —
Of all the farm and live stock, that she shall have her half;
For she has helped to earn it, through many a weary day,
And it 's nothin' more than justice that Betsy has her
    pay.

Give her the house and homestead; a man can thrive and
    roam,
But women are skeery critters, unless they have a home.
And I have always determined, and never failed to say,
That Betsy never should want a home, if I was taken away.

There is a little hard cash, that 's drawin' tol'rable pay, —
Couple of hundred dollars, laid by for a rainy day, —
Safe in the hands of good men, and easy to get at;
Put in another clause, there, and give her half of that.

Yes, I see you smile, sir, at my givin' her so much;
Yes, divorces is cheap, sir, but I take no stock in such.
True and fair I married her, when she was blithe and young;
And Betsy was al'ays good to me, exceptin' with her tongue.

Once, when I was young as you, and not so smart, perhaps,
For me she mittened a lawyer, and several other chaps;
And all of 'em was flustered, and fairly taken down,
And I for a time was counted the luckiest man in town.

Once, when I had a fever, — I won't forget it soon, —
I was hot as a basted turkey, and crazy as a loon, —
Never an hour went by me, when she was out of sight;
She nursed me true and tender, and stuck to me day and
    night.

And if ever a house was tidy, and ever a kitchen clean,
Her house and kitchen was tidy, as any I ever seen,
And I don't complain of Betsy, or any of her acts,
Exceptin' when we 've quarrelled, and told each other facts.

So draw up the paper, lawyer ; and I 'll go home to-night,
And read the agreement to her, and see if it 's all right ;
And then in the mornin' I 'll sell to a tradin' man I know,
And kiss the child that was left to us, and out in the world
      I 'll go.

And one thing put in the paper, that first to me did n't occur :
That when I am dead at last, she bring me back to her,
And lay me under the maples I planted years ago,
When she and I was happy, before we quarrelled so.

And when she dies, I wish that she would be laid ·by me ;
And, lyin' together in silence, perhaps we will agree.
And if ever we meet in heaven, I would n't think it queer,
If we loved each other better for what we have quarrelled
      here.

———◆———

THE VOLUNTEER'S WIFE. — M. A. Dennison.

" AN' sure I was tould to come to your Honor,
    To see if ye 'd write a few words to me Pat.
He 's gone for a soldier, is Misther O'Connor,
    Wid a sthripe on his arm and a band on his hat.

" An' what 'll ye tell him ?   It ought to be asy
    For sich as yer Honor to spake wid the pen, —
Jist say I 'm all right, and that Mavoorneen Daisy
    (The baby, yer Honor) is betther again.

" For when he went off it 's so sick was the childer
    She niver held up her blue eyes to his face ;
And when I 'd be cryin' he 'd look but the wilder,
    An' say, ' Would you wish for the counthry's disgrace ? '

" So he left her in danger, and me sorely gratin',
    To follow the flag wid an Irishman's joy ; —

O, it 's often I drame of the big drums a batin',
　　An' a bullet gone straight to the heart of me boy.

"An' say will he send me a bit of his money,
　　For the rint an' the docther's bill due in a wake ; —
Well, surely, there 's tears on yer eyelashes, honey !
　　Ah, faith, I 've no right with such freedom to spake.

"You 've overmuch trifling, I 'll not give ye trouble,
　　I 'll find some one willin' — O, what can it be ?
What 's that in the newspaper folded up double ?
　　Yer Honor, don't hide it, but rade it to me.

"What, Patrick O'Connor ! No, no ! 't is some other !
　　Dead ! dead ! no, not him ! 'T is a wake scarce gone by.
Dead ! dead ! why the kiss on the cheek of his mother,
　　It has n't had time yet, yer Honor, to dry.

"Don't tell me ! It 's not him ! O God, am I crazy ?
　　Shot dead ! O for love of sweet Heaven, say no
O, what 'll I do in the world wid poor Daisy !
　　O, how will I live, an' O, where will I go !

"The room is so dark I 'm not seein', yer Honor,
　　I think I 'll go home — " And a sob thick and dry
Came sharp from the bosom of Mary O'Connor,
　　But never a tear-drop welled up to her eye.

THE ROBBER.

ON the lone deserted cross-road,
　　Under the high crucifix,
Stood the robber, slyly lurking ;
In his hand his naked sabre
And his rifle, heavy loaded.
For the merchant would he plunder,
Who, with his full weight of money,

With his garments, and his rare wines,
Came to-day home from the market.
Down already had the sun sunk,
And the moon peers through the cloudlets,
And the robber stands awaiting
   Under the high crucifix.

Hark ! a sound like angel voices,
Soft, low sighing deep entreaty,
Coming clear as evening bells
Borne through the still atmosphere !
Sweet with unaccustomed accent
Steals a prayer upon his ear,
And he stands and listens anxious, —
   " O thou Guide of the deserted !
O thou Guardian of the lost ones !
Bend, O bend thy heavenly face,
Clear as sunlight, softly smiling,
Down on us, four little ones ;
Fold, O fold thy arms of mercy,
Which were on the cross extended,
Like two wings around our father,
That no storm destroy his pathway,
That his good steed may not stumble,
That the robber, still and lurking
In the forest, may not harm him.
O Protector of the abandoned,
O thou Guide of the deserted,
Send us home our own dear father ! "
And the robber heard it all
   Under the high crucifix.

Then the youngest crossing himself,
Folding his soft hands demurely, —
" O thou dear Christ," lisps he, childlike,
" O, I know thou art almighty,
Sitting on the throne of heaven,
   15 *

With the stars all glittering golden, —
As the nurse has told me often, —
O, be gracious, O thou dear Christ!
Give the robbers, the rapacious,
Give them bread, and bread in plenty,
That they may not need to plunder
Or to murder our good father!
Did I know where lived a robber,
I would give this little chainlet,
Give to him this cross and girdle,
Saying, ' O thou dear, dear robber,
Take this chain, this cross, and girdle,
That you may not need to plunder
Or to murder our dear father!"
And the robber hears it all
   Under the high crucifix.

From afar he hears approaching
Snorting steeds and wheels swift rolling.
Slowly then he takes his rifle,
Slowly does he seize his sabre,
And he stands there deeply thinking,
   Under the high crucifix.

And the children still are kneeling, —
" O thou Guide of the deserted,
O thou Guardian of the wanderer,
Send us home our own dear father!"
And the father came home riding
All in safety, unendangered;
Clasps his children to his bosom, —
Happy stammerings, kisses sweet.

Only the bare sabre found they;
Found the rifle heavy loaded;
Both had fallen from his hand
   Under the high crucifix.

KIT CARSON'S RIDE. — Joaquin Miller.

RUN? Now you bet you; I rather guess so.
But he's blind as a badger. Whoa, Paché, boy, whoa.
No, you would n't think so to look at his eyes,
But he is badger blind, and it happened this wise : —

. . . . .

We lay low in the grass on the broad plain levels,
Old Revels and I, and my stolen brown bride.
"Forty full miles if a foot to ride,
Forty full miles if a foot, and the devils
Of red Camanches are hot on the track
When once they strike it. Let the sun go down
Soon, very soon," muttered bearded old Revels
As he peered at the sun, lying low on his back,
Holding fast to his lasso; then he jerked at his steed,
And sprang to his feet, and glanced swiftly around,
And then dropped, as if shot, with his ear to the ground, —
Then again to his feet and to me, to my bride,
While his eyes were like fire, his face like a shroud,
His form like a king, and his beard like a cloud,
And his voice loud and shrill, as if blown from a reed, —
"Pull, pull in your lassos, and bridle to steed,
And speed, if ever for life you would speed ;
And ride for your lives, for your lives you must ride,
For the plain is aflame, the prairie on fire,
And feet of wild horses hard flying before
I hear like a sea breaking high on the shore ;
While the buffalo come like the surge of the sea,
Driven far by the flame, driving fast on us three
As a hurricane comes, crushing palms in his ire."

We drew in the lassos, seized saddle and rein,
Threw them on, sinched them on, sinched them over again,
And again drew the girth, cast aside the macheer,
Cut away tapidaros, loosed the sash from its fold,
Cast aside the catenas red and spangled with gold,
And gold-mounted Colt's, true companions for years,

Cast the red silk serapes to the wind in a breath,
And so bared to the skin sprang all haste to the horse,
As bare as when born, as when new from the hand
Of God, without word, or one word of command,
Turned head to the Brazos in a red race with death,
Turned head to the Brazos with a breath in the hair
Blowing hot from a king leaving death in his course ;
Turned head to the Brazos with a sound in the air
Like the rush of an army, and a flash in the eye
Of a red wall of fire reaching up to the sky,
Stretching fierce in pursuit of a black rolling sea,
Rushing fast upon us as the wind sweeping free
And afar from the desert, bearing death and despair.

Not a word, not a wail from a lip was let fall,
Not a kiss from my bride, not a look or low call
Of love-note or courage, but on o'er the plain
So steady and still, leaning low to the mane,
With the heel to the flank and the hand to the rein,
Rode we on, rode we three, rode we gray nose and nose,
Reaching long, breathing loud, like a creviced wind blows,
Yet we broke not a whisper, we breathed not a prayer,
There was work to be done, there was death in the air.
And the chance was as one to a thousand for all.

Gray nose to gray nose and each steady mustang
Stretched neck and stretched nerve till the hollow earth rang
And the foam from the flank and the croup and the neck
Flew around like the spray on a storm-driven deck.
Twenty miles ! thirty miles ! . . . . a dim distant speck . . . .
Then a long reaching line and the Brazos in sight,
And I rose in my seat with a shout of delight.
I stood in my stirrup and looked to my right,
But Revels was gone ; I glanced by my shoulder
And saw his horse stagger ; I saw his head drooping
Hard on his breast, and his naked breast stooping
Low down to the mane as so swifter and bolder
Ran reaching out for us the red-footed fire.

To right and to left the black buffalo came,
In miles and in millions, rolling on in despair,
With their beards to the dust and black tails in the air.

As a terrible surf on a red sea of flame
Rushing on in the rear, reaching high, reaching higher,
And he rode neck to neck to a buffalo bull,
The monarch of millions, with shaggy mane full
Of smoke and of dust, and it shook with desire
Of battle, with rage and with bellowings loud
And unearthly, and up through its lowering cloud
Came the flash of his eyes like a half-hidden fire,
While his keen crooked horns through the storm of his mane
Like black lances lifted and lifted again ;
And I looked but this once, for the fire licked through,
And he fell and was lost, as we rode two and two.

I looked to my left then, and nose, neck, and shoulder
Sank slowly, sank surely, till back to my thighs ;
And up through the black blowing veil of her hair
Did beam full in mine her two marvellous eyes
With a longing and love, yet a look of despair,
And a pity for me, as she felt the smoke fold her,
And flames reaching far for her glorious hair.
Her sinking steed faltered, his eager ears fell
To and fro and unsteady, and all the neck's swell
Did subside and recede and the nerves fall as dead.
Then she saw that my own steed still lorded his head
With a look of delight, for this Paché, you see,
Was her father's, and once at the South Santafee
Had won a whole herd, sweeping everything down
In a race where the world came to run for the crown ;
And so when I won the true heart of my bride, —
My neighbor's and deadliest enemy's child,
And child of the kingly war-chief of his tribe, —
She brought me this steed to the border the night
She met Revels and me in her perilous flight
From the lodge of the chief to the north Brazos side ;

And said, so half guessing of ill as she smiled,
As if jesting, that I, and I only, should ride
The fleet-footed Paché, so if kin should pursue
I should surely escape without other ado
Than to ride, without blood, to the north Brazos side,
And await her, — and wait till the next hollow moon
Hung her horn in the palms, when surely and soon
And swift she would join me, and all would be well
Without bloodshed or word.   And now as she fell
From the front, and went down in the ocean of fire,
The last that I saw was a look of delight
That I should escape, — a love, — a desire, —
Yet never a word, not a look of appeal,
Lest I should reach hand, should stay hand or stay heel
One instant for her in my terrible flight.

Then the rushing of fire rose around me and under,
And the howling of beasts like the sound of thunder, —
Beasts burning and blind and forced onward and over,
As the passionate flame reached around them and wove her
Hands in their hair, and kissed hot till they died, —
Till they died with a wild and a desolate moan,
As a sea heart-broken on the hard brown stone.
And into the Brazos . . . . I rode all alone, —
All alone, save only a horse long-limbed,
And blind and bare and burnt to the skin.
Then just as the terrible sea came in
And tumbled its thousands hot into the tide,
Till the tide blocked up and the swift stream brimmed
In eddies, we struck on the opposite side.

Sell Paché, — blind Paché?   Now, mister, look here,
You have slept in my tent and partook of my cheer
Many days, many days, on this rugged frontier,
For the ways they were rough and Camanches were near;
But you 'd better pack up!   Curse your dirty skin!
I could n't have thought you so niggardly small.
Do you men that make boots think an old mountaineer

On the rough border born has no tum-tum at all ?
Sell Paché ? You buy him ! A bag full of gold !
You show him ! Tell of him the tale I have told !
Why he bore me through fire, and is blind, and is old !
Now pack up your papers and get up and spin,
And never look back. Blast you and your tin !

———◆———

THE VOICE. — Forceythe Willson.

A SAINTLY Voice fell on my ear
    Out of the dewy atmosphere :
"O hush, dear Bird of Night, be mute ;
Be still, O throbbing heart and lute !"
The Night-Bird shook the sparkling dew
Upon me as he ruffed and flew ;
My heart was still almost as soon,
My lute as silent as the moon ;
I hushed my heart and held my breath,
And would have died the death of death
To hear, — but just once more, — to hear
That Voice within the atmosphere.

Again the Voice fell on my ear
Out of the dewy atmosphere.
The same words, but half heard at first,
I listened with a quenchless thirst,
And drank as of that heavenly balm,
The Silence that succeeds a psalm ;
My soul to ecstasy was stirred,
It was a voice that I had heard
A thousand blissful times before,
But deemed that I should hear no more
Till I should have a Spirit's ear
And breathe another Atmosphere.

Then there was Silence in my ear,
And Silence in the atmosphere ;

And silent moonshine on the mart,
And peace and silence in my heart;
But suddenly a dark Doubt said,
" The fancy of a fevered head ! "
A wild, quick whirlwind of desire
Then wrapt me as in folds of fire ;
I ran the strange words o'er and o'er,
And listened breathlessly once more ;
And lo, the third time, I did hear
The same words in the atmosphere !

They fell and died upon my ear
As dew dies on the atmosphere ;
And then an intense yearning thrilled
My Soul, that all might be fulfilled :
" Where art thou, Blessed Spirit, where ?
Whose Voice is dew upon the air ! "
I looked, around me, and above,
And cried aloud, " Where art thou, Love ?
O, let me see thy living eye,
And clasp thy living hand, or die ! "
Again, upon the atmosphere,
The selfsame words fell, " *I Am Here !* "

" Here ? Thou art here, Love ! " " *I Am Here !* "
The echo died upon my ear ;
I looked around me, — everywhere ;
But, ah ! there was no mortal there !
The moonlight was upon the mart,
And Awe and Wonder in my heart !
I saw no form ! — I only felt
Heaven's Peace upon me as I knelt ;
And knew a Soul Beatified
Was at that moment by my side !
And there was Silence in my ear,
And Silence in the atmosphere !